REDEFINING GEEK

REDEFINING {GEEK}

BIAS AND THE FIVE HIDDEN
HABITS OF TECH-SAVVY TEENS

Cassidy Puckett

THE UNIVERSITY OF CHICAGO PRESS

Chicago and London

The University of Chicago Press, Chicago 60637
The University of Chicago Press, Ltd., London
© 2022 by Cassidy Puckett
Published 2022
Printed in the United States of America

31 30 29 28 27 26 25 24 23 22   1 2 3 4 5

ISBN-13: 978-0-226-73255-8 (cloth)
ISBN-13: 978-0-226-73269-5 (paper)
ISBN-13: 978-0-226-73272-5 (e-book)
DOI: https://doi.org/10.7208/chicago/9780226732725.001.0001

Library of Congress Cataloging-in-Publication Data

Names: Puckett, Cassidy, author.
Title: Redefining geek : bias and the five hidden
  habits of tech-savvy teens / Cassidy Puckett.
Description: Chicago : University of Chicago Press,
  2022. | Includes bibliographical references and
  index.
Identifiers: LCCN 2021038166 | ISBN 9780226732558
  (cloth) | ISBN 9780226732695 (paperback) |
  ISBN 9780226732725 (ebook)
Subjects: LCSH: Technology and youth. | Technical
  education—Methodology.
Classification: LCC T65.3 .P83 2022 | DDC 620.0071/
  1—dc23
LC record available at https://lccn.loc.gov/2021038166

⊗ This paper meets the requirements of
ANSI/NISO Z39.48-1992 (Permanence of Paper).

To the warriors, artists, and scholars

Contents

Introduction

A TECH CLASS IN CALIFORNIA

It's May 2004 and I'm standing next to a whiteboard at the front of a technology class in a small public middle school called Urban Promise Academy (UPA, or "ooo-pah"). The school is located in the predominantly low-income Latinx Fruitvale neighborhood of Oakland, California. Walking to UPA from the Fruitvale Bay Area Rapid Transit (BART) station, I pass clusters of men in dusty work boots—day workers— waiting for the trucks that pick them up and women selling tamales from red coolers on the corner. Vibrant colors adorn most buildings, street signs, and even the trash cans on the street. Music calls out from busy *pupuserias* and *panaderías*, the delicious scent of Salvadoran stuffed corn cakes and Mexican sweet breads filling the air, and families smile and wave as they notice neighbors across International Boulevard.

It's the second of the six years I will teach technology classes (web design and robotics) at UPA, and I'm close to completing a master's degree from Stanford's Learning Design and Technology program. I'm standing at the whiteboard, chattering away at a breakneck pace, scribbling hypertext markup language (HTML) tags on the board to explain how to format pages of a yearlong web project celebrating the school's first graduating class. We've collected photos and quotes from each eighth grader about their experiences at UPA and are now formatting the individual student pages and populating the website with content. We are close to completing the project, my students are almost ready to move on to high school, and I am just about to graduate as well. It's an exciting moment.

Around me, the class munches on snacks. I explain how to hand code to structure each page, including where to add `<table>` tags. I say, "First you need the opening `<table>` and closing `</table>` tags, then you add code for the row, and each cell within that row like this..." I scribble on the board with dry-erase marker:

```
<table>
    <tr>
        <td></td>
        <td></td>
        <td></td>
    </tr>
</table>
```

"That's a table with one row with three cells. Get it? Anyone have any questions?" I look around the room and turn to Amairani, a quiet Latinx student with bright observant eyes, to whom I had just demonstrated the same task using a web design program called Dreamweaver.[1] I opened the explanation up to the entire class, using hand code and drawing on the board rather than having the software create tags for them. I ask Amairani if this approach is more confusing than using the software and she says no—in fact, it's simpler than figuring out the extra tags automatically added by Dreamweaver. With that, the class sets to work in pairs—one hand codes and types while the other reads off content to add into the tables.

I look around the room. Given the demographics of science, technology, engineering, and mathematics (STEM) education and occupational fields, everyone here could be viewed as an unlikely participant.[2] This disparity is particularly true in computer science, where sexist, racist, and classist assumptions about "natural" differences in technological competence and "ambient" cues about who belongs in these spaces shape participation.[3] Although not by design, we are all female. We are all from low-income backgrounds, my students much more so. Almost all of my students are first- or second-generation immigrants and come from homes where their first language is something other than English, primarily Spanish. The school and neighborhood have limited resources—which isn't to say it isn't a lively, thriving place. But based on the gender, racial, and socioeconomic makeup of my class, the school, and the neighborhood, we should (supposedly) not be engaged in what we are doing—playing with computers and coding—given that research shows we are the least likely people to be included in these aspects of STEM.[4]

Still, here we are—contrary to the statistics and what stereotypes might suggest—and here I am, a new teacher in a relatively new field, trying my best to lead my students toward an ill-defined end goal: technological competence. With so much potential around the room—the kind that I later come to understand as systematically unseen and undervalued—I want them to be able to pursue *any* form of technology learning to get them to wherever they want to go. But I don't know how to support them. I need to know: *What does it mean to be good with technology, how can I help my students achieve it, and how can I ensure that others recognize their potential?*

REDEFINING *TECHNOLOGICAL COMPETENCE*

This book offers an answer to these questions, based on what became a decadelong journey to understand what successful technology learners do, including a way of completely rethinking what it means to be good with technology. The project started out as a way to better understand and support my students and other students like them. That remains a goal: to provide tools for parents and educators to help students learn. But I also want to shake up our broader cultural assumptions about "natural" technological ability—assumptions that devalue the talent of low-income, minoritized, and female students and push them out of STEM. We do that by redefining *technological competence* as something that can be learned. Tech skills and literacies are not natural gifts. Instead, there are learning habits that help skills and literacies grow. These habits are especially important as technologies and the skills and literacies needed to use them change. So, what it really means to be good with technology is to develop skills, literacies, *and* technology learning habits.

These habits are critical but up to this point have gone unrecognized. In the chapters that follow, I describe the five habits I identified through a mixed-methods study that started with more than three hundred hours of observation and interviews with a diverse group of about one hundred tech-savvy teens in award-winning out-of-school and in-school technology programs and classes across the United States. Three of the habits connect to what research shows helps people learn in general, which I translate to the context of technology learning:

1. A willingness to try and fail
2. Management of frustration and boredom
3. Use of models

The other two habits are more technology specific:

4. Design logic (thinking about why technology is designed the way it is and how to use it for one's own purpose)
5. Efficiencies (identifying shortcuts)

When we reinterpret technological "instinct" as a set of learning habits and systematically describe these habits, we can then peer into what science and technology scholars call the "black box" of scientific and technical work. Black boxing hides what scientists and technologists actually do and makes it seem as though being tech savvy involves no learning at all but is instead the lucky ability of the talented few.[5] When we are unclear about what it means to be good with technology, popular opinion, public policy, and even many scientists default to the cultural myth that being good with technology is natural or instinctual.[6] This idea of natural ability is easily linked to other things considered natural or biological, such as age, race, and gender. In the tech world at this historical moment, assumptions about good "instinct" are often attached to young, white or Asian, and male bodies—an idea that disadvantages women and other racial and ethnic groups.[7] These assumptions make it harder for us to see what real technological ability is, they make it harder to teach, and they make it harder to fight against inequities in tech.

In this book, I use an interdisciplinary approach building on research in the learning sciences, communication, social psychology, and sociology to explain what being good with technology really is. And I counter assumptions about natural ability with in-depth descriptions of the five habits that help people learn new technologies, highlighting in particular the habits of low-income, Black, Latinx, Native American, and female teens. I also show how to measure and build these habits—and demonstrate that many teens historically marginalized in tech already use the habits. In other words, they may be more ready for advanced technological skill development than assumptions about instinct might suggest, building on a growing body of research demonstrating the many missed opportunities for socioeconomic, gender, and racial equity.[8] Unpacking "instinct" in this way is essential not only for the reconceptualization of the goals of STEM education to better support students' readiness to respond to technological change but also to contest ideas about natural technological ability to combat inequities in STEM.

HOW WE HAVE UNDERSTOOD TECHNOLOGICAL COMPETENCE IN THE PAST

Researchers, industry leaders, and policy makers have been mired in local, national, and global debates about the definition of technological competence for decades. Yet, defining technological competence became a necessity for schools when, from 1996 to 2015, they had to create technology plans with learning goals for students to be eligible for the Federal Communications Commission "e-Rate" program for discounted technology infrastructure.[9] If schools didn't have a plan, they could not receive much-needed federal funding toward computers, internet access, and more. In 2003, as both a tech teacher and a member of a team tasked with developing a plan, I was initially surprised to encounter the debate over the meaning of technological competence. Given the rise of state and local standards and accountability policies, I expected to find well-established technology standards and assessments.[10] Instead, there were and continue to be ongoing deliberations and an ever-growing list of definitions of *technological competence*.[11]

Yet despite all these definitions, little attention has been given to a core aspect of technological competence: the ability to learn as technologies change and new ones emerge. One of the earliest definitions of what it means to be good with technology was outlined in the National Educational Technology Standards (NETS), introduced in 1998 and redefined in 2007 and 2016 by the International Society for Technology Education (ISTE).[12] ISTE initially described tech competence as being "literate" in (1) basic operations and functions; (2) social, ethical, and human issues related to technology; (3) technology productivity tools; (4) technology communication tools; (5) technology research tools; and (6) technology problem-solving and decision-making tools.[13] But this description did not include technology learning.

Instead, the primary focus of definitions at that time and since is *what* students should learn rather than *how* students learn. Various organizations offer other national and international standards and assessments like Educational Testing Service's iSkills assessment of information and communications technology literacy skills.[14] Other researchers provide a range of definitions of competence focusing on current literacies or skills (e.g., Warschauer's computer literacy, information literacy, multimedia literacy, and computer mediated communication literacy; van Dijk's operational skill, information skill, and strategic skill).[15] But these definitions and measures do not include how to prepare students for the new technologies, programming languages, and ways of accomplishing technological tasks emerging year after year. If students are skillful or literate in one set of "basic operations and functions," is the assumption that they are "naturally" able to learn new ones? That did not seem to be the case in my classroom, where students who knew how to use Photoshop, for example, struggled with Dreamweaver.

Not only do these definitions of competence not pay attention to the process of technology learning, but they are coupled with a general, dismissive assumption that kids born into the digital age are naturally skillful with technology, including all three versions of the national standards.[16] The most recent 2016 ISTE NETS briefly mentions that students should be able to "transfer their knowledge to explore emerging technologies," but they provide no details about what this looks like.[17] Early on, the 2004 National Educational Technology Plan, a report by the United States Department of Education, declared:

> Today's students, of almost any age, are far ahead of their teacher in computer literacy . . . with the increased use of new technologies and the motivated expertise of today's students, it means that 10 years from now we could be looking at the greatest leap forward in achievement in the history of education.[18]

Many scholars argue that this myth of the "digital native" runs counter to empirical data.[19] Yet the idea of "natural" ability persists, often through age-, gender-, and race-based stereotypes about who is naturally skilled with technology.[20] As a teacher reading the 2004 National Educational Technology Plan, I knew this was simply not the case— students were not "far ahead," and while perhaps motivated, many did not automatically have technological "expertise," leaving me with little guidance about what and how to teach my students.

GENDER-, RACE-, AND CLASS-BASED ASSUMPTIONS ABOUT INSTINCT

The assumption of "instinct" does more than fail educators. It also makes it difficult to counter biased ways of thinking about technical work. It was the underlying premise, for example, of former Google engineer James Damore's controversial 2017 memo about the company's diversity policy.[21] In the memo, he argued that fewer women work in tech because men are instinctively more interested in and competent with technology, using "scientific evidence" to support his claim. Indeed, walking around Silicon Valley, you might think the same—given its demographics, tech could appear to be a "guy thing." Without an alternate framework, assumptions about natural technological ability justify this attitude and make it difficult to address the fact that so few women, Blacks, Latinx, and Native Americans pursue educational and occupational pathways in tech.

But my technology class was never a "guy thing." In most years, the class had equal numbers of girls and boys—and in the year we designed the graduation website, only girls enrolled, temporarily making it a girls-only class.[22] In fact, one day while I was walking near the front office, Principal Montes called out to a boy also walking down the hall, "Hey, you might like Miss Cassidy's technology class!" The boy looked quizzically back at Montes and responded, "Isn't that a *girl thing*?" I remember thinking how odd that sounded given broader gender disparities in tech. Later I understood just how much local constructions of gender can influence beliefs and behaviors in revolutionary ways by calling into question predominant stereotypes about who belongs in these fields.[23] In fact, when I asked the class to draw a "computer type" of person as part of an initial study I conducted while teaching, they only drew pictures of females: me or (more often) Cindy, an outgoing Latinx teen with a generous smile who was my "youth facilitator" (teaching assistant) and one of my tech-savviest students.[24]

Recent studies show that gender-based performance in other STEM areas, such as mathematics, also depends on the context.[25] While there were roughly equal numbers of boys and girls in the school as a whole, the gender ratio in my course varied from year to year; it was not always a defining feature of the class. Stanford sociologist Cecilia Ridgeway describes this dynamic as the salience of the "gender frame," which becomes greater in contexts where there is a particular gender majority, as for men in computer science or women in teaching—rather than being the "natural" ability or interest of particular genders for particular educational or occupational activities.[26] In my class, gender simply did not explain differences in how easily students could learn. Some girls struggled, other girls didn't. Some boys struggled, other boys didn't. But, with no agreed-upon definition of *technology competence* and little attention paid to the importance of technology learning, there was (until now) nothing to counter the gender-, race-, or class-based assumptions about who is good with technology.

DIFFERENCES AND DIGITAL DIVIDES

Yet, there were differences among my students. For example, some students more easily engaged in technical aspects of the class, like hand coding `<table>` `</table>` tags. There were students like Amairani, who easily and enthusiastically learned HTML. Other students let more knowledgeable or willing peers do technical things for them or tried it and gave up, taking on other roles (e.g., photographer, content producer). While I considered all roles valued ways of participating, skipping tasks such as coding limited some students from fully engaging in the project and in their learning.

Research on the digital divide focused on who has access to technology suggests that limited access, particularly at home, might be the cause of such differences (called the "first level" digital divide).[27] But this wasn't the case with my students.[28] Everyone in the class had computer and internet access inside and outside school. Or, they found ways to gain access despite limited resources. For example, Meihong, a teen who was at first very quiet but quickly revealed her true fun-loving self, arrived from China two years prior and shared a single computer with her father and older sister. But she always figured out ways of getting more screen time. Over Instant Messenger—which I offered to students working on projects outside of class—she shared her strategy:

```
CASSIDY: r u on a computer in your room?
MEIHONG: naaa. . . . .mah dad'z room
CASSIDY: it's kind of late . . . do your parents mind?
MEIHONG: no he's sleep
CASSIDY: he's sleeping? your typing doesn't wake him up?
MEIHONG: no. he fall alseep easy :)
```

Many students did not have their own personal computers, but they still found creative ways to access technology and, especially, the internet.

While access is still a concern—especially in rural communities—scholars quickly turned to other explanations of differences in technology use.[29] Called the "second level" digital divide, researchers argued that differences in technology use beyond access may be explained by differences in skills and literacies.[30] In a 2004 article reframing the problem, Paul DiMaggio and colleagues further suggested that because skills shape technology use, defining and measuring competence—including skill—was an important first step. But, they said, this step was complicated by technological change that demands new skills and therefore new definitions and new measures. As a result, researchers of the second-level digital divide have added new definitions to the list of "literacies" and "skills," and introduced new or updated measures that respond to technological change.[31] But these studies still miss a central feature of technological competence: *continual learning. What helps people continue to learn and adapt to technological change?*

UNPACKING PERSISTENCE

Outside of technology education, researchers have been tackling a similar question about what helps people continue to learn or persist more generally. Some explanations emphasize the role of the individual. For example, one answer to this question is "grit" or a personality trait within individuals where a "passion and perseverance towards a goal" helps them persist and eventually succeed.[32] This was, in fact, the explanation given by my students—they thought that the individual ability to "not give up" made some students more tech savvy than others. Yet, many sociologists and social psychologists critique grit for its exclusion of cultural and structural forces, saying that it draws attention away from the barriers faced by disadvantaged students, placing the onus on individuals to solve social problems.[33] Also, grit seems unable to account for patterns of persistence in the specific context of technology education. Applying grit to this case would suggest, for example, that women are somehow less "gritty" than men in computer science while being simultaneously "grittier" than men overall, given their greater college attendance and completion rates.[34]

Grit also did not explain persistence among my students. On the (supposedly) nongritty end of the spectrum in my technology class was Maria, a high-achieving Latinx teen who was often lost deep in thought, who expressed less interest in activities that required technical skill development and eventually dropped out of the class. While there, she regularly blogged about Eminem and Nike shoes—an activity that could introduce students to basic HTML tags, if they changed their blog's design. Yet Maria did not touch the code despite lots of encouragement. During a field trip to the Tech Museum in San Jose, she did try out 3D design software to create renderings of lowrider bicycles. But, the majority of the time she participated in activities she already knew how to do. When, close to the end of the year a conflict elsewhere in school resulted in a brief suspension, she never returned to class. What made her quit? She said she just "didn't feel the same" about school, including the class, and felt like giving up. This explanation could be taken as a lack of grit, but she was part of the web design class for more than two years, and her stellar grades and later successes suggest otherwise (she graduated valedictorian and went on to earn a bachelors from UC Davis).

Other explanations of educational persistence (e.g., high school graduation, college attendance, college graduation) emphasize structural factors, notably socioeconomic status, which is the strongest predictor of educational attainment in general. But research in STEM education shows social psychological factors, or the ways individuals think about their fit in a field, are critical to persistence. These factors include self-concept (beliefs in their ability), interest, career aspirations, and STEM "identity," which are conditioned by social context.[35] In other words, in STEM we have to understand how people think about what they do and how learning contexts and broader structural forces shape their ideas and actions.

However, because STEM research focuses largely on mathematics and science rather than technology, it leaves out an in-depth understanding of the process of technology learning, which allows cultural assumptions about "natural" technological ability to go unquestioned. One argument suggests that the sociological concept of *alienation*, or a feeling of powerlessness (how much a context will respond to you), best captures the dynamics between individuals and social contexts, whereby individuals in "responsive" contexts experience less alienation, develop a greater sense of their ability to shape the future, and act accordingly.[36] Applying the concept of alienation to Maria's experiences, I believe that in an unusual moment of conflict and suspension, the school was unresponsive to her more typical self-concept as a "good student," and my class was unresponsive to her needs because I did not yet know how to support Maria's technology learning process. These experiences made her feel (unusually) alienated and want to quit. But only the class, not everything.

Other students persisted in the class until its conclusion but had difficulty persisting with certain types of technical work. Meihong, who was a good friend of Maria's, remained in the class despite her friend's departure. She, too, was not as involved with activities that required skill development *inside* class—but she did engage in increasingly more advanced activities *outside* class. For example, at the time, MySpace (an early social networking site) and "guestbooks" were popular, and Meihong obsessed about manipulating their design. Users could change aspects of how they looked and their interactivity using coding languages such as HTML and cascading style sheets (CSS), so Meihong asked for help with projects outside school, such as how to change the cursor from an arrow to a crosshair on her guestbook.[37] Meihong surprised me by sharing the guestbook for critique during class, but it disappeared afterward. What happened? Over email, she said:

```
i was changing it on sunday night,
then i think i messed up something.
and the whole thing was gone.
then todai i try to fix it something went wrong again.
just want to tell u dat i'm not those kind of person give up
    so easy.
maybe i'll give up later,
when i'm tired of it, i mean when i can't do it no more.
then i'll give up on that website.
any wayz have a nice spring break.
~*Meihong*~ :D
```

Meihong echoed the individualistic idea of grit (to not "give up so easy") and tied this idea to a "kind" of person—an innate fixed quality, not something that is learned. While it was good that she saw herself as a persistent person, it was troubling because it individuated a social process—a kind of person, rather than having the social supports to persist—and aligned with assumptions about "natural" technological competence, something that you inherently do or do not have.[38]

These ideas link to psychologist Carol Dweck's research on "mindset" whereby a "fixed mindset," like the one Meihong expressed, is the belief that ability is static rather than malleable, as it would be in a "growth mindset." Dweck argues that this general orientation to learning actually shapes learning and, therefore, knowledge and skill development.[39] Some observers critique mindset, like grit, as suggesting that individuals are responsible for their own problems. Dweck, however, does not see mindset as a personal attribute but instead a way of thinking that is shaped by subtle and explicit cues from social contexts.[40] Think, for example, of that boy's reluctance to join my all-girls class: based on who was in the class, he thought it wasn't a good "fit" for him. Mindset also does not function alone; beyond the belief that growth is possible, students need to know *how* to learn—for example, Dweck's research shows that educational interventions that combine mindset with math study skills increase mathematics achievement.[41] With the case of technology, many people hold an assumption that, like Meihong, combines "grit" with the "fixed mindset"—you are either the type of person who gives up with technology or not. Yet, we know little about how students actually learn technologies that are new to them.

Indeed, the problems Meihong encountered are not solved with a different mindset. Another one of my students seemed to demonstrate both "grit" and a "growth mindset" but still encountered difficulties. Cindy, one of my most engaged students, readily participated in all class activities but gave herself mixed reviews about her technological know-how. Despite the fact that she understood and worked with HTML in the class, she said it wasn't something in which she excelled. Cindy didn't think she was always a "patient" a person when coding, which is what she viewed as a requirement for being a true technological expert. Cindy elaborated on this distinction in an interview, reinterpreting a "computer type" of person as actions someone takes in the learning process—continuing to try to understand something and being patient:

CASSIDY: Do you think there's a computer type of person?
CINDY: I think so.
CASSIDY: You think so? What type of person is that?
CINDY: I think it's a type of person that's really into them. That enjoys, like, you might get frustrated in a while, when you try to do something. But you won't give up on what you're doing. *You continue to try to understand it.* You won't give up on what you're doing.

CASSIDY: Do you see yourself as a computer type person?

CINDY: Yeah, I think so.

[Later]

CASSIDY: What does it take to be good with computers?

CINDY: Just not giving up. I know some people . . . let's say you want to change something in PowerPoint. They can't decide what to do and they just give up on it. They say, "I'm frustrated with it. I don't want to do this no more." I think you really *need to be patient with yourself* and not give up.

[Later]

CASSIDY: Do you learn differently from other people in the class?

CINDY: Yeah, some people might get into something . . . learn it easier than other people.

CASSIDY: So some things might be hard for you and easy for other people, or easy for you and hard for other people?

CINDY: Yeah.

CASSIDY: Like what?

CINDY: I think the coding. Like, sometimes I'll do it and I'll forget to do something.

CASSIDY: So coding is kind of a little bit more difficult than Photoshop? [something she said she was good at]

CINDY: Yeah.

Cindy expressed a nuanced view on persistence—that while in general she wouldn't give up easily and believed she was capable of learning, there were times when she would stop trying to understand something and could no longer be patient. While at the time, I did not fully appreciate the implications of Cindy's words, I now interpret them to mean that what my students really needed was help developing habits that could support their technology learning process, even things they found more difficult.

Without understanding precisely what technology learners do, how social contexts shape what learners do, and how people respond to what learners do (that is, whether or not others see learning habits as a signal of potential), differences in technological competence might appear to be differences in innate talents. As a teacher, I was troubled by these views about natural ability presented in research, by public policy makers, and in conversation with many of my students. They suggested that competence is something you're born into; either you have it or you don't. Or, even if they held a more nuanced views like those of Cindy, they still didn't know *what to do* as they learned. But what if I could define it better? How might this redefinition help my students reorient their learning? And, how might a redefinition reshape public and academic understandings of technological ability—and the quiet justification of inequity in STEM?

THE BOOK: A ROAD MAP

This book started out as a project to answer the practical questions of an educator. But it became about much more. While it is for educators and their practical concerns, it is also for parents, policy makers, researchers, and the broader public—anyone wanting to help create a more equitable technological future. In what follows in the book, I address my initial questions about technological competence by redefining what it means to be good with technology—at its core, continual learning, persistence—not a personality trait but a set of five habits that help people learn new technologies. *Why is understanding technology learning important?* Because not understanding it does two things. It leaves educators empty-handed in terms of how to orient their teaching. And, it allows assumptions about natural technological ability to go unquestioned, undercutting efforts to address digital inequality.

In fact, we have known about and have tried to address digital inequality for a long time, but it continues to persist. In chapter 1 I describe three contradictory logics that have long been used to frame technology education—and how even despite good intentions, they often lead to the exclusion of tech-savvy teens like Amairani, Cindy, and Meihong. One logic views technology education as fundamental *for a democratic society*. The other two (*to serve market needs* and *for individual advantage*) accept inequality as part of their design and suggest that sorting and competition can serve the public good. Efforts to increase equity in tech have drawn from all three logics, including such recent efforts as the Hour of Code and Computer Science for All, confusing and combining goals that march toward very different ends. In this chapter, I clarify these logics—and in particular the digital inequality perspective that technological competence is fundamental to an *equitable society*. I also explain how the latter two logics inadvertently encourage gatekeeping to undermine the first and primary goal of technology education. I also describe a significant gap in digital inequality research described earlier—that is, *how* people develop technological skill—and show how addressing this gap can better support technology education for *an equitable society*, as well as push back against persistent gatekeeping motivated by the logics of *serving markets* and *providing individual advantage*.

In chapter 1, I also explain why I focus on habits—small things for big goals—and introduce the programs and some of the teens who allowed me to follow them through technology classes and programs across the country to understand what helps them "not give up." This approach takes seriously the expertise of predominantly low-income, historically marginalized, and mixed-gender tech-savvy teens.[42] As a technology teacher and educational researcher, I used my professional networks to target well-known, award-winning educational technology programs. These programs serve students from diverse gender, race, and socioeconomic backgrounds all across the country—including Youth Movement Records; the Bay Area Video Coalition's Bay Unity Music Project (BUMP) Records and Digital Pathways video production and game design programs; the Field Museum's WhyReef program; the Digital

Youth Network (DYN) collaboration with the Chicago Public Library at YOUmedia Chicago; Mouse/Geek Squad Summer Academy; I Dig Zambia at Global Kids and the Field Museum; Radio Arte; and Mouse Squad California (MSCA). In this process, I identified the five habits that I briefly introduce in chapter 1 and explain in greater detail in subsequent chapters.

Chapters 2 and 3 describe the five habits: *willingness to try and fail, management of frustration and boredom, use of models, design logic*, and *efficiencies*. The first three habits link to general approaches to learning applied to the context of technology learning, as explored in chapter 2, and the final two habits are more technology specific, as detailed in chapter 3. How to observe and measure the five habits is described in chapter 4, where I give examples of students demonstrating them. Here I introduce and describe a quantitative measure I developed called the *Digital Adaptability Scale (DAS)*, based on more than one thousand Chicago Public Schools students in schools serving large populations of low-income, first-generation, second language learners—in other words, students like Amairani, Maria, Meihong, and Cindy.[43]

No prior research defines or directly measures what people do as they learn new technologies and adapt to technological change. By describing the five technology learning habits and presenting a measure of these habits, this book makes it possible to reconceptualize the goals of STEM education. Because new technologies demand new skill sets, these technology learning habits are critical for adapting to technological change—perhaps more than particular skills. Therefore, this framework helps redirect STEM education to support readiness for an unknown technological future. Redefining tech competence to include the five learning habits and supporting their development can also lead us to a more equitable future.

Chapter 5 moves from the definition and measurement of the five technology learning habits to show how they connect to students' futures. We see from my studies in Chicago and a replication study in Boston that there is a clear link between the habits, the technology courses teens take in high school, their future educational plans, and what they aspire to be. We already know from prior research that these educational experiences and early career aspirations are prerequisites for STEM degree completion, and they play a part in race-, class-, and gender-based stratification in these fields.[44] Without seeing possible futures as computer scientists, tech entrepreneurs, or engineers, the door to these careers is closed. But shaping students' plans and aspirations can be difficult. While the relationship between the five habits and students' plans and aspirations is not a causal one—better technology learning habits may encourage aspirations in STEM and vice versa— teaching the five habits can help teens envision career paths that might otherwise seem impossible. Therefore, building students' habits may be an effective way of influencing students' futures and addressing equity by encouraging those otherwise disinclined to pursue STEM fields—so long as others recognize and reward their potential.

Chapter 6 describes how parents and educators can help develop teens' technology learning habits. This account includes advice about how to use the DAS and a set of measures that capture the nature of technology learning in school, at home, and among friends (the social context of technology learning). This information (teens' current habits and how they learn about technology in various social spheres) can be used for educational interventions, targeting teens who might need more support inside or outside school. The chapter also details the successful approaches of the award-winning technology classes and programs included in the study. For example, DYN in Chicago develops what one program director called a "renaissance learner" by engaging teens in a range of activities that require them to learn multiple types of technology within the same project. In a musical album project, teens create audio recordings with Pro Tools, design an album cover in Photoshop, and create a website for the album with Dreamweaver. Using multiple technologies in the context of the same project provides a rationale for this activity (why a person needs to use multiple types of technology), while it builds teens' technology learning habits as they move across technologies. This chapter speaks to exactly what I wanted as a teacher: practical tools and advice with concrete examples of how to support teens' technology learning habits. But it also describes the role that gatekeeping plays in perpetuating digital inequality and some ways to address this problem.

*

A belief in "natural" technological ability justifies and makes difficult to address educational and occupational inequities in STEM. This myth also stifles our collective need for a more innovative, equitable society. Instead, we need to redefine what it means to be good with technology the way one tech-savvy girl from a low-income immigrant family described in a chat message during my field research in Chicago:

> CASSIDY: what do you think it takes to be good with technology?
> SUMALEE: ahhh hard to explain
> it's the geek instinct xD
> CASSIDY: what's that geek instinct?
> SUMALEE: well to be good with technology is learn with ur experience . . .
> and mix with some new stuff that you learn
> and [try] to think of something new
> past experiences, mixed with new stuff, and try to find even newer stuff
> and geek instinct is my term o.o because i learn technology with my common sense + my experience, so i figured that that thing goes here, there, or there[45]

Teens—or anyone—can acquire new skills if they develop habits that help them continually learn technologies that are new to them. We must redefine *technological competence* to include these habits to point ourselves toward a more equitable future.

The book ends with a word of caution: simply developing students' technology learning habits will not solve all deeply ingrained inequities in STEM. But understanding technological competence as learnable makes a significant contribution by reorienting societal assumptions about what it means to be good with technology—and, therefore, who is or can be good with technology in the future. In fact, findings from this study suggest there may be many hidden techies like Shuri from *Black Panther*—Black, or Latinx, or Native American students otherwise marginalized in STEM who already use these habits, who go unrecognized—who can be better supported with further learning opportunities and other supports to realize their potential.[46] This book therefore walks a fine line between techno-optimism and techno-pessimism. As Alicia Headlam Hines, Alondra Nelson, and Thuy Linh N. Tu note in *Technicolor: Race, Technology, and Everyday Life*, it is too common and easy to talk about people of color as victims when talking about race and technology. "After all, if people of color are seen only as victims, then there is very little reason to entrust them with the tools of the future." They urge us to instead affirm the roles of people of color "as producers and innovators, as members of various technological communities, and as participants in the creation of a wired world."[47]

This book pushes back against assumptions of natural technological ability, to see the "geek instinct" as a set of habits that are teachable and learnable *by everyone*, to intervene where support is needed, and to recognize and reward existing talent. Doing all this includes the difficult but necessary task of confronting systemic racism, classism, and sexism in tech.

[1]

Why Does Digital Inequality Persist?

> No question under discussion in education is so fraught with consequences for the future of democracy as the question of industrial education. Its right development will do more to make public education truly democratic than any other one agency now under consideration. Its wrong treatment will surely accentuate all undemocratic tendencies in our present situation, by fostering and strengthening class divisions in school and out.
>
> John Dewey, *The Need of an Industrial Education in an Industrial Democracy* (1916)

In the spring of 2020, a global pandemic forced rapid adaptation to technological change. Students and educators at all levels, from early education through graduate school, went online, making clearer than ever the importance of technological infrastructure and learning. Prior to that moment, it may have seemed that technology learning was only essential for "techie" people going into tech fields—but in fact, it was already central to so much more. Certainly, my students' technology learning mawttered to me, as I wanted them to be able to fully participate in our class activities and feel confident in their ability. But more than that,

I wanted them and other historically marginalized groups to more fully participate in the many and powerful ways technology is used in society, within and beyond science, technology, engineering, and mathematics (STEM) fields. To ensure that everyone has full agency in all aspects of contemporary life—and, like education as a whole, help support an equitable and more democratic society. Who wouldn't agree with that?

In fact, for decades, research and educational technology policies have suggested as much—that how we think about and organize technology education is pivotal to a more egalitarian society, just as John Dewey advocated with industrial education back in 1910.[1] More specifically, *digital inequality* scholarship—research that emerged in the first decade of the twenty-first century while I was teaching at Urban Promise Academy—has focused on concerns about digital technology learning and use and its relationship to society. This scholarship shows that tech use is influenced by and influences existing social inequalities, with negative implications for a democratic society.[2] These concerns have only increased as more affluent white and Asian males have come to dominate tech fields and occupations. Such unequal representation allows a sliver of the population to hold sway over our technological infrastructure—shaping everything from how Medicaid benefits are determined to how policing happens.[3] Thus, making the claim that who has access to technology learning and who plays a powerful role in technological development matters *for an equitable society* might seem utterly obvious.

But if we've known about this problem for so long, why and how does it persist? One reason that I already touched upon in the introduction is that we do not yet fully understand what it means to be good with technology. Research identifies some dimensions of technological competence. But as I explain in further detail in this chapter, it leaves out a central feature: how people continually develop their technological skills and literacies as technologies change. This constant adjustment makes it difficult for well-intentioned teachers to support all students because it mystifies the technology learning process, making it seem as though some students pick things up more easily while others struggle—defaulting back to the idea of natural ability. This book addresses this issue with a redefinition of *technological competence* based on what tech-savvy people actually do. My revised definition includes a key set of five technology learning habits—detailed in subsequent chapters—that support continual technology learning.

This reconceptualization can help address an important but less emphasized second reason digital inequality persists: *gatekeeping*, whereby only some students are supported and recognized for their gifts. For example, gatekeepers (e.g., educators, employers) may fail to fully cultivate, see, or make use of the budding talents (i.e., the technology learning habits) of groups historically marginalized in tech and continue to exclude them, while at the same time blaming them for their lack of adequate training. This failure hurts our collective well-being—we miss out on the benefits of their talents. So, it is crucial for the gatekeepers within schools and workplaces to pay attention to how they understand, teach, and reward technological competence and to who they assume is tech savvy. The concrete tools in this book are designed to help gatekeepers develop and recognize five technology learning habits in students. In doing so, this book can help democratize tech use and support equitable benefits from tech.

Yet, a redefinition of what it means to be good with technology only solves part of the gatekeeping problem—it might let some students through, but there are always new ways to justify social hierarchies, opportunity hoarding, and exclusion.[4] In fact, the reason such gatekeeping exists is because two of the three historical logics that structure education push us toward an unequal society: to serve the *needs of markets* and to help *individuals get ahead*.[5] It is easy for the third one—to create *an equitable society*—to get lost. In fact, as a technology teacher, I unknowingly drew upon all three of education's logics in how I thought about my students: I thought everyone should develop their technological competence, I wanted to help my students fill much-needed roles in tech fields, and I hoped they could get ahead by entering higher-earning career paths. Couldn't technology education readily address all three?

Unfortunately, I found out that the answer is no. The ways I thought about technology education were ultimately incompatible because of the ends they aim to produce. Only one (tech learning *for an equitable society*) aims to support democratic ideals, whereas the other two (*for markets* and *for individual advantage*) instead rely on inequality in their function.

These logics applied to education more generally are called *democratic equality* (for society), *social efficiency* (for employers/markets), and *social mobility* (for individuals)—and are very much at odds, producing inequality in education as a whole.[6] Linking these ideas to technology learning, in this chapter I explain why understanding technology learning *for an equitable society* is so critical—and what digital inequality research shows that supports this position. I also argue that using the *market* and *individual* perspectives has undermined the greater good by accepting inequality and fueling gatekeeping, helping to perpetuate digital inequality despite efforts to address it. Because these perspectives rely on competition and stratification, they privilege certain types of technical work and match more advantaged groups to more prestigious forms, while diminishing others. Thus, while the *market* and *individual* perspectives are concerned with how technological competence might benefit *some of us*, to create an equitable future we should focus on how technology learning can benefit *all of us*.

FOR SOCIETY: TECHNOLOGY USE AND DIGITAL IN/EQUALITY

How is technology learning key to an equitable society? This "democratic equality" perspective on the purpose of education, as historian David Labaree explains, views schooling as a way to create an informed citizenry and "counteract the growth of selfishness (arising from a burgeoning capitalist economy) by instilling in their charges a personal dedication to the public good."[7] Media literacy scholars have long argued the same; that technology learning is essential to the functioning of our country and, ultimately, the greater good. For example, early media literacy scholar Len Masterman argued in 1985:

Media education is an essential step in the long march towards a truly participatory democracy, and the democratization of our institutions. Widespread media literacy is essential if all citizens are to wield power, make rational decisions, become effective change agents, and have an effective involvement with the media. It is in this much wider sense of "education for democracy" that media literacy can play the most significant role of all.[8]

Applying these ideas to technological competence suggests that being good with technology is foundational to full democratic participation and an equitable society. But is there evidence to support this perspective? The answer is yes. Digital inequality research has confirmed an empirical relationship between technological competence and inequality, using both macrolevel evidence from *the top down (society to individual)* and microlevel evidence from *the ground up (individual to society)*. While incomplete in some ways that are addressed in this book, this scholarship supports the democratic equality perspective that is essential to ending digital disadvantage. So let's take a closer look.

Digital Inequality from the Top Down

Research examining the relationship between technological competence and inequality from a top-down perspective comes primarily from economics. This scholarship looks at the characteristics of society at a macrolevel: for example, the gap between rich and poor. Since the 1980s, economists have observed a trend where income inequality has increased, and part of the explanation is about technological change. For example, computers and automation have displaced "middle-range" workers and polarized the labor market into "low-skill" low-wage jobs and "high-skill" high-wage jobs—a dynamic called "skill-biased technological change."[9] As more machines can do the jobs of factory workers, we simply don't need as many factory workers.

But this was not the first time technological advancements displaced workers. In fact, the same thing happened 150 years ago in the United

States during industrialization, when the introduction of new (non-digital) technologies such as machinery that enabled mass production displaced artisans, increasing economic inequality. But, economists argue, as workers increased their skill through education, inequality subsequently decreased—a phenomenon depicted visually as a "Kuznets Curve," where inequality first increases with new innovations, then decreases.[10] Yet, there has been no decrease in inequality since the 1980s, as expected by the Kuznets model.[11]

Scholars continue to debate why inequality has not decreased. One of the major theories is that the US educational system has failed to meet the demand for technological skill in the labor market—it just isn't training enough people to be tech savvy.[12] As a result, we have more high-tech high-skill jobs than people sufficiently educated to fill them. So, if we better educate people, including moving those already in the labor market in "low-skill" low-wage jobs to "high-skill" higher-wage jobs (called "upskilling"), it could help address inequality—although so could better recognizing the skill and valuation of all forms of technological work.[13]

Overall, research supports the idea that technology learning matters for inequality. Using macrolevel evidence from the top down, these findings motivate other digital inequality scholarship using microlevel evidence to examine the relationship between technological competence and inequality from the bottom up. While the top-down approach suggests that differences in people's technological skill explain ongoing social inequalities ranging from income to health, it doesn't directly measure individual skill. Nor does it account for differences in people's technological access or in the benefits they receive for equivalent access and skill. So, the bottom-up approach asks: How do differences in technological access, competence, and/or reward for technology use shape inequality (and vice versa)?

Digital Inequality from the Bottom Up: The Three Levels of the Digital Divide

Scholars who research digital inequality from the bottom up call these three concerns—about access, competence, and reward—the three "levels" of the digital divide. The first-level divide is the most well-known. But it's worth revisiting because digital divide rhetoric emerged just as the dynamics of gatekeeping took hold. And understanding that history in a new way helps explain how digital inequality persists. The second- and third-level divides may be less familiar, as the term *digital divide* is often used to refer simply to issues of access. This book focuses primarily on the issues of competence and reward: the habits that help build skills and literacies (explained in chapters 2 and 3) and the extent to which people are recognized for their talents.

THE FIRST-LEVEL DIGITAL DIVIDE

Discussion of the first level of the digital divide, about technological access, first appeared in the 1980s and grew in prominence through the late 1990s.[14] While not previously understood this way, it was the moment when technology use first became intertwined with the three conflicting logics of schooling, which had long fueled gatekeeping in public education.[15] In the early 1980s, an unusual combination of public officials, corporate executives, vendors, policy makers, and parents together advocated for a robust digital infrastructure and increased technology use in public schools.[16] Their interests were not all the same. Businesses sought profit by selling equipment and software and expanding their consumer base. Public officials hoped technological access could solve difficult social problems. Educational reformers wanted to bring new practices into schools. And both policy makers and parents argued that children should not be left behind because future jobs would require of students "technological knowledge and skills and . . . a far more demanding workplace than their parents faced."[17] Despite their competing goals, these arguments suggested that increasing access could solve all problems—merging the competing goals of democratic equality, social efficiency, and social mobility into one simple formulation: bridge the digital divide.[18]

Scholars then and now criticize this idea as both contradictory and overly simplistic. By focusing narrowly on access as a quick fix for more complex problems, interest groups across the political spectrum stopped paying attention to the inequality caused by other structural forces.[19] Emphasizing access also followed historical patterns wherein policy makers or private companies suggest "easy" technological fixes (including the use of the calculator, the radio, cable television) to address much deeper issues of educational equity. As technology historian Jennifer Light and others argue, while it may be "comforting to imagine that the diffusion and use of a particular technology will remedy complex social problems," these problems have deeper fundamental causes.[20]

Others further argue that concerns about students having access to individual machines (e.g., laptops) was, in fact, a social problem created by the tech industry. As Joy Lisi Rankin describes in her 2018 book *A People's History of Computing in the United States*, the dilemma of individual access was produced by industry in the 1980s. In the decades before, computing was a shared endeavor. While limited in number, in early computing, K-12 schools and universities participated in a networked form of "time-sharing" technologies that were "created for— and by—students and educators . . . as civilian, civic-minded projects."[21] Rankin explains:

> The developers of these systems viewed access to computing as a public good available to a collective body, whether that body consisted of a university, a school system, a state, or even a country. For the students and educators, sharing was a feature, not a bug, of the networks. By design, time-sharing networks accommodated multiple users, and multiple users meant possibilities for cooperation, inspiration, community, and communication. Personal computer purveyors and boosters later insisted on the superiority of personal machines. They celebrated not having to share a computer; rather, they praised the individual access of one person to one computer. Ultimately, in the Silicon Valley mythology, the personal computer became the hero, the liberator that freed users from the tyranny of the mainframe and the crush of corporate IBM."[22]

Ultimately, the design and marketing of personal computers encouraged the idea that access to technology serves the needs of the individual—which readily mapped onto the already well-established logic of *individual advantage* in schools. Technological competence could help individuals get ahead; sharing and cooperation (democratic equality) stood in the way of that goal. As individualized computing came to be the dominant paradigm within and beyond education, it prompted concerns about *individual access* and *individual advantage* through that access.

These ideas might seem compatible—if all individuals gain access, everyone wins! But the policy implications of viewing access as a public good versus something for individual competition are quite different. When individualized, access can be privatized, which is precisely what happened in the United States.[23] During the 1990s, the US government adopted the goal of universal internet access, but rather than treating it as a public utility, corporations were given control of its provision.[24] Early reports showed that whites were more likely to have internet access, even when controlling for socioeconomic background.[25] Even as the use of technology has expanded since the beginning of the twenty-first century, studies continue to show gaps in access by race, class, and language background.[26] Indeed, a 2015 study found that Black and Latinx internet access was still lower than whites'.[27] Most recently, as the country shifted to online learning during the COVID-19 pandemic, digital inequality scholars, policy advocates, and news media made clear that the lack of universal access to reliable technological infrastructure persists and continues to threaten full participation in social institutions, from schooling to politics.[28]

THE SECOND-LEVEL DIGITAL DIVIDE

As noted in the introduction, as access increased in the first decade of the twenty-first century, digital inequality scholars identified a new level of the digital divide: differences in technology use that are shaped by and contribute to inequality.[29] Research on the second-level divide explores how inequality persists after access is addressed, by investigating why some people are better at using technology than others. What could explain differences in tech use? The primary answer digital inequality scholars have landed on is disparities in people's skills and literacies. But they haven't been able to agree on the definition of *technological competence*, especially as technologies change. So, over the past twenty years researchers have tried to identify and measure the skills and literacies that comprise technological competence—and document the benefits these skills and literacies provide. The list continues to grow, with early definitions including new media literacies; information, media, and technology skills; computer, information, multimedia, and computer mediated communication literacies; "participatory culture" skill; Web 2.0 skill; operational, information, and strategic skill; computer skill; web use skill; and internet skill.[30] Scholarship concerning the second-level divide shows that better skills, literacies, and technology use are associated with a range of benefits, such as access to health information, teachers' inflated perception of students' academic skill, and increased earnings.[31]

Further, scholars of the second-level divide argue that disparities in skills and literacies are the result of unequal experiences with technology education.[32] This disparity can be a result of structural barriers, whereby some schools can afford to hire and effectively utilize technology teachers, whereas others cannot. Or, technology classes get taken over by other priorities, such as standardized testing. For example, in *Stuck in the Shallow End*, Jane Margolis and colleagues showed that even when underresourced predominantly Black schools try to offer technology courses, schools are pushed to focus on standardized testing.[33] But even when schools successfully provide technology courses, there are inequities in enrollment, especially in advanced courses. Margolis and colleagues also showed that even in higher-resourced schools, Black students are systematically marginalized in computer science.[34] Similarly, in *Unlocking the Clubhouse*, Margolis and coauthor Allan Fisher (then associate dean for undergraduate education in the School of Computer Science at Carnegie Mellon) showed that women are systematically disadvantaged in undergraduate computer science because introductory courses advantage male students' early exposure.[35] More recent research shows surprisingly little change.[36]

What all this research suggests is that technological competence and technology education matter for an equitable society. But it misses the critical issue of technological change identified by the top-down approach: digital inequality research has not yet investigated how people become and remain technologically competent. As technology changes, individuals must continually learn and adapt to maintain or expand their skills and literacies. Early research on the second level divide noted this challenge—that defining and measuring competence would be difficult, given technology's changing nature.[37] Consequently, researchers adopted proxy measures such as education level—which is problematic because it does not directly measure learning.[38] Some have tried to address this problem by updating measures of skills and litera-cies to reflect technological change.[39] While helpful, this modification still fails to capture the technology learning process and how individuals learn something new. Being skillful with PowerPoint, for example, may not help someone learn to code.

This omission is a significant gap in second-level digital divide research because, like the top-down approach, both bodies of research suggest that inequality in the digital age hinges on the ability to adapt, but they fail to define and directly measure how people learn. Educa-tional interventions then can exacerbate preexisting differences by fail-ing to support students in their learning process—for example, by add-ing new computer science high school graduation requirements without addressing students' readiness for technology learning.[40] Conversely, without a definition and measure of the ability to learn new technol-ogies, technological competence may be unfairly underestimated, similar to how academic skills are often underestimated by race.[41] The challenge is to separate adaptability from other factors that might shape inequality, such as racial or gender biases pushing marginal-ized groups out of technology-related pathways—a challenge taken up here.[42]

The third-level digital divide is about results. Once we have achieved equal access for all, and once everyone is technologically competent, is the reward for technology use still unequal?[43] In other words, this research seeks to understand: Do people reap the same reward for their talent? And, if not, why not? This work so far shows that more-advantaged groups reap greater reward. For example, studies of internet use show that users who have similar access and skill do not have the same returns on their internet use.[44] People who start off with more advantage reap greater financial, governmental, and educational rewards from technology use than those who are less advantaged, suggesting that technology can amplify preexisting forms of inequality. In summary, then, research at the first-, second-, and third-level digital divides shows that social stratification shapes all three divides: more-advantaged groups are better equipped to gain access, develop skills and literacies, and reap benefits from their technology use.

Yet, a major flaw at all levels of digital inequality research is that it largely suggests the fix is to change disadvantaged groups. The idea is to give the "less privileged" more access to technology, make them more competent, and show them how to reap greater reward. But as some scholars doing research on the second- and third- level divides show, it is the gatekeepers who are the problem; they shape the differences in the ability to access technology education and reap rewards. Entire occupational fields or individual organizations, for example, can frame technology uses as more or less valued and match activities to status groups. They are the ones who, for example, perceive coding as "administrative" when done by women, but "technical" when done by men.[45]

The same happens in schools. In a comparative study of three technology-rich middle schools in California, Matthew H. Rafalow shows that organizations value equally skilled students' technology use in different ways, depending on their racial and socioeconomic background. This disparity in perceived value ultimately shapes whether students' skill translates into reward. One school serving predominantly lower-income Latinx students framed technology use as irrelevant, while another serving middle-class Asian students viewed technology use as risky, and a third serving primarily wealthy white students framed technology use as essential to success. While students in all three schools were skillful and used technology in similar ways, the benefits of access and skill translated in disparate ways depending on the social and organizational context.[46]

Furthermore, this research and other studies show that gatekeeping matters in terms of not just the beneficial development and use of technology but also the harmful use of technology. Exclusionary organizations can create technologies that surveil, control, discipline, punish, or ignore groups marginalized in tech fields. For example, Safiya Umoja Noble explains that Google algorithms mirror deeply embedded societal racism by presenting racist tropes in search results that reinforce and substantiate systems of power.[47] In fact, early search results for the query "Black girls" brought up hypersexualized and pornographic images. Other studies show that facial recognition software, often trained on white male faces, misidentifies female and darker-skinned users—making everything from automated entry into housing and automated policing more prone to error.[48] In other words, unequal power relations are often embedded in the conceptualization, design, and use of technologies that intersect with and exacerbate preexisting inequities. Therefore, we need to cultivate and support innovators who draw from a wider range of experience to inform their designs, who can push back against these biases. More equitable access to technological fields and occupations matters for the democratic design of our technological futures.

FOCUSING ON THE GREATER GOOD

Overall, digital inequality research shows that the three levels of the digital divide are shaped by and continue to shape inequality in the digital age. We should care about unequal technology access, competence, and technological benefits because they quietly apportion power and social control in vastly unequal ways. If, as the logic of democratic equality suggests, a common set of broad competencies in a nation's citizenry is necessary for full participation in a democracy, then technological competence is needed to ensure equitable engagement in an increasingly technological world—and a focus on equalizing its development and recognition is necessary.[49] The next logical question is: How?

To answer this question, this book investigates better ways of understanding and supporting technological competence and equitably recognizing and rewarding ability. Overall my research shows that some groups could use more support—in particular, girls, like Maria, Meihong, and Cindy. But I also do not observe any class- or race-based differences in students' technology learning habits. These students do not need to be "fixed," as a large body of research might suggest. Instead, it is the *perceptions* of these groups and the meaning of technological competence that need to be changed in order to better see their capabilities, as well as the engines that fuel gatekeeping. That's a different take than digital inequality research that primarily argues their marginalization is because of their own deficits. But, it would be impossible to know where the problem lies without identifying and measuring how individuals develop new skill and adapt to technological change—and how gatekeeping systematically excludes perfectly competent people from technological futures—which is exactly what this book addresses.

ALTERNATE LOGICS: FOR MARKETS AND INDIVIDUALS

We've established that technology learning matters *for society*. But before launching into the rest of the book, it's worth understanding the two alternate arguments used to make the case for the importance of technology learning because these competing logics are actually what fuels gatekeeping. As noted earlier in this chapter, the idea that technology learning can serve the *needs of markets* and help *individuals get ahead* have often been confused with and embedded in arguments about *the greater good*. They will likely sound familiar and can be difficult to pull apart, given the common practice of combining these alternate visions with arguments about equity. Policy makers seeking funding for technology in schools, for example, will often combine these threads in ways that make them seem compatible.[50] They say things like, "To make the US more competitive in the global economy and to help students compete in the labor market, schools need to develop students' twenty-first-century skills." But the logics of *serving the needs of markets* and *for individual advantage* ultimately rely on competition and stratification, which work against the goal of equity. Their continued dominance, particularly the logic of *individual advantage*, is why digital inequality persists.

For Markets

The first of these two alternate perspectives focuses on how to keep the country competitive in the global economy, a stance which commonly suggests that a benefit to private companies via skilled labor and consumption is the same as public benefit. This perspective asks, "How does technological learning help meet the needs of private industry?" It echoes and expands on the idea that the country's "economic well-being depends on our ability to prepare the young to carry out useful economic roles with competence."[51] Wouldn't a technologically competent workforce help create a strong economy, with skilled workers and ready consumers, and therefore benefit the greater good? On the surface, it might seem so. But in the end, this perspective focuses on the benefit to industry, not society, and views learning as a "public good in service to the private sector."[52] The private sector, though, relies on inequality whereby certain groups of people are funneled into low-wage jobs and others into high-wage jobs, to the benefit of industry, not everyone. Sure, the country's finances may get better, but this improvement does not mean workers will profit; inequality between the rich and poor has only expanded in the United States, even during recent economic booms.[53]

Educational policies often reflect this market logic. For example, the 1983 report *A Nation at Risk* proclaimed that the United States, with its "once unchallenged preeminence in commerce, industry, science, and technological innovation," was at risk of "being overtaken by competitors throughout the world."[54] More recently, a 2007 report by the National Research Council, *Rising above the Gathering Storm: Energizing and Employing America for a Brighter Economic Future*, argued that economic "vitality" in the United States is "derived in large part from the productivity of well-trained people and the steady stream of innovations they produce." To keep a competitive edge, the United States must "optimiz[e] its knowledge-based resources, particularly in science and technology, and . . . [sustain] the most fertile environment for new and revitalized industries and the well-paying jobs they bring."[55]

Researchers and policy makers often use this justification—some citing these reports—to argue for a greater focus on STEM and to rationalize costly technological investments. The idea is that emphasizing technological skills in schools will help historically marginalized groups by moving them from lower-skill, lower-wage jobs into higher-skill, higher-wage jobs—rather than importing higher-skilled workers from other countries.[56] This notion combines and confuses arguments about technology learning for the public good with arguments for the private *benefit of markets* and for *individual advantage* (described in the next section), suggesting that all interests can point in the same direction.[57] It might seem as though increasing STEM learning will benefit all of us—but it is unclear exactly how being more competitive economically provides broad social benefits when this competition still relies on a large pool of low-wage labor.

The perspective of markets instead relies on not everyone developing technological skill; only some people should be technologically competent, while others should work in other fields and in lower-status positions to meet all market demands. The market perspective would say that to keep the United States competitive, we must fill the job skills that employers need and increase consumption. Applied to technology education, this perspective ultimately assumes stratified learning for a stratified society. For everyone to be equally skillful would run counter to how free market capitalism works, where "the pursuit of competitive advantage is the driving force behind economic behavior."[58] Policy makers and researchers have for decades used the social efficiency perspective to argue for more funding for technology learning to address the exclusion of groups historically marginalized in STEM, but this claim rests on contradictory premises.[59]

On the one hand, we need technologically skilled labor to support the economy. On the other hand, there are only so many skilled positions to fill—although there's a current demand, that does not mean this demand will always be there or that there are STEM jobs for everyone.[60] Social efficiency's fundamental position is that only those best "suited" for these roles undertake them; that we invest only in technology learning for those with the best fit. In other words, there should be inequality. Maybe funneling people into different roles is acceptable, but then how do we select who is best suited to do particular jobs, especially as things change and "competence" is a moving target? And, how can we ensure that individuals don't game the system to their benefit, even if they are not best suited for the work—to ensure true "meritocracy"?[61]

This was the challenge faced by companies that needed to identify "good" potential programmers during the mid-twentieth century. In line with the social efficiency perspective, employers developed a suite of ostensibly "objective" aptitude tests and psychological profiles to screen large numbers of applicants.[62] These tests and profiles filtered for "innate" cognitive and personality traits "thought essential to good programming, such as the ability to think logically and do abstract reasoning."[63] The tests and profiles "embod[ied] and privilege[d] masculine characteristics," particularly items measuring mathematical ability that in the 1950s and 1960s required coursework largely unavailable to women and racial and ethnic minorities, despite the fact that women had been at the forefront of computing during World War II and in spite of a growing industry consensus that mathematical training was irrelevant to most commercial programming tasks.[64] Personality profiles also "reinforced the ideal of the 'detached' (read male) programmer."[65]

This legacy of the social efficiency perspective, whereby advantaged male bodies were systematically linked to technology-related fields while others were excluded on the basis of "scientific" measures, continues to this day.[66] As computing historian Nathan Ensmenger explains in *The Computer Boys Take Over*:

> The primary selection mechanism used by the industry selected for antisocial, mathematically inclined males, and therefore antisocial, mathematically inclined males were overrepresented in the programmer population; this in turn reinforced the popular perception that programmers *ought* to be antisocial and mathematically inclined (and therefore male), and so on ad infinitum. . . . This bias toward male programmers was not so much deliberate as it was convenient—a combination of laziness, ambiguity, and traditional male privilege. The fact that the use of lazy screening practices inadvertently excluded large numbers of potential *female* trainees was simply never considered. But the increasing assumption that the average programmer was also male did play a key role in the establishment of a highly masculine programming subculture.[67]

While at the time and later recognized as highly flawed, these tests helped reduce uncertainty for gatekeepers, promising "at least the illusion of managerial control."[68] Once these sorting mechanisms for social efficiency were established, technology fields and occupations grew more exclusionary than ever.[69] Indeed, the inequities we see in tech today fully support the idea that technology learning should meet the demands of the market, thus sorting and arranging people into social hierarchies. I had hoped with my teaching to address this issue, even in a small way, to help move historically marginalized groups into high-skill positions—but even training a select few for coveted jobs still assumes a fundamental inequality wherein many are left behind.

For Individuals

When we think about any kind of learning, it is commonly understood as a means *for individual advantage*.[70] To ask, for example, "What will earning a high school diploma versus graduating from college mean for where I end up in life?" This idea is what education scholars call a "social mobility" perspective. It suggests that education is a "commodity, whose only purpose is to provide individuals . . . with a competitive advantage in the struggle for desirable social positions."[71] The same could be said for technology learning—arguments are often made that technological skill development can move people ahead in life. Indeed, research in STEM education suggests as much: early experiences and skill development help students' pathways into these fields. As a technology teacher, I thought the *individual advantage* perspective made sense: technology classes could encourage my students to enroll in future technology classes (if offered) and prepare them for college technology courses, becoming majors in technology fields, and pursuing higher-skill, higher-wage technology jobs.[72] I wanted my students to get ahead, which technology pathways might help them achieve.

Yet, this perspective does something most people do not think about—something I did not realize as a tech teacher. It also assumes individual competition that, like the perspective of markets, must result in an unequal outcome. Could getting ahead help my students? Sure, if nothing blocked or pushed them out along the way. But unfortunately, research shows that women and historically marginalized students are systematically discouraged from entry and persistence in tech.[73] Advantaged groups, particularly those already dominant in particular educational and occupational fields, will always be better positioned—even before they are born—to win this competition. They can signal their "fit" to gatekeepers with little effort. They can also shift their attention to whatever educational experiences and jobs are considered "prized" at a given historical moment, which makes competition sharper and more difficult for those starting with any form of disadvantage. And, at this historical moment—though it hasn't always been this way—the prize is tech.

Affluent students and their families already know that many jobs in tech fields are well rewarded and have positioned themselves for fiercer competition. For example, in 2014, almost 25 percent of Stanford graduates said they planned to work in tech.[74] The reasoning behind this?

Tech jobs now afford status and financial stability.[75] You don't always have to go to an elite school to acquire a tech job; Silicon Valley companies do hire from less elite local institutions, such as San Jose State University.[76] But, as the prestige of a field increases, what often occurs is what's known as the "elevator effect," whereby requirements to secure positions increase, advantaging those already better poised in educational and occupational markets.[77] In tech-related fields, this upward movement has been a relatively recent phenomenon, constructed over time and *with intention* to professionalize the field and, in doing so, match certain bodies (white, Asian, male) to what are now but have not always been viewed as higher-status positions.[78] In such a competition, those already in the lead often win the race.

The dominant perspective that learning and education are *for individual advantage* is highly problematic—and this is a common perspective even among those hoping to create equity in technology education and occupational fields. When individual benefit is emphasized, it heightens competition for resources and increases the perception of their value. Labaree argues that as a result of a focus on social mobility in education, schooling "has increasingly come to be perceived as a private good that is harnessed to the pursuit of personal advantage; and on the whole, the consequences of this for both school and society have been profoundly negative."[79] Competition ultimately creates barriers for those who are already disadvantaged, leaving out and devaluing the skill of disadvantaged groups while at the same time offering the illusion of an open playing field.

These alternate logics, I now understand, fuel gatekeeping and are the opposite of what I'd hoped for my students. Given these competitive dynamics, applying the logic of *individual advantage* to technology learning means that even when women or historically marginalized groups are technologically competent, they are at a disadvantage—and that those in advantaged positions will continue to "win" the competition. While wanting my students to get ahead, accepting this logic ultimately means that some kids win and others lose, and not on their merits. This way of thinking also undermines the collective benefit of having a more technologically competent citizenry.

For these reasons, I emphasize the first perspective on the importance of technology learning *for society*. This perspective takes the position that everyone should develop some level of technological competence and that it should be equitably rewarded. In other words, how we end digital inequality is not to "fix" those left out but to stop the engines of inequality that keep them out. Think about it like this: Why insist that everyone should know how to read? It's not just for the benefit of employers or individuals but because we understand that democracy requires equality of "democratic agency" and that agency includes a common set of broad competencies.[80] Should technological competence be included? As the 2020 pandemic made strikingly clear, technology is indeed central to how our society functions, including how children are educated, the ways we work, how we socialize, how we participate in politics, and so many other facets of life. It is easy to see that technological competence is a part of democratic agency in the twenty-first century and matters *for the greater good*.

WHY HABITS?

You might wonder, with an emphasis on broad social equity, why focus on *habits*? It might seem like zeroing in on habits reverts back to the idea that to address digital inequality, educators need to "fix" people. Or, you might wonder why examine habits when second-level divide research already identified other aspects of technological competence (skills and literacies). The first reason is practice- and policy-oriented. While digital inequality research thus far has been helpful, it has not accounted for technological change. Because new technologies demand new skill sets, technology learning habits are critical for adapting to this change. These habits, which support the acquisition of skills and literacies, compose a key unstudied dimension of technological competence. Therefore, this book can help educators focus on a core aspect of competence—necessary for all members of a changing, and equitable, digital world.

When I began to identify and measure the habits I describe in the next two chapters, I drew on research in learning and cognition. Studies in these areas show that observing expert learners can reveal important information about how people develop their skill and knowledge. Expert learners "display planfulness, control, and reflection; are aware of the knowledge and skills they possess, or are lacking, and use appropriate strategies to actively implement or acquire them."[81] They can articulate what helps them learn. I identified these learners through their participation in the award-winning technology programs I introduce in the next section, observing and interviewing them to understand what helps in the learning process.[82]

The second reason I focus on habits is to reorient how we think about who is "naturally" gifted in tech to help address systemic racism, classism, and sexism in this field. Reinterpreting technological "instinct" as learning habits and systematically identifying and describing these habits unmasks the process of technological knowledge production, including what scientists and technologists do and, especially, how they become skilled. Rather than being the result of "natural" ability, technological competence is an accomplishment gained by habits that are learned and practiced. But, in order for these habits to convert into benefits, they have to be seen. Indeed, social theorists from Thorstein Veblen to Max Weber to W. E. B. Du Bois to Pierre Bourdieu argued that examining habits can reveal not only how and why individuals and groups behave the way they do but also how society—and inequality— functions.[83] So, throughout the book I argue that a redefinition of technological competence as skills, literacies, *and habit*s is fundamentally political, not only to identify students in need of support but also to ascertain which students have gone unrecognized due to biases about who has good tech instinct.

The purpose of identifying and describing these habits is to make them visible—and to make these abilities seen by both gatekeepers and technology learners in themselves. Stereotypes can suggest technological incompetence, even when a person might have great potential. Many observers believe that tech geeks are male, nerdy, introverted— but this idea may not be the case at all. These stereotypes can make women and historically marginalized groups feel like they have less competence because they don't fit the mold.[84] This book pushes against this bias by showing what it is that tech-savvy people actually do—and how continual learning is central to what they do. To teach these habits and equally reward them will help develop a technologically competent citizenry who can use and create new technologies to help contend with the broad challenges we face in the digital age, to all our benefit.

WHOSE HABITS?

You might think that the best way to understand expert technology learners' habits would be to study professional people in tech fields. But, we can learn more by looking at *everyone* who is tech savvy, not just those currently overrepresented in tech fields.[85] Taking a broader look can help us disentangle successful technology learning habits from class-, race-, and gender-biased styles of learning. Doing so also means believing that marginalized groups are capable and that there is much to learn about technological expertise from them. Prior to engaging in this research project, it meant starting with the simple assumption that tech-savvy Black, Latinx, Native American, female, and low-income teens *exist*.

Certainly, listening to arguments about the digital divide or look-ing at the face of the tech industry might suggest there's a "pipeline" or "supply" problem whereby these groups are "underrepresented" in tech fields because they lack the skills to enter. This rhetoric can easily lead to the assumption that these groups are underprepared and lack technological competence and therefore would be inappropriate for this study. But groups currently not well represented in STEM are better understood as *historically marginalized*, erased from typical narratives about STEM and systematically *pushed out* of pipelines, their potential going unrecognized.[86] This means that instead of needing to fix kids, the challenge is to fix the lens through which potential and technological expertise is understood.

Like fireflies hiding in plain sight whose glory you can only see when looking carefully—in certain places and at certain times—tech-savvy girls and historically marginalized teens are scattered all across the country, participating in tech programs, flashing their brilliance. How did I know where to look? By using a broader definition of *technology-related* programs to include *all* forms of creative technology learning under the more inclusive STEAM umbrella (adding an *A* for the arts), it was easy to find many programs that attract diverse talent.[87] In these programs are Black, Latinx, Native American, female, and low-income students—and, to a lesser extent, white and Asian students—who, contrary to the stereotypes, are excited and curious about technology learning.[88] To know what helps *all* tech-savvy teens learn, I sampled just ten of many programs that occur after school, during the summer, and some during school, all across the United States.[89]

More specifically, I visited five programs in the San Francisco Bay Area, three in Chicago, one in New York City, and one cooccurring in Chicago and New York. Programs varied in their structure: most had formal projects and attendance policies, but a few others operated on a drop-in basis. In all programs, technology education was a primary focus (e.g., learning how to build computers) or secondary focus (e.g., learning Second Life software to simulate an archaeological dig), delivered in person and online. Many of the organizations offered programs in multiple formats (e.g., during school, after school, summer). The Methods Appendix at the back of this book provides greater detail about how I identified programs and collected data. The following is a brief summary of the programs in the formats I observed them.

DURING AND AFTER SCHOOL:
- Mouse Squad California (MSCA; Bay Area): Technology program for fourth through twelfth grades, offered through a partnership with various schools and out-of-school providers. Workshops involved a range of technology activities, including

computer building and maintenance, information technology (IT) networking, visual and audio production, web design, and gaming. Workshops met in schools and out-of-school spaces.

- Digital Youth Network (DYN) at YOUmedia (Chicago): Audio and video production workshops for high school students provided by DYN, a digital technology–based youth development program that includes activities in school, outside school, and in an online space called Remix World. Workshops met at the Harold Washington Public Library just south of the "Loop" downtown.
- WhyReef at the Field Museum (Chicago): Named for the museum's simulated coral reef, program composed of biology and ecology workshops for younger teens (generally sixth through eighth grades) created as part of an effort to understand and advocate for aquatic ecosystem conservation and restoration. Workshops met at the museum and involved hands-on in-person experiences (e.g., scientist visits) and virtual experiences (WhyReef).
- Bay Area Video Coalition (BAVC; pronounced "Bay-Vac") Next Gen Digital Pathways video production (Bay Area): Ten-month introductory video production workshops for high school students. Workshops focused on in-depth media projects and met at BAVC in the San Francisco Mission District.
- BAVC Next Gen Digital Pathways game design (Bay Area): Ten-month introductory workshops for high school students involving the creation of digital video games. Workshops met at BAVC and other San Francisco locations.
- BAVC Next Gen Bay Unity Music Project (BUMP) Records (Bay Area): Advanced music performance and production program for Bay Area youth ages fourteen through nineteen. Workshops included composition, DJing, and producing original music using "industry-standard" technologies, as well as

training in branding and promoting albums. Workshops met at a studio in downtown Oakland.

- Youth Movement Records (YMR; Bay Area): Audio and video production program for youth ages thirteen through nineteen. Program organized as participation in a music company, with all-company meetings. Workshops focused on long-term student-led projects and training in entrepreneurship and were conducted in the Fox Theater building at the Oakland School for the Arts.
- Radio Arte (Chicago): Radio production training program for teens and young adults. Workshops involved producing radio segments to be aired on the youth-run bilingual (Spanish/ English) radio station in the predominantly Latinx neighborhood of Pilsen.
- I Dig Zambia (Chicago and New York City): Multisited program focused on archaeology, global leadership, and civic engagement for high school teens. Workshops involved hands-on in-person experiences (e.g., museum visits) and virtual experiences (using Second Life) and met at the Field Museum in Chicago and the Global Kids (GK) office in Manhattan.
- Mouse/Geek Squad Summer Academy (New York City): Technology program for younger teens (sixth through eighth grades), offered through a partnership between Mouse and Best Buy's Geek Squad. Workshops engaged students in computer building, IT networking, visual and audio production, web design, and gaming. Workshops met aboard the USS *Intrepid*, location of the Sea, Air, and Space Museum on the Hudson River.

Students in these programs didn't fit obvious stereotypes or reflect the demographics of tech, but they were equally passionate about it.

Take, for example, Christine (not her real name), an African American Skyline High School student who, when I met her, had participated in BUMP Records for two years.[90] Smiling enthusiastically, Christine said the program helped her develop technological skills, like "mixing and mastering." She had become so skilled she said she could easily fix songs if they "sound[ed] a little flat" and "touch [them] up with a couple buttons." She started with no experience, yet with the mentorship of a professional music producer at BUMP who taught her how to use the audio production software ProTools, when I met her she proudly explained she could now develop her own musical tracks. She came to understand technical skill and software as essential tools, she said, "important for all beat makers, writers. It's like typing—it's a *must* do. You do it over and over again until you get good at it." Although not stereotypically tech savvy, Christine was excited, deeply engaged, and highly skilled at technological activities—and tech learning.

Overall, I observed and/or interviewed 111 teens, or about 11 per program. Nine programs served a small number (about 10) per session. Mouse/Geek Squad Summer Academy served about 100 teens, organized into smaller cohorts of 10 to 15 students meeting together in the morning, lunch, afternoon break, and the program's end. There, I followed one cohort identified by program directors. Programs served a range of teens in terms of racial/ethnic background, socioeconomic status, home language background, and ages. The group of teens I followed was roughly gender balanced, with about 40 percent Latinx, 30 percent Black, 18 percent white, 10 percent Asian, and 2 percent Native American. I oversampled students whose home languages were something other than English (about 35 percent) to take into account English proficiency. What this means is the habits I describe in the upcoming chapters are not based on groups overrepresented in tech in most industrialized countries today. Instead, they describe what helps a broader range of tech-savvy teens develop technological competence.

Carefully watching and listening to the teens in these programs, I looked for (1) moments when students learned technologies that were new to them or used technologies in new ways; (2) instances where students encountered difficulties and how they responded; and (3) expressions of how they felt about the learning process (happiness, frustration). For example, at Mouse/Geek Squad Summer Academy, I observed Julia, an Asian female who was asked by an instructor to do a task she had never done before: identify why a computer would not start. I watched and videotaped what she did (laughed, persisted, and failed to identify the problem but appeared to enjoy and learn from the experience). Immediately afterward, I asked what helped her in that process. Wherever possible, I videotaped activities for later analysis and in short interviews asked questions about program activities. In longer interviews, I asked for more detailed information about what helped students learn in the program and in other contexts. I then scoured my notes for the learning habits (behaviors, thoughts, and feelings) that helped these diverse teens learn new technologies.

For example, in my visit to MSCA at Campbell Middle School I met a tech-savvy Latinx eighth grader named Miguel who had been in the school's Mouse Squad through most of middle school.[91] What had he done with technology? He said he fixed programs by rebooting them, worked on operating systems, and was "good with video." Where did this interest in technology start? "My parents stuck me on a computer pretty young and then in sixth grade we had a computer class, and then in the seventh grade I did TV production, and now [video production]." What was he learning when I visited? How to use Movie Maker to create a video about baseball. What was his favorite thing to do with computers? "Fixing programs! It's interesting and seems like a good use of my time—it's like a puzzle." What about when he encounters problems?

MIGUEL: In the seventh grade, I had to fix tons of mistakes with something I was making in iMovie. I screwed up so much, so I had to redo the audio, video, and remix it. What helped was [keeping at it] and screwing around until I fixed it. I focus on one thing at a time and try to learn more about the background of the problem. I'll say to myself, "Okay, if I look under File, are there any options there that might help me?"

CASSIDY: That sounds very systematic!

MIGUEL (laughing): You could say that. I would say "screwing around."

Did he think he'd work with computers in the future? "No," he said, "I think it would be a side job. Who knows? In my old age, I might make a hobby out of it."

I tried to conceal my sadness at this statement—perhaps he didn't quite see his potential and understand how remarkable his skills were, despite his teacher saying he was one of the tech-savviest in the squad. More hopefully, maybe he was being humble about his skill. But the exchange made me wonder: Would his aspirations be different if his potential were clearer to him and clearer to gatekeepers beyond his school, in high school, college, and the broader world? What if they would see, cultivate, and equitably value his technology learning habits?

THE FIVE HABITS

This diverse group of teens, just a small sample of many teens across the country, helped me understand what supports their learning process and (as Cindy described) to "not give up." As I observed these programs, I heard about and noticed teens using a similar set of habits— the same thoughts, feelings, and actions—over and over again. These habits formed the basis of their technological competence; they were the tools they used to get better at the things they loved. The habits were the reason that even in challenging moments they could continue to learn. Although some teens started out with a primary interest in technology, most were like Christine: they had a passion (in her case, singing) but found they could live up to their potential by developing technological skills. It was their passion that led them into these programs, where they developed their technology learning habits. So, what are the habits?

Let's get to them.

[2]

What Helps People Learn

THREE GENERAL TECHNOLOGY LEARNING HABITS

> I didn't start out a "tech" person. But now I have all kinds
> of tricks.
>
> Christine, teen at BUMP Records

At the Bay Area Video Coalition's Bay Unity Music Project (BUMP) Records, I sit in a small recording studio listening to Christine—a student who has been in the program for two years and whom instructors have identified as particularly tech savvy. She tells me about her experiences; it's been exciting but challenging to learn new technologies and improve her audio production skills. She explains:

> You get thrown in, you have to force yourself to learn to record your own music. If you make a mistake, you learn to hear that. They teach you the business, how to know your own work and understand all aspects of the industry. It's a great program for musicians of any sort. The networking that happens; I never would've met these talented people. And, I'm a really independent person. They showed me how to open up and take critique. At first I was scared to record; I really didn't

like hearing myself. Had to put myself out there—and then, just like anything else, you gotta work at it.

Christine thinks for a moment and adds that what pushes her forward is trying to realize her goals. She says, "If I'm passionate about it—if I love it—music, whatever I have to do to get it, I will. If I have the drive [to start] . . . really, it's about passion, not even using technology. But what you can get with the technology is amazing."

Not quite sure what I'm looking for, I ask for more specifics. What does she do when she's learning? She says what really helps her is trying "different things." Thinking about what it is that she does, she searches for words to explain her learning process:

> [I try] different things; my drive to do it keeps me there. If I look around me at other people who are better, I try to think "They're good at this . . . but I'm good at that" rather than "I'm not good at this." Then you can exchange [with that person] what you're good at. After you get through the challenge, you feel so accomplished. Part of it is building confidence. One thing that I wasn't confident about was being in a cypher [a group of rappers in a circle performing for each other].[1] Being female should have nothing to do with it [but few women participate]. Now I can hop in and just spit it.

Maybe she was already somewhat "techie" before the program? She smiles and laughs:

> I didn't even know how to burn a CD! I was scared to do it. I had hardly any access to technology at home. All I had was my Sidekick [cell phone]. I'd type in lots of lyrics in there and email it to myself and print it out. . . .
> *I didn't start out a "tech" person. . . . But now I have all kinds of tricks.* [When recording], in the studio, I turn on the music loud with a pen and paper in one hand, lyrics in the other. I try to have someone in the studio recording, and an iPod to change up what you're listening

to. I walk back and forth, and also try to hear what other people are doing [in the studio for inspiration], if it sounds good. And, I think when you're in the booth, you can record and then share with people around the world!

[When editing], there are all these layers. Something might be off. So, you can press "mute" to hear each layer. Sometimes your main and double might be off. Your main is singing or rapping, that's the heart of the song. Everything else is structured around that. Double is doing it over again with a different song—some thicker, some thinner. You press mute to see if the main or double is off. Sometimes when you record it, there's something that's not right. You can also do panning with the instruments in your right or left ear. Maybe it's not weighted evenly, so you have to adjust it.

Christine's words gave me pause—I could tell that I was on to something. It was not just passion, although certainly she had plenty. It was these *tricks*—the things Christine did, like listening to others' music, thinking about design and structure of the audio (as layers)—that helped her and many other tech-savvy teens not give up.

To make technology learning more explicit, observable, and teachable (as well as to counter the idea that being good with technology is a "natural" ability), in this chapter and the next chapter I describe the five technology learning habits—the "tricks" that Christine described. I identified these habits by observing and interviewing teens in the programs I introduced in chapter 1, whom I consider expert technology learners.[2] Whereas these teens are not experts in technological fields per se, they are learners who demonstrate an ability to persist through their engagement in award-winning technology curriculum. Research on learning shows learning habits can be (1) general and applied to any kind of learning, (2) domain-specific and helpful within a specific field, or (3) more narrowly "task-limited" and only helpful with discrete tasks, such as using a mnemonic to learn a musical scale ("every good boy deserves fudge" for EGBDF).[3] Understanding these research findings, I looked for general and domain-specific technology learning habits. Overall, I identified three general technology learning habits I describe in this chapter (*willingness to try and fail, management of frustration and boredom,* and *use of models*) and two domain-specific habits I describe in the next chapter (*design logic* and *efficiencies*).

The habits described in this chapter are not entirely new—previous research already identified these types of habits as important for all kinds of learning. So then why include them in this book? The reason is that these habits have never been previously identified as key to technology learning, and general learning habits can have technology-specific nuances. Like the literacy strategy "talking to the text," whereby learners keep track of what they are thinking as they try to comprehend something new, a learning habit may be helpful in English, science, and math but can look very different depending on the subject. There is also research that shows knowledge production can have general as well as specific characteristics for different disciplines and fields of study—learning habits can operate the same way.[4] Together, this unique combination of five learning habits add to the redefinition of what it means to be good with technology—based on the practices of a diverse group of tech-savvy teens.

"KEEP AN OPEN MIND"—WILLINGNESS TO TRY AND FAIL

New York City. Aboard the USS *Intrepid*, I follow a group of teens to the Mouse/Geek Squad Summer Academy. Laughing and playing, they run across the sunlit deck of the ship, weaving through and pointing out details on brightly painted airplanes lined up in rows around us. An African American male instructor with a Geek Squad T-shirt bellows, "Below deck!" and the teens scurry toward a small, darkened door. Inside, they are escorted into the depths of the ship, to two windowless rooms with gray flooring and whitewashed metal walls. It seems a bit strange to be in such a barren, windowless space in the middle of the bright freedom of summer, but the teens are energized to be there.

One of the larger rooms is the cafeteria, where video game stations are set up along rows of foldable cafeteria tables. Some girls cluster around a station with Guitar Hero and start to play. An instructor joins in. Isabella, a Puerto Rican girl with spiky brown hair, does well, hitting all the right notes in the right rhythm; it appears she's already an expert at this game. Yesenia, a Dominican girl wearing a bright yellow T-shirt, sits watching nearby and comments on Isabella's skill. After twenty minutes, the girls move on to another game and a group of boys takes over the Guitar Hero station. At another station close by, two African American girls are using Wii boxing, giggling as their hands punch the air. Everyone seems ready and willing to play; those sitting watching from the sidelines comment and laugh, waiting their turn.

At about 10:00 a.m. after an hour of free play, instructors gather groups together for the first morning session. I'm with a group called the "F-emails" (females), roughly a dozen middle-school-aged girls, whom I follow into a smaller room with empty desktop computer towers perched atop a set of white folding tables. Joe, a white male instructor with a buzz cut who led the workshop the previous day, stands over one table in the middle of the room and yells, "Welcome to PC Build!" He seems as excited as the group and enthusiastically calls out the names of various computer parts, reminding the girls of the previous day's activity, while holding up the parts for everyone to see. His arm pumps up and down as he draws the next component into the air and shouts, "Power supply! Screws! Motherboard!"

Then he tells the class to take the motherboard and insert it in the tower and lock it in place with the screws. Two other instructors move from table to table helping the girls identify which screws to use. Joe then calls, "Now, RAM [random-access memory]! Hold up your hard drive!" Yesenia, in the corner, makes a mistake by holding up the wrong part and Joe smiles at her. Teasing, he shouts, "*No!* You fail!" Kevin, an Asian male instructor standing near the back of the room, coaxes Joe, "What about a little *positive* reinforcement?!" Joe nods and smiles. He plugs small speakers into his laptop computer, turns up the volume, and plays hip-hop—his form of encouragement. He moves on, showing where and how to place the optical drive and modem.

I stand to the left side of the room, near two Dominican girls named

Jessie and Erika. I ask if they've ever put a computer together before this workshop and they shake their heads no. Jessie, dark hair expertly smoothed back into a tight bun, says, "It's faster than I thought. Easier." Next to us, Joe shouts to the group, "Plug in your drives! The USB [universal serial bus] is the big white one! The next one is the CPU [central processing unit] cable. It's a square! It gets plugged in right next to the processor!"[5] I hear a "bloop bloop" sound as Joe turns up the music on his computer, singing at the top of his lungs in a deep New York accent the words of a popular summer song, played throughout the week of the program:

> We fly high, no lie, you know this (ballin'!)
> Foreign rides outside, it's like showbiz (we in the building)
> We stay fly, no lie, you know this (ballin'!)

The girls laugh and call out the lyrics at the end of each phrase ("ballin'!!"). Some girls dance and most stand as they move around their tables, slowly building their computers.

Kevin sets up a computer and projector behind Joe with instructions, but it's difficult for some girls to see the wall with the projection now that almost everyone is standing—yet that doesn't seem to stop them from trying things out. Kevin then moves to work with Yesenia and Julia, an Asian girl with bright pink cheeks, as the duo finish building their computer. He tells the girls he's going to give them an extra challenge. He says to Julia, "Close your eyes!" She does and Kevin scurries around their computer trying to keep Julia from knowing what he's doing. After a few moments he quietly pulls out the power cord, smiling at Yesenia and calling to Julia, "Okay, open your eyes!" He explains to Julia that he changed "only one thing" and that she has to figure out what he did and fix it. Yesenia watches with a smile.

Julia looks over the computer, now open and flat on its side. As instructed earlier in the program, she starts by grounding herself with an antistatic wristband. She touches the edge of the case with one hand and inspects one side of the tower, carefully checking each component's placement and connections, working her way to the other side. She then tries to turn on the computer by pushing the power button. It fails. She checks the connections again, looks around the tower for missing pieces, then checks a one-page instruction sheet with a diagram that I now notice is on all of the tables next to a box of computer parts. She again systematically checks each piece. She tries powering up the computer. It does not hum to life. Yesenia giggles. Kevin smiles at Julia and asks, "Do you give up?" Julia shakes her head no. She goes back to inspecting all of the pieces of the computer, but Joe calls out that it's time to go. Julia looks at Kevin and he shrugs, "I unplugged it." All three start to laugh. Julia nods, understanding (and enjoying) the lesson, "Ahhhhhh!"

Sine Qua Non of (Technology) Learning

Watching Julia and all the girls in the room build their computers, it was clear they were ready and willing to jump in and try—again and again—regardless of whether or not they failed, no matter if they succeeded in the task in front of them or not. A simple attempt was a success. This behavioral pattern was the first habit I noticed and heard about in interviews, over and over again. What helped these teens learn technologies that were new to them was first being willing to try. Their excessive and celebratory willingness to plunge in, take risks, and fail defined them as technologically competent. It was the *sine qua non* ("without which, nothing"—i.e., the essential feature) of technology learning and helped teens self-identify as tech savvy: being willing to try technologies others might be unwilling to learn symbolically distinguished those who were more tech savvy from others.

This willingness to fail ties to several bodies of research on motivation and affect in learning, particularly research on what scholars call "self-efficacy." Albert Bandura defined *self-efficacy* as "the conviction that one can successfully execute the behavior required to produce the outcomes."[6] Research shows that self-efficacy (an estimate of potential success) is intertwined with a person's willingness to try things and often measure the two together.[7] My observations and interviews with teens seemed to suggest that their willingness to try and fail with technology was a distinctly pivotal aspect of their technology learning self-efficacy. For example, Alex at Radio Arte (a Latinx student who wore emo black, head to toe) said he joined the program because a teacher in his high school (Hubbard) encouraged him to "get a summer job" to give him something to do.[8] Alex said the job jumped out at him because he was interested in radio, but he had "no skills with sound editing." He explained that at first learning how to do sound editing was "intimidating," but he was willing to "play around with it." Circling back, he explained, "The main thing that was intimidating was just to start." He had to be willing to take that leap.

Stefani and Beatriz, also Latinx teens at Radio Arte, described a similar experience and used much of the same language as Alex. Stefani, who met my gaze through a set of thick black-rimmed glasses, said that when she started learning the audio editing software Audacity it was "intimidating," but she was willing to try. She kept close track of the purpose of all of the buttons, writing down notes as she learned new things so she could later remind herself of their functions. Beatriz, who earned a scholarship to attend the private Catholic St. Gregory High School on the Far North Side, explained that one of the key things that seemed to help her learn new technologies in the program was "keeping an open mind about learning something," even if she didn't do it very well at first.

This habit—*willingness to try and fail*—is central to technology learning because it is an ongoing practice.[9] Whereas *willingness to try and fail* is important for learning in general, because new technologies persistently replace old ones, continual learning and risk of failure is a regular feature rather than a once-in-a-while experience in tech.[10] In fact, the tech-savvy teens I interviewed said that failure is so much at the core of technology learning that even if they simply attempt to learn a technology or solve a problem, they *define the attempt as a success*. Therefore, being good with technology means that you expect and even get excited about engaging in failure—over and over again. Research shows that this type of "growth mindset" is a feature of learning in general but suggests it is an underlying rather than explicit belief that shapes learning.[11] Instead, in my observations and interviews I found that a *willingness to try and fail* is an explicit—and even celebrated—habit of tech-savvy teens.

Failing in a Safe Place

Of course, the willingness to try and fail is shaped by the learning context, where some contexts are more "responsive" to students than others.[12] In the programs I visited, instructors carefully crafted learning environments to help teens get beyond their initial level of intimidation, making it safe to fail. For example, at Youth Movement Records (YMR), a white male instructor named Chris treated his Pro Tools class like an open-ended investigation of that software, posing questions that encouraged students to "try" out their ideas, moving from simpler questions that students could identify by reading drop-down menu titles, to more difficult questions.

In the very first session of his class, Chris asked, "Does anyone want to *take a stab* at how to get tracks into your session?" Moving her mouse to the tabs she might use, Rae, an African American female teen who had announced her intention to learn Pro Tools in the first all-company meeting, guessed, "Tracks>Add Tracks?" Smiling at her, Chris laughed, "I love people who can read!" He asked another question and again Rae was ready to try out some ideas.

> CHRIS: What do we do with a MIDI track?
> RAE: Use instruments?
> CHRIS: A special kind.
> RAE: Keyboard?
> CHRIS: There's no sound generated by the keyboard; it's coming out of the computer.

RAE: So, MIDI is an electronic instrument?

CHRIS: Yes, I like that.

Later, when Chris recapped the class, he asked about the function of several parts of Pro Tools—and again multiple students tried out ideas.

CHRIS: What do we do with [the] mix [window]?

MICHAEL (African American male sitting near Chris): Blending instruments.

CHRIS: What do we do in the edit window?

FATIMA (African American female next to Chris): Delete, rearrange, shorten, make longer.

MICHAEL: Remaster the track?

CHRIS: No, that's more mixing, blending. I always ask this in the first class, but there's no way [for you] to know because we haven't done anything, just want to see how you think.

By asking questions, Chris encouraged teens to "take a stab" and practice *willingness to try and fail,* and explicitly said the answer was not something they should know "because we haven't done anything." He told students he wanted to understand "how you think" when learning something new, and they should reflect on that, too. By the end of the class, like Rae, Michael, and Fatima, everyone practiced trying out their ideas at least once and was willing to learn more.

In terms of a hierarchy of habits, the first—*willingness to try and fail*—is most fundamental, given that without it, little technology learning is possible. While true for any area of learning, the words and actions of Isabella, Yesenia, Jessie, Erika, Julia, and the other F-emails at Mouse/Geek Squad Summer Academy; Alex, Stefani, and Beatriz at Radio Arte; and Rae, Michael, and Fatima at YMR made clear that "keeping an open mind" takes on a specific definition in the context of technology learning. It means explicitly (and often loudly) celebrating any attempt at technology learning as a success. To be tech savvy is to expect to laugh and cheer at failure—to say, "This might go badly, but watch me try. . . . Look how badly that went! . . . Watch me try again!" This iterative process of repeated failure and interpretation of simply trying as a success can only start with a *willingness to try and fail*—and continued with the next habit.

"YOU'RE GOING TO SUCK": MANAGEMENT OF FRUSTRATION AND BOREDOM

In a small concrete building in a formerly industrial section of San Francisco, a group of adults and teens gather and sit on brightly colored chairs in an empty open office space, turning their attention toward a Bay Area Video Coalition (BAVC) game design instructor who is welcoming them. He introduces an Asian male teen named Jeffrey, who, like many other students in the program, says he attends Balboa High School ("Bal," a predominantly low-income school south of the Mission). Jeffrey has a mop of black hair combed to one side, a broad bright smile, and rectangular dark-rimmed glasses. He talks about the video game he designed, which focuses on cooking challenges. He explains that it was inspired by the first dish he learned to make when he was young—fried rice. From the third row, his parents chuckle, knowingly.

After the presentations, Jeffrey stands talking to friends, family, and BAVC staff. I interrupt to ask some questions. Does he want to design more games in the future? He shakes his head no and laughs, repeating what he said during his presentation to the group, "Actually, I want to be a chef." This goal is surprising, given what others in the room have said about him. Zack, a tall white teen and friend of Jeffrey's who also attends Bal, advised me to "talk to Jeffrey, he has lots of interesting tricks to help him learn." I approach Jeffrey and ask: What are these tricks? Are they specific to technology or will they help him with anything, like his goal of being a chef? He nods, explaining what helps him learn:

> JEFFREY: Well, sometimes I'm happy, but sometimes I get frustrated. If I'm frustrated with what I've done, I'll try to redo it,

find another way or start over. I'm never really sure, but I'm okay with that feeling [of frustration].

CASSIDY: Where do you think that comes from?

JEFFREY: I think it's from playing video games. You're obviously not going to get it. *You're going to suck.* So, you keep doing it over and over again. My family is like that; I think that contributes.

CASSIDY: What helps when you get stuck?

JEFFREY: I think of everything as a game, like life as a game. You find things that you know for sure are correct and focus on the things that are correct. Things that are messed up, you reverse engineer; you break the problem into parts, leave things that you're sure are working fine.

Switching the conversation back to cooking, Jeffrey says this way of reverse engineering is "kind of like peeling the layers of an onion," where you keep peeling back until you get to the good parts. Is the expectation and management of frustration unique to technology learning? No, it's true of cooking—and it's true for life in general. But it definitely helps when failure is a central part of the technology learning process.

This habit connects to Cindy's idea of "not giving up" as well as starting with a *willingness to try and fail,* but it's used during the learning process. It includes reflecting on the experience of frustration and boredom (being aware of these feelings) and having an entire repertoire of techniques to work through it. I saw this habit in examples such as the game that Mouse/Geek Squad instructor Kevin and Julia played (described earlier in this chapter), and I heard about this habit many times during interviews. Teens explained that they had many "tricks" to manage frustration and boredom, like simply sitting in front of a computer and returning to projects and technologies again and again or pivoting to something enjoyable while experiencing frustration.

This technology learning habit—the *management of frustration and boredom*—connects to well-established research on *self-regulation,* which is the process through which learners direct their thoughts, feelings, and actions to meet their goals.[13] Self-regulation develops over time. As Bandura describes, it is not "an act of will" but rather a "skill that must be developed." Developing self-regulation involves helping learners (1) monitor their thoughts, actions, and feelings, and (to the extent they can) situate themselves in an environment that supports their learning; (2) focus on short-term goals; (3) utilize a range of "coping strategies" rather than just one; and (4) draw on personally meaningful incentives to persist in their efforts. Bandura described this process as difficult—that "it is one thing to possess self-regulatory skills but another to get oneself to apply them consistently and persistently in the face of difficulties, stressors and competing attractions."[14]

In other words, being able to manage frustration and boredom is not a "natural" ability—one you have, or you don't—instead, it must be explicitly taught and practiced, repeatedly. It also requires creativity, given that a person must draw from a range of strategies. With practice, these strategies become habits. It also means there are lots of ways to manage frustration and boredom. In fact, having a range of possible ways to *manage frustration and boredom* helps more than one single "best" technique. So, what does this range look like?

Framing to Learn

One technique tech-savvy teens used to manage their frustration and boredom was to frame technology learning in distinct ways. One framing was understanding technology learning as a *process* rather than a question of "Can I do this or not?" For example, at the Mouse/Geek Squad Summer Academy in New York City, two African American girls named Taysia and Imani, wearing matching pink bracelets, were playing Guitar Hero during lunch. Imani had difficulty with the game. She pushed her glasses farther up her nose and sighed, then turned to give her guitar to Rishi, an Asian male instructor who was sitting nearby. Frustrated, she said to him, "I can't do it." He gave her a slight tilt of his head. She smiled back and then said, loudly, "I can't do it *at this time!*" Later, when instructors gave out junior agent certificates at the end of the program, Rishi reminded the group, "When someone asks you something you don't know about technology, don't say 'I don't know.' Instead say, 'I'll find out.'"

Several other teens said the same. At Radio Arte, Alex framed technology learning as a "learn as you go process." Beatriz agreed; she said technology learning was "something you have to get used to." But, once practiced, feelings of frustration become more recognizable and comfortable. They become "easier." Tucking a strand of her long ombre-dyed hair behind her ear, Beatriz continued, "You'll always have to learn [new technologies] in the future." At Mouse Squad CA (MSCA) at Campbell Middle School in California, one of the students identified by teacher Carrie Tibbs as "very tech-savvy" (Miguel) said he'd "advise people . . . [that] everything's a learning experience." This framing of technology learning as a process helped students manage their frustration and boredom.

Another way to frame problems that come up in the process of learning a new technology is to understand issues as technical, rather than personal shortcomings. For example, Beatriz said that what helps her learn is to define difficulties as technical issues. She said that by understanding the problems she encounters as an issue with the technology, not a problem with her capability, "I don't give up [because] it's something technical." With this idea in mind—that the problem is somewhere in the technical aspects of a design or code—teens would reverse engineer their work, as Jeffrey at BAVC game design described in the previous section, trying to isolate the root cause rather than dissect how they might not be the type of person who could figure it out. Other teens said the same, like Miguel at MSCA, who said that when he encountered problems, it helped him to think of them as a technical challenge to be solved.

Understanding difficulty as a technical puzzle rather personal failing is something practiced—it does not develop "naturally." Often, teens first learned this way of thinking through the help of their families, as Jeffrey described ("My family is like that"), and it was reinforced in the programs they attended. Miguel said it took some time for him to understand the problems he encountered as technical ones needing identification—and to develop a method for identifying the cause. When I interviewed him, he said he had "lots of experience fixing computers." But it took him time to understand his frustrations as technical puzzles that he could identify and address by systematically working to uncover the issue. Like Jeffrey, Miguel said his parents helped; they gave him a computer when he was very young and encouraged him to tinker. His involvement in MSCA also helped; in seventh grade they did television production, which helped him solidify this method of managing his frustration. He explained that he made lots of mistakes in iMovie, but his teacher Carrie coached him to think about the problems he encountered as technical rather than personal deficiencies and to identify their cause—to learn more about "the background of the problem." While Miguel insisted he mostly "screwed around," what he described was a systematic understanding and approach to addressing problems both technological and emotional. He managed his feelings of frustration by framing difficulty like a game that required reverse engineering to find and fix problems—and helped him continue to learn.

Practicing Imperfection

Another technique for *managing frustration and boredom* was to practice imperfection. Students were encouraged to avoid perfectionism in all programs, and instructors shared various methods. For example, at YMR Tony, an African American beat-making and audio production instructor who was a professional engineer at Avid Technology and helped create Pro Tools audio production systems for professional clients (e.g., Sony, Disney, Lucas Arts), encouraged a lanky white male teen named Kyle not to strive for perfection:

TONY: I've been doing this [beat making, audio production] for six years. [To make a song now] it takes from five to ten minutes or up to an hour.

KYLE: Me, it takes weeks!

TONY: You gotta let it go. Perfection is debatable. Move on. The more you move, more beats you make. You won't run out [of ideas].

Kyle nodded and continued to work on Reason, an audio production software, accepting Tony's encouragement to "let [perfection] go." Likewise, in a YMR practice recording session, Latinx band and digital recording instructor Ricardo announced, "Don't correct past mistakes. It's already in the past. Just keep it going." In other words, he did not want them to get hung up on mistakes—it was all just practice.

Other students and instructors described similar techniques to practice imperfection. In her presentation at BAVC game design, an Asian teen named Jia who was a junior at Galileo High School and wanted to be a graphic designer or programmer, said she "had to re-create her board three times."[15] She designed a game where players traveled all over the globe. There was an area in her game she made into a lake that "took a long time to make a fish and flowers move"—and it still wasn't perfect. But that was okay; she would try again in future work. Though not perfect, through the process of creating her game, she still learned how to use Cinema 4D (a 3D modeling, animation, and rendering application), something she had never done before.

At BUMP Records, Christine said she was now proficient in how to "write and perform," but when she first sat down with Pro Tools there were "so many buttons and screens" that it scared her. It could also get frustrating. She said, "It will fail you. I had a song deleted. With everything, there's a downside." But, with practice it became "like a home, a part of you." She explained, "It takes patience and time. I thought it was just going to come to me—I could be a genius, just not yet discovered! (*laughs*). . . . People forget, nothing is perfect in life. Don't just shut stuff down before you've tried it." In other words, to manage frustration, teens had to practice and get comfortable with being imperfect. Miguel in MSCA said the same—when he's trying to learn a new technology, the most important thing he can do is to "keep trying," not to be perfect. Beatriz at Radio Arte agreed, saying what was key to her technology learning was to "just try things" and practice being comfortable with the mistakes she would inevitably make, which helped her become more skillful.

Both framing learning as a process and practicing imperfection link to research on students' goal orientation. These tech-savvy teens focused on what researchers call "mastery-oriented" thinking, wherein they would shoot for incremental improvement, often connecting their learning to real-world contexts and goals. This viewpoint contrasts with "performance-oriented" thinking, wherein learners focus on managing the *impression* of their ability rather than developing learning strategies that help them persist in the face of difficulty.[16] Rae in the Pro Tools class at YMR demonstrated mastery-oriented thinking. She said that her father, who was involved in music and took classes in Pro Tools, told her that she "need[ed] to learn it to be in the music industry," which is what she wanted to do. Stefani at Radio Arte said that her goal is to work in film and that radio was like "playing a movie in your head," so she saw it as preparation for her larger goal. Gisela, a Latinx teen also at Radio Arte, felt the habits she was developing by learning to create radio segments would help her with jobs in general, so making incremental improvements—even if she wasn't perfect—helped with her long-term goals.

Managing Frustration and Boredom: Building a Repertoire

While all teens seemed to use the two techniques of framing to learn and practicing imperfection to *manage frustration and boredom,* other techniques varied. Yet, all teens seemed aware that they needed a range—a management repertoire—to maintain their focus during the process of technology learning. In the following sections I explain a sampling of the myriad ways tech-savvy teens managed their frustration and boredom.

PIVOTING

Many teens used *pivoting*—that is, shifting purposefully to doing something else or trying another technique—when frustrated or bored. For example, Zack in BAVC game design said his management repertoire included having another game open while designing his own game, so he could take a break to play another game and wouldn't get too overwhelmed when something went wrong in the game he was designing. Pivoting temporarily to something else—and something related to what he was doing—helped him calm down in the face of frustration and maintain focus on the goal of designing a high-quality game. Miguel in MSCA likewise said, "Sometimes I'll want to give up, so I'll try something different and improvise a little."

BREAKING DOWN TASKS

Another technique that teens used to manage frustration and boredom was *breaking down tasks into smaller pieces*. This method was something several instructors instilled in their students. For example, at YMR a white male DJ instructor named Zane, wearing long gray shorts and black high-top Air Jordans, started his class by explaining to students, "It takes work to get to where you're having fun. But, stick with it! You should break things down into smaller goals." He cued up some records and walked the class through a demonstration of how to scratch a record. Then, he had students come up three at a time to try it out, slowly. After the initial experience of just touching the record and moving it once he asked, "How'd that feel? Good?" Students nodded. He explained they should keep track of the record and not let it go, connecting their brief touch with the larger process of learning how to DJ. Then he demonstrated how the one scratch turns into eight per beat. Zane said, "I keep saying stay on the beat—eight scratches per beat.

The basic move is back and forth, that's the basis for everything else." Showing students this technique, Zane modeled how to break tasks down into their simplest components.

BLOCKING OUT DISTRACTIONS

Many teens also used techniques to manage frustration and boredom that involved *blocking out distractions*—for example, using headphones to maintain their focus. This practice helped them continue to work and not get distracted when frustration or boredom set in. For example, in Tony's Beat Making class at YMR, Myesha, a tall African American female with short purple hair, sat working on a song. Kyle turned to her and asked, "Can I take a listen?" But Myesha had headphones on and was so focused that she didn't hear him or even notice him wave at her. Kyle said aloud, "Yeah, she's into her beat!" (*laughed*) "I had a whole conversation with myself!" Kyle couldn't distract her from her song because, through these techniques, she was able to give her full attention to the task at hand—and achieve what scholars call "flow."

Flow is a psychological state in which an individual experiences deep involvement and absorption in a task—because the context for action allows a person to meet or exceed their present capabilities.[17] Flow has six qualities. First is action without awareness, wherein a person has a sense of knowing exactly what to do and how to do it without having to think about it. Second is concentration on the present moment. Third is a complete loss of self-consciousness—no critical self-talk or social comparison—and, relatedly, fourth, no fear of failure. Fifth is loss of a sense of the passage of time. And finally, sixth is "autotelic motivation," or pleasure in simply doing the work, rather than for external reward or obligation.[18] The primary obstacles for flow are anxiety and boredom. Anxiety (which I include in the umbrella term *frustration*) stems from situations wherein individuals perceive challenges to be greater than their ability. Conversely, boredom occurs when individuals perceive their ability to be greater than given challenges. Both can occur during the learning process, with some aspects beyond a learner's current ability and other aspects repetitive or detail-oriented, such as learning to edit lines of code. And either can invite distraction. Therefore, to achieve a state of flow like Myesha did, learners must develop techniques to manage frustration and boredom and make sure that nothing gets in their way.

ENLISTING OTHERS TO HELP WITH FRUSTRATION MANAGEMENT
Finally, teens often would *use others to help manage their frustration* (especially instructors), to understand how to monitor and change how they felt in the learning process. For example, in Tony's class another African American female student clad in a tie-dye shirt named MJ tried to use Reason, but she thought it wasn't doing what she wanted it to do (bring the volume down on the tracks she was working on). She asked Tony how to turn the volume down.

> TONY: Level is how loud it is. Slide that.
> MJ (*tries this but appears frustrated*): It's not doing it.
> TONY: It's doing it slowly.
> MJ: Oh.
> TONY: Bring it up slowly. See, you can make it slow or really big.
> And, pitch, that makes it sound like a devil or a chipmunk.
> (*MJ smiles at Tony.*)

While MJ was in fact doing the correct thing, she used Tony as a way to understand her actions as correct ones and his encouragement as a way to manage her frustration.

In BAVC game design, Cai, a female Asian student with a short angled bob, stood in front of the group to talk about her game in the final program celebration. She said a theme in the game was "pain" because it took her five tries to make it. So, she included elements such as a sign that says "Pain This Way" at the beginning of the game and then a treasure box, where "all ideas come from—some are good, but some lead you in the wrong direction." Later, when I interviewed Cai, she described all the struggles she encountered. She said, "Whenever I would move files, Unity [a game development engine] would wipe out the graphics, like when I was importing from Cinema 4D [an animation, modeling, simulation, and rendering software] to Unity . . . I had to make a different texture inside and outside of the room." What would she do when she encountered problems? "I'd start over in a different way, get myself to try a little harder, or go to the instructors for help." She continued, "There were lots of times when I wanted to give up. But I invested my time and I don't like leaving things unfinished. It leaves a little hole in my heart." Fortunately, Cai had developed a strong set of technology learning habits—including the last general habit of using models I describe in this section—and it was unlikely she'd leave anything unfinished.

While not an exhaustive list, what seemed crucial was that tech-savvy teens developed multiple techniques for helping them move through frustration and boredom. Raul, another Campbell Middle School MSCA student identified by teacher Carrie Tibbs as among her savviest students, said that when he encountered problems, he would acknowledge the difficulty, then draw on various techniques that he learned would help him. He said, "Yeah, you put so much effort into it. Sometimes I do give up—well, not give up—I'll try something different. You come out of it with a sense of accomplishment and figure out what works for you." With practice, teens noticed they became used to the feelings of frustration and boredom that came with learning new technologies, so much so that they could "sit" with those feelings and eventually figure out what was holding them back. For example, Zack in BAVC game design explained, "Even if in the middle of it, I'd feel like *oh shit*. I'd just sit there until I'd figure it out. There were times I needed to ask for help. I'd say [to the instructor], 'Could you come here?' But I'd figure it out before he got there."

In terms of a hierarchy of technology learning habits, this second habit—*management of frustration and boredom*—is critical to ongoing technology learning. Like all the habits in this chapter, it also applies across many areas of learning. Translated to the case of technology learning, this habit includes a repertoire of management techniques, including but not limited to

- Framing technology learning as a process,
- Practicing imperfection,
- Pivoting,
- Breaking down tasks,
- Blocking out distractions, and
- Using others to help with repertoire development.

This last technique links to the third and final general technology learning habit in this chapter: using models to guide the learning process.

FIND EXPERTS: THE USE OF MODELS

It's the second day of the Beat Making class at YMR and Tony reintroduces a method of keeping all elements of a song (sounds, instruments, etc.) on beat. He reminds everyone that this method is called *quantizing*, which he introduced the first day of class. He explains that if they want to record something, it's "as simple as clicking the red button [in Reason]. But it has to be on beat. You've heard of a metronome—that's the beat. We can put [instrumentals] on the beat by quantizing." Sitting in a chair by the side of the classroom, I look to see what students are doing.

Myesha peers over her computer and watches Tony's movements. Tony demonstrates with his screen projected on the wall: "Okay, to quantize, just highlight, click, and drag to select. Then, in the tools window, click here to put it on the beat." She nods and sits down to try what she just observed. An hour and a half later, Myesha finishes her song and asks Tony to listen. He puts her headphones on and nods to the beat. He takes them off and says to her, "All you gotta do is solo export each. For drums, you gotta mute the others." Myesha asks, "I don't need to edit more?" Tony replies, "Nope." Myesha smiles and says, "Cool."

Later, I ask Myesha about how she gets help when she has problems. She says that one of the main things she does is exactly what she did in the class: look to more knowledgeable people. But her *use of models* extends far beyond student-teacher roles. She also identifies and asks a wide range of people who are knowledgeable about technology, including peers and other adults, as well as goes to online forums where "experts have put information online" that she reads. She tells me no single person has complete mastery of absolutely everything, so she instead gleans what she can from a range of models—sources of in-person or online information—based on their advice about what to do or where to go for help. She explains, "I ask Tony or any of my friends. If they don't know the answer, they'll tell me how to go online [to find it]. Nobody has mastery. But they know places to go." Seeking out help from multiple sources, Myesha and other tech-savvy teens find and use models to learn new technologies.

Apprenticeship in the Digital Age

One of the most powerful things I watched students do while learning how to use a new technology was to stand next to another student or teacher and watch what they did; to *use models* to help them learn. This habit might seem like an obvious one—if you want to know something, you ask someone more knowledgeable. But what I observed was a complex process. It included (1) being aware that models (more knowledge-able people, online resources) can help in the learning process, (2) being able to identify models, and (3) accessing and observing models to gather information and work toward the standards set by the model. To identify these models, teens looked for cues from their instructors, peers, or both to understand a potential model's level of knowledge. Then, as Myesha described, they would "listen to more knowledgeable people" and "get around experts" to observe and mimic their behaviors or gather their advice—either in person or online.

Myesha's use of multiple models recognizes what is known as *distributed cognition*, the idea that knowledge is not located entirely within one person or object—as Myesha explained, "nobody has mastery." Instead, technology learning is facilitated by drawing on a range of resources: from people who know the content, who know how to learn technology, or who can suggest other resources; or from nonhuman resources, such as examples of code or online information. Observing and connecting to multiple models—treating knowledge as a distributed system—is crucial for learning.[19]

Because new technologies are always emerging, technological expertise is ephemeral; this constant change makes understanding and treating knowledge as distributed particularly helpful for technology learning. For example, in a study of industry experts, Christian Sandvig found that many tech workers continually feel outdated, uncertain of their own expertise as new programming languages emerge and make knowledge of older languages obsolete: "They constantly [feel] inadequate" and "[worry] about the same question, 'What do you really know about technology?'"[20] Because of these feelings, Sandvig reports, "consultants tell CEOs that they should estimate the useful lifespan of any particular technological skill as two years."[21] Similarly, Gina Neff and David Stark argue that all technologies are in "permanent beta" and that "individual users and employees bear a greater responsibility for adaptation to change."[22] To keep up, people must continually seek various sources of information.

How did the tech-savvy teens I observed identify people who could be models in a changing technological environment? They used indicators of certified knowledge ("they're the instructor") or social knowledge ("those teens were in the program last year"). Once identified, they knew these people could be essential resources, but only if they put forth the effort to use their expertise. For example, in Mouse/Geek Squad Summer Academy, during one lunch I interviewed Ty, an African American teen with freckles across his nose. As he sipped on a juice box, he told me, "Instructors are trained professionals, so I ask them [for help]. You demonstrate to the instructor what you know, and then where you're stuck." In other words, instructors are an easily identifiable possible source of information because of their training, but it takes additional negotiation for them to be a useful resource for a given situation—that is, Ty's technique of demonstrating his knowledge and where he was stuck.

Teens across all programs practiced this habit. At WhyReef at the Field Museum in Chicago, a group of nine students worked on a simulation to understand how to restore a virtual reef. Alexis, an African American female from the south suburbs with a keen interest in science and especially fish, turned to ask instructor Beth Sanzenbacher a question about how she should interpret what was going on in the game. Beth, a white woman with a dry wit she used to playfully engage students, explained that they were simulating changes in the reef's ecology to see how it responded. Alexis still seemed a bit confused, so she tried out an interpretation with Beth to check whether it was accurate:

ALEXIS: Okay, I think I got it. This one (*pointing*) increased?
BETH: Look at the simulation, click here. Which way did it go?
ALEXIS: Down.
BETH: So it . . . ? (*smiling, rolling her eyes a bit to tease Alexis*)
ALEXIS: Decreased.
BETH (*throwing her arms in the air*): Yes! You have two more left. (*with a serious and excited tone*) You're getting good at this.
ALEXIS (*smiles*): Thanks!

By checking her understanding with another person, Alexis used Beth as a model of how to think about the technology she was learning. But using others as models wasn't unique to Alexis, Ty, or Myesha— students across other programs did the same.

Peers are another important potential source of information.[23] Studies show that both peers with greater mastery and peers of any mastery level who are "coping" well can help other learners.[24] By observing how these groups of peers overcome challenges, learners can pick up on ways of thinking, acting, and feeling that help in the learning process.[25] Raul in MSCA said that asking for help from peers is key. How does he know whom to ask? He turns to friends who are good at whatever he might be trying to learn—and he can tell they're good because "they're learning fast" (which links to the habit of "efficiencies" to be explained in chapter 3). Miguel, also in MSCA, said that because of his advanced technological skill, he was often a model for his peers, especially to those not in the program. He said, "When my friends' computers break, they call me. I'm the only one into them—they're into sports."

Beyond instructors and peers, many teens said that they go to other people and online resources, just as Myesha described. Miguel said to get help he'd even "gone to neighbors" with technological expertise, like how to fix computers. He said people don't necessarily know everything but can help by pointing to good resources online. He explained, "Maybe they know where good advice might be on YouTube. . . . You won't know most components [of a computer or piece of software]. So, ask someone else who might be able to guide you. If you still don't get it, there's always Google!" Students also said learning and using key technical terms made it more likely to find these resources. For example, in BAVC game production, at the end of the program, students presented their games and reflected on their work process. Zack said that when he encountered problems, he would look things up online by using terms he learned in class—for example, the word *primitives* to describe 3D shapes. Using that term, he looked for online resources as models and that helped him in the learning process.

Many programs promoted the idea of using models by building it into the program structure. Jayden, a tall, Black-white biracial teen who attended Bal, explained that he was in video production as well as BUMP Records. As he worked on editing a soundtrack for a film, he described his experiences with BAVC. Expressing a seriousness in his work he said, "I might not be able to compare to other programs, but the instructors [here] are always positive and constructive and it's clear what instructors want us to get out of it." He explained that the setup for the class was helpful because they would listen to one another's work and everyone got "feedback from people coming from different perspectives." Working with other people helped him learn. Smiling as he described the program in detail, he said, "You kind of discover [the software] together. You talk with somebody, then you listen to something else than what you're working on—it changes the way you're reacting." In other words, everyone in the program wanted to increase their technological skill, and they worked together to move everyone forward. He said he'd also listen to "more knowledgeable people" and that learning happened "through relationships." His eyes sparkled as he described these experiences—he clearly considered himself lucky to be in the program, learning from instructor and peer models and being a model for others.

Many programs also crafted students' learning experiences as real-world apprenticeship by hiring professional filmmakers, musicians, and videographers to teach classes who showed that they, too, used multiple sources of information in their work. At YMR, the video production workshop began with an interview with professional singer-songwriter Goapele just three weeks into the class. Instructor Gabe, a tall African American male with a tan cap twisted slightly to the side, said to the class, "It'll be you guys with me and Evan [a white male teen teaching assistant] as support." The project included all steps for pre- and postproduction, from learning how to use cameras and microphones to editing video with Final Cut Pro. Through these apprenticeship experiences, the entire program provided a model of how to do real-world video production.

Using Multiple Models

But teens said using one or two models—a teacher and a close friend, for example—just wasn't enough. As with *management of frustration and boredom*, for *using models*, teens noted that they could not rely on just one model. Like Myesha, Gisela in Radio Arte explained that her identification of a range of models was an ongoing process. What Gisela found helpful was listening to what other students created, identifying the features she might want to emulate, and using a range of peers (and peers' work) to learn technologies and craft her own radio segments. For example, she noticed an audio effect another teen used in their radio segment where the music would fade in and out at the beginning and end of their piece. She approached the person and asked how they created the fading effect and they helped her re-create it in her radio segment. But, that was just for that particular goal. Gisela would continually work to identify multiple models by listening to peers' work or, if in the studio at the same time, she would note whether they "look like they know what they're doing" with a particular program or in their learning process. She would observe whether they continued to work at things, found new effects or techniques, and did not give up. Gisela also said she used industry standards as models—for example, creating radio segments that sound "like *This American Life*."

Research supports the idea that using multiple models helps learning, especially since access can depend on the availability of resources and people willing to share their knowledge and expertise, so the more sources, the better.[26] Understanding the benefit, instructors in many programs encouraged students to use multiple models—not just one. At YMR in Beat Making class, Tony encouraged students to emulate industry models, in the same way Gisela described her use of *This American Life* as a model. For example, in another interaction with Kyle, Tony listened to a few of the songs he was working on and encouraged Kyle to try to emulate industry producers, in much the same way beginning authors might emulate other writers' style to develop their skills and find their own voice.

> TONY (*listening to Kyle's song*): [It's] really Neptunes-ish [music producers Pharrell Williams and Chad Hugo]. Good percussion, lots of good ideas. Needs something to tie it together. Reverb. Smooth it out. Something you can do with mixing.
> KYLE: Maybe, yeah, compression . . . ?
> TONY: What do you listen to?
> KYLE: Mos Def.
> TONY: Listen to things. That's a way to get better. Mannie Fresh, Neptunes, Just Blaze. Not to copy, but to see what they do.

In this interaction, Tony encouraged Kyle not only to listen to specific music but also to incorporate the technique of using multiple models as a method for learning—"not to copy, but to see what they do."

In several programs, activities and structures encouraged students to identify and use multiple models, not just rely on instructors. For example, at Radio Arte, a Latinx teen named José, who was a Columbia College student and involved in the training program for two years, said the program was designed to help encourage participants to use peers as models. Teens who had gone through the program were invited to return to further their skills as well as to mentor new students. So, more knowledgeable peers were often around. Alex at Radio Arte also said he identified models by watching whom other people would go to besides the teacher; that was often the best person to ask for help. Because of its structure, more knowledgeable peers likely had gone through the program before—but sometimes they came with prior skill. For example, at one point while Alex was working on a radio segment about gang violence and trying to incorporate the sound of a gunshot, he turned to a more knowledgeable peer named David, another Latinx teen, for "pointers" about which buttons to press to make a sound fade in and out. Alex knew he should go to David by observing others asking him for help, as well as hearing when David shared a radio segment that included the fading sound.

In fact, Radio Arte's structure encouraged teens to use a range of models by having them formally share work in critique sessions, which is where Alex heard David's work, and encouraging them to give and receive help from past and current participants. Doing so helped teens understand not only *what* they could do with the new tools they were learning but also *how* to approach their learning. Further, throughout the production process, students worked in teams and shared work with other teams who would help identify what worked and what needed improvement. For example, close to an editing deadline, while I was interviewing Stefani at Radio Arte, an African American student named Carla called across the room to Stefani and asked if she would listen to her *radionovela*. In my notes I scribbled:

> Stefani walks across the small room and accepts a pair of headphones offered by Carla. Stefani sits, closes her eyes and listens as Carla clicks the play button. She breathes deeply. Opening her eyes to look

at Carla, she smiles and says, "I really like it!" Carla smiles back and asks if she can play her another track. Stefani nods and listens again, this time saying, "I think I can hear an echo." Carla says, "Yeah, that was probably caused in the recording process." Carla thanks Stefani and returns to work on the track.

Returning to our interview, Stefani explained that Carla was working on a "really interesting" project imagining Chicago in one hundred years, when "it'll still be segregated, but more by class than by race." Next to us Laura, another Latinx teen in a black hoodie, chatted with her neighbor Manuel about her project. They discussed the need for ambient noise. Manuel, fiddling with his button-down shirt, argued, "The city *bustles*." Laura—who had been hesitant to add the sound, partly because she didn't know how to do it, relented and said, "Okay, I'll ask you how I can get those sounds onto my computer."

Developing Mental Models

Programs also encouraged teens to develop mental models toward which they could direct their learning. This way of prompting students to use models also happened through the program's formal critique sessions. For example, on my second day of observations at Radio Arte, sixteen students in smaller production teams of two to four presented their work to other teams and four instructors. The radio segments they developed focused on topics of their choosing, including gentrification in the local neighborhood, an art exhibit based on Sandra Cisneros's book *The House on Mango Street*, interracial love, steroid use in sports, Chicago Public School closings, army recruiters in schools, the use of medical marijuana, police violence, growing up bilingual, and what teens do in their spare time. Students critiqued the work based on the content of the segments and the quality of audio mixing (e.g., "the music is too loud, I can't hear the narration"). José, the Columbia College student, explained that these sessions—in which students shared segments, gathered feedback, and critiqued other teams' segments—

made him "more conscious of what goes into a radio segment" or his mental model of high-quality work, which he was learning how to create.

Other programs also encouraged students to similarly develop mental models to guide their learning. In BAVC's video production program, instructors led students through sessions wherein teens learned to explicitly define *quality*. As they listened to songs, students were asked to identify things they thought were "good," and instructors would translate these observations into larger categories students could use to develop a mental model of how a song should sound, such as a song's "technical" and "aesthetic" qualities. The same was true of BAVC's BUMP Records program. During an interview, an African American instructor named Dan who had been a program participant as a teen explained that the program encouraged students to listen closely to their favorite albums to "see if [their own] album can go toe-to-toe with that. We encourage and build that in the program, tell students to listen to influencers—there's often a formula."

Digital Youth Network (DYN) and YOUmedia Chicago (which at the time was led primarily by DYN instructors) did the same. During video production classes, for example, students were asked to critique professional videos as they worked on their own projects and developed their technical skill. In one video production class, an African American instructor and professional videographer named Raphael asked students to critique a professionally produced public service announcement (PSA) while the class worked on their own PSAs about their neighborhoods, linking the activity to *The House on Mango Street*. Raphael showed the video and then turned to the class and asked, "What did you think of [the PSA]?"

TYLER (AFRICAN AMERICAN MALE TEEN, LONGTIME DYN PARTICIPANT): Anticlimactic.
RAPHAEL (*encouraging them to say more and to use technical language*): Okay . . . what are the themes?

SASHA (AFRICAN AMERICAN FEMALE TEEN, ALSO PREVIOUSLY INVOLVED IN DYN): Coming-of-age.

RAPHAEL: What about the setting? Would it be the same in a rural town?

TYLER: It's in the inner city.

SASHA: You could still have a coming-of-age story in a rural town.

RAPHAEL: Okay, so coming-of-age. What else is a major force?

SASHA: He is trying to find a girl.

RAPHAEL: What else?

SASHA: He kept going even though they kept telling him to go away.

RAPHAEL: Persistence, good.

They went on to talk about how the story unfolded—what happened at the beginning, middle, and end of the story to create a story arc. Raphael then broke the class into small groups to discuss how they could apply the idea of a story arc to their PSAs, using the example and the overall idea of a story arc as a mental model to guide their work.

In terms of a hierarchy of habits, the third habit—*use of models*—is critical to the ongoing learning process because it helps learners understand the many possible methods to achieve their goals. Seeking out multiple models helps so that if one fails, learners have an ever-growing list of other models to try, opening many possible ways of learning new technologies. Like the other habits in this chapter, using multiple models can benefit any area of learning, but it is particularly essential for tech learning because of tech's ever-changing nature. As Myesha so astutely pointed out, "*Nobody has mastery. But they know places to go.*" As technologies shift and change, "mastery" as an end point doesn't exist. Instead, mastery is defined by continual learning and being able to go out and find many new ways of approaching things—by gathering ideas from multiple human and technological resources.

CONCLUSION: GENERAL TECHNOLOGY LEARNING HABITS

In this chapter I identified three habits previous research suggests are helpful to learning in general that are especially so for technology learning: *willingness to try and fail, management of frustration and boredom*, and *use of models*. I also described why these three habits are so central to technology learning and what they look like in this context. For example, I noted that *willingness to try and fail* is a central habit for technology learning—so much so that when practiced to its fullest extent, tech-savvy teens would (loudly) celebrate the process of failure and redefine even the simplest attempt as a success.

Given the centrality of failure, it is also crucial for individuals to develop a range of techniques to manage frustration and boredom. Will these techniques look the same for everyone? Probably not. The array will likely differ from person to person, and the efficacy of methods will likely change based on a given situation. If one technique is unhelpful, as long as people develop a range of techniques, they will have other ways of managing frustration and boredom (e.g., framing, practicing failing, pivoting, breaking down tasks, and blocking out distractions). The list of techniques presented in this chapter is a start, but not exhaustive. The key is to understand that learning technology can be frustrating and boring—and to develop multiple ways of managing these experiences.

Finally, it's important to note that all the habits I describe in this chapter and the next—especially the *use of models*, the third habit presented in this chapter—are contingent on teens' access to people and online resources that can help teens build these habits. The tech-savvy teens described in these chapters have that social support, but not every teen does, as I note later in the book. Lack of knowledge of learning opportunities, limited availability or space in programs, or being located in less technology-rich neighborhoods or in rural areas with limited resources can limit teens' ability to develop or enact these habits.[27] Further, access to more advanced computing is also contingent on a learning context in which talent is recognized and encouraged. In too many cases talent is devalued or policed—something this book is designed to address by redefining what it means to be good with technology to help better identify our hidden tech talent.[28] Later I discuss how parents, educators, schools, and policy makers might be able to address these issues. But first, in chapter 3, I describe the final two technology-specific habits.

[3]

Techie Tricks

THE TWO TECHNOLOGY-SPECIFIC HABITS

> Often, tech skills are hidden. You might know how to use
> MySpace, but not Microsoft Word. Or, you know how to use
> Fruity Loops, but you're scared to touch the hardware.
> That's part of the process. [I] have to remind [students]
> constantly that they're learning—and that it'll be appli-
> cable to other areas.
>
> Dan, former student and instructor at BUMP Records

As Dan describes in this chapter's opening quotation, the process of
technology learning is often a hidden part of tech savviness. This hid-
denness makes technology teaching and learning more difficult, and
it makes inequities in tech easier to justify. As I argued earlier, if certain people (white, Asian, male) are viewed as "instinctively" skilled,
there is no explanatory room for systemic racism, classism, or sexism
in tech. The differences in computer science participation by gender,
for example, can appear to reflect "natural" differences between men
and women.[1] So to make technology learning more explicit, observable, and teachable, in this chapter I continue to unpack the black box
of skill development by describing the five technology learning habits.
This unpacking is grounded in what learners actually do—not what past

research suggests or what technology "experts" do. If we follow the "experts," we might conflate what affluent/white/Asian/male techies do as the "correct" approach to learning, further emphasizing the limited assumptions about who is technologically competent.

In chapter 2, I began with the three general habits that help tech-savvy teens learn new technologies. To complete the set, in this chapter I describe two technology-specific habits: *design logic and efficiencies*. These two habits are the key facets that, like a secret passcode, open the door to technological learning.

DESIGN LOGIC

August 2009. It's the end of the first year of my sociology PhD program at Northwestern and I am in the midst of studying tech-savvy students. I travel to observe and interview a group of teens in a technology-related program in Chicago's Pilsen neighborhood. I've been to the area before, hovering over *conchas* (shell-shaped sweet rolls) in Panaderia Nuevo Leon. The neighborhood is reminiscent of the Fruitvale in Oakland where I taught, but with small brick buildings and a Romanesque cathedral instead of California 1920s bungalows and Mission Revival buildings. Through the large glass street-level windows of a small brick building on a triangle corner, I notice what looks like a radio station: a counter with a control panel and microphones hanging above. I realize I'm here, at Radio Arte.

I am visiting this historically Latinx neighborhood to observe the radio station's youth media training program to make sure the study includes teens with a range of home language backgrounds. Research suggests that there are many tech-savvy, low-income students of color, including from homes where languages other than English are spoken.[2] Unlike research on styles of learning that seek to explain disadvantage, such as low-income students being hindered by their help-seeking behaviors, I instead want to know what helps tech-savvy lower-income youth of color succeed in their technology learning.[3] In other words, I'm trying to better understand what would help students like mine in Oakland.

Inside, Tania Unzueta, the director of youth training, welcomes me with a broad smile and leads me into a small room above the radio station. She asks for clarification about what I'm there to observe, even though she's already welcomed me to visit the program. I tell her I want to understand what helps her students learn. Typically, researchers pursuing this question are more interested in what teachers do, to evaluate their "effectiveness."[4] What and how Radio Arte and other technology programs teach their students is useful information, but I'm not here to evaluate. What I want to understand is what helps teens in their learning process—which they may pick up in these programs, or at school, at home, or among their friends.[5] Tania thinks for a moment and walks me to a room near the stairs where about five students sit in front of computers, some clustered together. She introduces me to a seventeen-year-old Latinx teen named Gisela sitting alone, who is a senior at the selective enrollment magnet high school Lane Tech, which she attends because of her interest in technology, art, and architecture.

Gisela first got involved with Radio Arte after her dad saw an ad in *Hoy*, a Spanish-language newspaper, about the summer radio program. She applied online and now is paid to participate, which involves learning new software and producing radio segments with other program participants. Her current project is a short radio segment about language development. She explains:

> We did this writing exercise about our past experiences. It hit me: At five years old, I didn't speak English! So, I'm doing a story about people's experiences with that—stories of having to interpret for family members and the struggle of losing your language. What I want people to get from it is an awareness of this issue, that there are youth—second grade, third grade—they might get to a point of realization when speaking two languages where it's like, *What part of yourself do you keep?*

Gisela is learning about all kinds of audio recording equipment and software through the program, including the open source audio editing software Audacity. The Radio Arte instructors gave her an explanation of the software, but she feels as though she only half heard the first time and that she primarily learns as she goes.

Can she identify anything that helps her in that process, for this new software—or any new software—I ask? Gisela hesitates and I wait, shifting in my seat. She cocks her head slightly and meets my gaze. "Well, I always *look for things in certain places*," she explains. "Certain things are similar. Like, File and Edit are usually there in the same place, so [I look for] similar things." This strategy also helps her learn "computer English," by looking for the ways computer programs mirror their designs, so she can transfer her understanding of how one program functions in Spanish to an entirely different program in English.

Gisela's "reading" of how software is designed is a perfect example of the technology-specific habit, *design logic*. This habit is:

1. An awareness of and ability to identify patterns embedded in the design of technological tools,
2. Thinking about how to decode the logic of these patterns, and
3. Reading the purpose behind the design against one's own goals.

It is a type of "meta" awareness in the sense that the students are cognizant of the symbolic systems they are decoding within and across technologies that may (or may not) build on one another. This habit is similar to past research on digital literacies in the sense that it involves "reading" the logic of how a designer created the technology.[6] But it's different because *design logic* focuses more centrally on the learning process, the changing nature of technological tools, and what the learner brings to the table—the story Gisela wanted to tell.

Reading Technologically

How does technology learning connect to language development? Scholars such as Renee Hobbs and James Paul Gee have long framed media and technology use as "literacy" or "multiliteracies" because it involves decoding a symbolic system.[7] This framing strategically connects media and technology use to English, a subject area central to schooling.[8] Yet, while scholars seem to agree on this general framing and the importance of media and digital literacy, they disagree about how to define, measure, and develop it in children. For decades, scholars have argued over "new" and ever more fine-grained definitions of the types of literacies students should develop.[9] At the same time, few scholars have looked at *how* students learn technology—the habits that support literacy and skill development. For this reason, research fails to capture the differences I observed among my students—why Cindy liked most of our tech class activities but found coding difficult and why Maria barely engaged in the more technical aspects of class activities.

But, literacies research does offer a starting point. In his book *What Video Games Have to Teach Us about Learning and Literacy*, James Paul Gee argues for a broad definition of *literacy* beyond print to other domains where meaning is constructed, like tech.[10] In each domain, there are what he calls internal and external "design grammars." The *internal grammar* is how we recognize something as being part of a domain—the principles and patterns that identify it. This regularity is how, for example, we can recognize a reggae song immediately—it has a distinctive rhythm. The *external grammar* is understanding how something fits into the world—what is acceptable or typical in terms of how it is used—such as knowing not to play a wedding march at a funeral. In other words, *internal grammar* is reading how something is designed, and *external grammar* is understanding the socially acceptable way of using it.

As we see with Gisela and other tech-savvy teens like her, the learning habit of *design logic* is in some ways remarkably similar to Gee's design grammar. More precisely, it is similar to the idea of an internal grammar, where technologies are understood as "designed by someone" who "appl[ies] certain principles, patterns, and procedures to the construction of [things like video games], [and] the content . . . comes to have recognizable shape."[11] Understanding technologies as designed systems is precisely what helped Gisela learn: reading the internal design grammar by identifying the principles, patterns, and procedures of Audacity helped her figure out how to use it. She also read the design grammar through the *use of models*, described in chapter 2, comparing what she knew about other programs (where the File and Edit tabs might be located) to the new software she was learning.

But, there was something more in what Gisela described. First, she wanted to tell a story. This consideration of her own goals is different from Gee's idea of an external grammar, which he characterized as essentially reading what others already deemed acceptable use; a more passive stance than what Gisela expressed. She read the design logic of a technology *against what she hoped to do with it*. She might realize a software or hardware was designed for her exact purpose, that there were limitations, or that it was designed for a completely different purpose— which would shape how she could use it to accomplish her own goals.[12] That negotiation is embedded in technology learning and therefore a central feature of *design logic*.

Second, Gee's idea of design grammar suggests that once a person can "read" a particular type of media, learning is required only when moving to "new" media. But what Gisela expressed suggests very little is fixed, both within and across media. For example, she said "dealing with audio [in Audacity] is different" from other technologies she learned in the past, including software she called "basics" such as Word and Excel and design software such as Photoshop and Illustrator. Therefore, this "reading" cannot be generalized across technologies (as Gee argues). *Design logic* is something that must be deciphered over and over again because it involves thinking about how a tool can be used for a particular goal and decoding logics within and across media *that may or may not build on the logic of other technologies*.

In these ways, though *design logic* draws from design grammar, it **is** different—most centrally, it more explicitly takes into account the changeable nature of technology and what the learner brings to the table in terms of how they wish to use the tool. In some ways, *design* *logic* is closer to research on designing games rather than playing them. Constance Steinkuehler explains it this way:

> To make a game is not only to decompose a system, understand its structure and parts, but then also reassemble a model of that system using algorithms (code). It also means to express an idea explicitly for others, to create for them a first-person experience that one believes is worth having. It is to share a viewpoint inside. Thus, game creation is emancipatory. Like all art mediums, game making fosters individual autonomy by forcing designers to examine how technical, material, and social systems work, take a position or stance on their operation, and express that outlook for others as a first-person experience.[13]

This powerful view of technology learning can extend beyond game design to other technologies. In Gisela's case, she learned Audacity to tell the story of her struggle to figure out who she was as the language she used to express herself changed. "*What part of yourself do you keep?*" Her goal was to create a radio segment to bring a broader awareness that language acquisition involves identity shift. To use new technological tools to tell that story, Gisela used *design logic*.

Later in the program, in a meeting with other Radio Arte students and staff, Gisela and her peer coproducer shared their radio segments for critique. Everyone listened intently as they queued up the audio on a computer, projecting the sound through a pair of speakers. Ambient noise of young children running around a schoolyard calling out to one another *en español*—an image of naïve childhood play—filled the room. Soon after, Gisela's narration confronted this idyllic image with the challenge of language acquisition "facing many immigrant children in Chicago Public Schools" who must "forge a new identity" far from their parents' country of origin. The segment ended and Gisela's peers and program staff nodded and smiled, telling Gisela and her coproducer that it sounded "really professional"—"like NPR." Gisela seemed pleased by the comparison to National Public Radio.

Seeing the Logic

Gisela was not alone in this approach. In interviews and observations, many tech-savvy teens articulated an awareness of the designed nature of technology and worked to decode logics to achieve particular goals. At Radio Arte, other students also reported they use *design logic* to move between software programs, looking for similarities and differences using a combination of this habit with *use of models* as Gisela did. For example, Stefani at Radio Arte explained that to learn Audacity she successfully applied the logic of other programs she used in the past. To make a sound fade in and out, Stefani said, she used her knowledge of Pro Tools (another audio engineering program) to figure out how to create a fading effect in Audacity. Alan, an Asian male with spiky short hair in Mouse Squad CA at Giannini Middle School in San Francisco, smiled when asked what helps him learn. He said, "Oh, I've got tricks!" One of the main things he does, like Gisela and Stefani, is look for things in certain places, like System Preferences or other things that might be similar in design across technologies.

Many student-teacher interactions in programs—as will be described further in chapter 6—focused on *design logic*, where teachers helped students read the internal grammar but then very quickly encouraged students to use the tools for their own purposes. For example, at Youth Movement Records (YMR) in Oakland, the African American male instructor Tony (whom we met in chapter 2) encouraged students to use *design logic* to learn the audio software Reason to create "beats" or musical compositions. Tony walked around the small, windowless classroom and checked in with an African American teen named DJ, who was clicking rapidly with his mouse, an Oakland A's hat sitting neatly on the computer table next to his hand.

TONY (*glancing at DJ and then looking at his screen*): You use any instruments besides N-19?

DJ: I just used whatever *they* pick.

TONY: Okay, but don't only use them [instruments provided by the program].

In this case, DJ articulated an understanding that software is designed (that designers make choices and "pick" sounds) and that the design logic shapes what he could do with Reason. Tony encouraged him to move beyond software defaults to mix sounds and make his own product. Later, during an interview, DJ explicitly said that what helped him learn new technology was "to put myself in the [designer's] shoes." To be able to learn how to use a new piece of technology is to read its purpose and think about how that shapes what you can do; instructors like Tony encouraged students to be aware of and think through this logic, but only in order to accomplish their own goals.

In other programs with a similar curricular focus on audio production, instructors and students also emphasized the use of *design logic*. For example, the African American instructor Dan at BUMP Records said that the things instructors did that helped him as a teen in the program also helped the students he now taught in the program. This list included building the habits described in previous chapters—a *willingness to try and fail, management of frustration and boredom*, and *use of models*. And, it also involved the development of one particularly helpful habit: seeing the logic of the design, especially through comparison with other technologies, he said, is key to learning. Dan explained:

> I tell students, they can apply what they learned in Pro Tools [to] any programs. For example, at home I have Acid and Adobe Audition. They're similar to Pro Tools. It was easy for me to learn them because I had seen the format before. You take what you've learned here (*gestures to computer*) and you can apply it elsewhere. Lots of students that see similarities between programs understand things faster.

In other words, students who read the logic of the design and apply similar logic to another computer program (through the *use of models*) have an easier time learning new technology.

Students in other technology programs with a different curricular focus also used *design logic*. For example, in Mouse/Geek Squad Summer Academy in New York City, I followed another group of girls called the "Digital Divas" to a session on computer networking. I watched, sitting at a table with two African American girls named Maya and Sierra, as a white male instructor named Kenneth explained in a deep Bronx accent how cables for a digital subscriber line (also known as DSL, an internet connection that uses telephone lines) should be plugged in to a network terminator (a box that connects data equipment to a line from the service provider).[14] Kenneth said to the students, "First goes the striped orange, then orange, then striped green, blue, striped blue, green, striped brown, brown." He explained why that particular order was important and told the girls to plug the cables into the network terminator in the correct order. He then turned on some music and he and the girls sang along (repeating the same, popular song: "*We fly high, no lie, you know this—ballin'!*") while other instructors handed out equipment.

As the girls worked diligently, I turned to the one sitting next to me and asked what she thought of the exercise. Maya smiled brightly, "I like this. It's like the circuitry we did in science last year." I expected her to find the task too simplistic, but instead she found it exciting to make a connection between circuitry and networking. In doing so, Maya combined the *use of models* with *design logic* to understand that technologies have logics that may be transferred across technologies. Like Dan at BUMP Records, Maya recognized that the logic of circuitry was "applicable to other areas."

Later, as I watched the Digital Divas in a PC Build class, instructors led them in a "speed build" whereby they raced each other to put the pieces of a computer together. How did the winning team (Taysia, who was still wearing the pink bracelet I'd seen her wearing playing Guitar Hero, and another African American girl named Samra) pick things up so quickly? Samra, not missing a beat as though she'd been asked the question a million times before, explained that a big part of learning new technologies is "recognizing patterns." These patterns are the *design logic* of both software and hardware—understanding the logic made it easier to learn new technologies and use them with greater proficiency. Turning back to their pile of equipment, Samra and Taysia continued to work, practicing putting the computer together to sharpen their understanding of the logic of how computer parts fit, taking it apart and putting the computer back together, again and again, smiling all the while. Other groups did the same, asking instructors to time them so they could get faster and make the logic second nature.

This habit and the second technology-specific learning habit I describe in the following section complete the set of five habits. Some of these habits are previously known from research on learning in general, applied to technology learning (*willingness to try and fail, management of frustration and boredom, use of models*). This one (*design logic*) is modified from past work on digital literacies to more centrally address the process of learning, the changing nature of technological tools, and the goals learners bring to the task. *Design logic* is an awareness of and ability to identify patterns embedded in the design of technologies, thinking about how to decode the logic of these patterns, and reading the purpose behind the design against one's own goals. The last habit (*efficiencies*) is unlike the others in that it is completely new.

EFFICIENCIES

The second of the two technology-specific habits I identified during observations and interviews is something I call *efficiencies*. It has three components. First is awareness that software and hardware often (but not always) have shorter ways of accomplishing tasks (like keyboard commands vs. pull-down menus). Second is thinking about how to find these shorter pathways to make work and learning faster. Finally, there's the behavior of trying out and practicing these efficient ways of accomplishing tasks. It includes things like hot keys as well as ways to shorten work like "batch" functions (for example, recording an action in Photoshop and repeating this action with an entire folder of image files). While the general notion of efficiencies could be applied to anything—

faster ways of cooking, for example—this habit is key to technology learning because efficiencies are often embedded in technological systems with the expectation that users will seek them out and their use is a core feature of technological competence (that is, figuring out ways to be faster).

The CoolSwitch

In Oakland in late June 2009 I'm again at YMR observing Chris, the Pro Tools instructor (a white male, whom we met in chapter 2), teach in a small computer classroom. There are five students: one Latinx male, two African American males, and two African American females. Chris says he's going to teach them some "tricks." He walks the students through some of the functionality of the program. After explaining how "copy and paste" works in Pro Tools, he says, "The only thing I didn't give you is the commands."

Chris continues, "You can hold down the option key and drag it [to duplicate]. And, if you want to add a sound, you can make a selection by right clicking or hitting the control key. Then, you hit copy and paste to add the sound." Students gaze up to their left where Chris has projected his computer's screen on the wall. He repeats his instructions and demonstrates these actions, an additional track appearing below his original track. Chris says, "Now, you know the tools—the selector tool and the grabber. But you really only need selection. Shortcuts *make you faster*." Chris then launches into one more shortcut, explaining that the plus and minus keys function in the same way as the hand tool in Pro Tools. "Hit the plus key until you see something," he explains, demonstrating that this shortcut moves his selection. "So, that took all of the functionality of the hand tool." In other words, using these shortcuts will allow the students to use the program more easily.

Chris's extended explanation of keyboard commands strikes me as odd—I circle it in my notebook. Are shortcuts really that important? As Chris finishes, students practice keyboard commands to manipulate the software. They smile as though they had just learned a big secret.

I remember this same feeling when I learned something known as the "CoolSwitch"—holding the Command key on a Mac or the Alt key on a PC together with the Tab key to switch between running programs.[15] Using the shortcut felt like magic. I think: *Maybe there's something to this.* Rae, the African American female teen we met in chapter 2 who had announced her intention to learn Pro Tools, looks up from her computer and asks Chris if there is a way she can move her selection up and down. Chris shows her where to find more keyboard commands and says, pointing, "There's A-Z at the top which you can use for keyboard commands. The P [key] makes it move up, semicolon moves you down." Rae, now equipped with the answer to her question, as well as a way to find more shortcuts, tries this trick and says, "Niiice!"

The Importance of Tricks of the Trade

These kinds of tricks to be faster using technology are important for learning for three reasons. First, students said knowing there are things like keyboard commands and looking for shortcuts helps them figure out how to manipulate technologies faster and makes them feel more confident in their ability to learn, which in turn makes learning less laborious because learners don't have to consciously navigate every step when using hardware and software. When these steps become effortless, it allows the learner to focus on more advanced technology use—it helps learners feel and be more efficacious using technology. For example, an African student named Bisi at Global Kids' I Dig Zambia in New York City explained that things like keyboard commands "make the learning process shorter" and give him the general sense he can easily learn any type of technology, if he looks for these shortcuts.

Second, students said learning tricks not only helps them become faster and more proficient with a particular program, it also helps them move across multiple technologies when they look for similar shortcuts across programs, using a combination of *design logic*, *use of models*, and *efficiencies*. For example, Jeffrey, an Asian teen in BAVC's game design program who hoped to be a chef and designed a video game about cooking, explained that finding shortcuts was one of his most helpful learning habits. He said he looks for "hot keys" or "shortcuts" which help him "figure things out" and understand technologies with greater ease.

Third, combining the *use of models* and *efficiencies*, students can identify more knowledgeable peers by those who use these kinds of tricks—and it is also how teachers identify more knowledgeable students. For example, in BAVC game design when I explained my interest in what helps students learn new technologies to Zack, he recommended that I speak with his friend Jeffrey because he had "all these little tricks." Jeffrey's tricks included using efficiencies. He would find things embedded in the technologies (e.g., shortcuts) as well as figure out creative ways of making work faster that might be outside of the technology's original purpose. For example, someone might use Instagram to get a particular filter effect for an image and use it for something like designing a game, rather than posting the image to social media. Using tricks signals insider knowledge, so the habit of *efficiencies* works as an identifier of "techie" group membership and belonging—like knowing the secret club handshake.

Based on my own experiences learning the CoolSwitch, I was vaguely aware of this habit, but I had not realized how essential it could be for student learning. Neither has research; unlike *design logic* and the general habits described in chapter 2, this habit appears nowhere in prior literature. The only existing written materials describing *efficiencies* are how-to manuals explaining shortcuts for particular software. For example, Pro Tools manuals devote pages and pages to explain how keyboard commands work. One advanced manual has an entire section (thirty-four pages) on "Tactile Control of Pro Tools," including this introduction:

> Using a keyboard to access the functions you use regularly increases both speed and precision. As you become more familiar with Pro Tools (and dedicated to implementing these shortcuts into your workflow), you will start to develop "strings" of key combinations that will allow you to "touch-type" routine tasks. Just like standard typing, becom-

ing efficient at controlling Pro Tools with an alphanumeric keyboard requires time and practice. In this lesson you'll explore seldom used keyboard commands, review the general theory behind modifiers, and learn focus key functions you may have not known even existed in Pro Tools. . . . Many common modifier and key combination listings are directly available through Pro Tools by clicking on the menu Help > Keyboard Commands. However, numerous key combinations do not have menu equivalents and some are contextual in nature.[16]

In other words, shortcuts are a core way of becoming proficient—but they can be hard to find and difficult to learn. In fact, they are so foundational that the book recommends special color-coded keyboards (or "skins" to go over keyboards) to identify the keyboard commands for Pro Tools, Adobe Premiere, InDesign, and other software.

Becoming an Insider

All the programs I observed explicitly taught *efficiencies*, through teacher-student instruction and peer interaction, because it is a key part of becoming an insider. To be seen and feel like a techie, you must use *efficiencies*. Instructors repeatedly explained shortcuts and encouraged students to look for and use them. They taught keyboard commands for computer use in general (such as Command+C for copying on a Mac or Windows+D on a PC for minimizing all windows) or commands specific to the particular software students were learning. For example, in the Pro Tools class, Chris showed students how to "toggle" between windows using Command+. In the Reason class, Tony explained:

> Let me show you a trick. . . . Draw in a bunch of octaves (*demonstrates on an overhead projector*). Now, get a different instrument, don't draw it in—hit Tab to go behind it (*demonstrates*) [this displays the back of what looks like a "rack" of audio equipment]. Then *click and hold* it (*demonstrates*), drop it in the second spot (*demonstrates*). So, if you want to have two instruments doing the same thing, that trick works.

Instructors told students that tricks like these could help them use technologies more proficiently and were especially useful when moving from technologies they already knew how to use to ones they were beginning to learn (with *use of models*), as a way of trying to build on prior knowledge (if possible).

This emphasis on *efficiencies* communicated to students that a central practice of technological competence and a way of signaling membership as a tech insider is knowing "secret" tricks. In DYN workshops at YOUmedia Chicago, instructors explained and repeated keyboard commands many times to students—especially Command+S (using Macs; Ctrl+S on a PC) to save their files. They would also quiz students on keyboard commands. For example, in music production, African American instructor and professional musician Simeon asked the group about a shortcut in GarageBand (on a Mac), "Anyone remember how to make this a keyboard?" Maurice (a teen who went on to study film in college) offered, "Shift+Apple+K?" Simeon nodded. In video production, Raphael explained how to use keyboard commands in iMovie: "Let's say you want the first clip to be two seconds. The bar that scrolls is the *play head*. Go earlier in the first clip, then hit Apple+T, that slices. Now you have two clips. To get rid of one, you click it and hit Delete. If you make a mistake, you hit Apple+Z [to undo it; this command corresponds to Ctrl+Z on a PC]." A bit later, Raphael gave a shortcut for applying transitions, such as fading in and out between scenes, across clips. "Next, let's go to transitions. Find two clips and make sure play head is in between the two. You could take one of the transitions and drop it. You can also hold the Shift key and click on the clips you wanted to apply the same transition to all of them." Students followed along and tried the tricks Raphael suggested, some students scribbling commands in their notebooks.

Students also helped other students learn *efficiencies*. For example, during an editing session at Radio Arte, students put together *radio-novelas*, following scripts written in prior weeks. Teams moved through each line of their scripts, making sure they could find various recordings and editing to cut extraneous time and ensure that there was sufficient space between speakers so listeners could follow the storyline. Roberto, a Latinx teen with neatly combed back hair and black horn-rimmed glasses, sat working on one segment. He turned to Laura, another Latinx teen in a black hoodie—who I later found out had been in the program the previous year—and asked how to get rid of a section of audio. Laura said, "Click twice and hit Delete." Roberto tried this trick and succeeded, then said, "Got it, thanks!"

To summarize, *efficiencies*—the last of the five habits that help teens learn new technologies—means understanding that technology often has shorter ways of accomplishing tasks, thinking about how to find short pathways to make use more efficient, and trying out and practicing more efficient pathways. Teens reported that finding shortcuts was one of their most helpful habits—something completely left out of previous research on technology learning. This habit was also a central feature of how students and teachers defined *technological competence*—teens said people who are good with technology are "fast" in their technology use and learning process, and that this habit helped them feel more confident and more like a tech insider. It was so ubiquitous that my notes were crammed with example after example of teachers and students explaining secret tech tricks. Certainly, as a learner, if you didn't know these efficiencies, you might look around and feel like you're missing something that everyone around you seems to know and therefore that you don't belong. These types of secret insider tricks symbolically mark who is a "techie" and, from an outsider perspective, might make some people appear as though they have a "natural" ability with technology while others don't.

GENDER AND TECHNOLOGY-SPECIFIC HABITS

Are people who are using these habits—particularly *efficiencies*—necessarily doing good work, or might they be rushing toward mediocrity? It is true that a student might learn to use shortcuts using software to create a video game or compose a song but nevertheless craft low-quality products. These habits do not take into account the quality of what teens do with computers—that is taken up by research on skills and literacies, which are honed over time. Learning habits, skills, and literacies are intimately related, but they are not precisely the same. Habits support the development of skills and literacies within particular technologies, as well as the transfer of these abilities across technologies.

In fact, other studies looking at the development of technical skill in the digital realm have identified similar habits for *analog* (nondigital) technologies. For example, in a 2004 study of technical work, describing how a Malaysian mechanic learned his trade, Ulf Mellström did not describe them as such but identified four of the five habits: *use of models, a willingness to try and fail, management of frustration and boredom,* and *efficiencies*:

> Ah Teong's father seldom told him explicitly how to perform the different tasks in the workshop. "*Observe* and *try*" was always the implicit message, through practical interaction with the materials. . . . Then the apprentice moves on to increasingly complex tasks that require a combination of occupational skills and tenacity. During this phase of learning, the apprentice must endure tedium. . . . It is a time of proving that one can stand *the boredom of certain tasks* and the mild indignity of continually being bossed around. . . . Another important part of the learning process is [finding shortcuts]. . . . Ah Teong says, "*You have to find the shortcuts*. By a good ear you can always find the shortcuts. *Finding shortcuts is the most important!*"[17]

Whereas Mellström characterizes these experiences as *phases* of vocational skill development through technical apprenticeship, I argue that they are *habits* necessary for continual technological learning.

Mellström goes on to show how these habits are mapped to masculinity because boys are taught to embody these thoughts, feelings, and actions, but girls are not. To enact these habits is to embody masculinity. With digital technologies, too, there are gender differences. Although it might seem surprising given all the tech-savvy girls described in this chapter (Gisela, Stefani, Laura, Samra, Taysia, Rae, and Maya), in a later survey of almost 900 Chicago Public School eighth-grade students (and another survey of almost 1,300 high school students in the Boston area), I found significant differences in the five habits by gender.[18] Although there are techie girls—some even more so than boys—girls use fewer technology learning habits on average, and differences seem to hinge on the two technology-specific habits described in this chapter: *design logic* and *efficiencies*.[19] In his work Mellström argues, "What this shows . . . is that the gender codification of technology starts early and runs deep and that it is based on an early embodiment of machines.[20]

How gender is constituted through technology use in childhood has profound implications for later professional life, but its form depends on cultural context." Whereas Mellström's 2004 research on vocational technologies suggests a deep divide in the socialization of boys and girls that might be difficult to address, his 2009 article on computer science shows that women in Malaysia actually dominate this field. Therefore, he argues that gender and technology relations are always "deeply embedded in cultural contexts shaping the use, design and production of technologies, and their co-production of gender and technology."[21] I take these findings to mean that gender-based inequities in tech are difficult to address (as are other types of inequities)—but none of them is fixed. Or, more pragmatically: teach girls technology-specific habits, which seem to be specialized gender-coded insider knowledge, and see how they do. Maybe a girl like Cindy, who was highly skilled in many general learning habits, would benefit from these technology-specific habits and more readily assert that she is exactly the kind of person who can code. But it is also crucial to shift our general assumptions away from the idea that people either have a "natural" ability or they do not, in order to change the broader cultural context.

To understand these gender-based differences—and an important lack of race-based differences discussed in the next chapter—it is necessary to measure the five habits. A measure makes technical learning explicit, observable, and potentially explainable across a wider sample of students—as well as provides a tool for educators, policy makers, and researchers. But measures can be biased, depending on the group with which they are developed. So I deliberately piloted and tested a measure of the five habits with a group of racially, socioeconomically, linguistically, and gender diverse teens—so as to again avoid conflating successful technology learning habits in ways that devalue the practices of those historically marginalized.[22] I explain the process of developing the measure and describe findings with regard to race, class, and gender differences in the five technology learning habits in the next chapter.

CONCLUSION: THE FIVE HABITS

So what is technological competence and how can we help students achieve it? By studying a diverse group of successful technology learners, we can redefine what it means to be good with technology in a more equitable way, with five technology learning habits at its core: *willingness to try and fail, management of frustration and boredom, use of models, design logic,* and *efficiencies.* The first three habits link to general approaches to learning applied to technology learning, and the final two habits—the keys to the clubhouse—are technology specific. Table 3.1 summarizes all five habits.

This answer does three things. First, redefining technological competence to add the set of habits as a central feature provides a way for educators, parents, and policy makers to rethink the goals of technology education. Second, describing the five habits (and offering a measure of the habits, presented in chapter 4) gives educators and parents a concrete way to observe technology learning readiness and identify where to intervene. Finally, and most critically, redefining technological competence to focus on learning habits—rather than a magical "natural" ability—demystifies the process of technical work. It counters the idea of "instinct," which essentializes technological competence in ways that perpetuate racism, sexism, and classism. Instead, it redefines technological competence with a focus on continual learning—and describes how diverse, tech-savvy teens learn new technologies.

TABLE 3.1. The five technology learning habits

Willingness to try and fail	1. Developing the attitude that it is okay to try new things and make mistakes
	2. Trying new things and using failure as an opportunity for learning
Management of frustration and boredom	1. Developing the attitude that it is okay to be frustrated and bored with learning
	2. Reflecting on feelings and physiological responses to frustration and boredom
	3. Enacting behaviors to manage frustration and boredom (e.g., persisting by taking breaks but then going back to tasks, placing oneself in a nondistracting environment, actively rejecting potential distractions)
	4. Monitoring focus
Use of models	1. Developing an awareness of and ability to identify different types of models for learning technology and comparing one's approach to these models
	2. Placing oneself in proximity to models, watching and asking questions
	3. Trying out models' approach to learning technology
Design logic	1. Developing awareness that technology is designed with a system of logic
	2. Decoding logic to achieve goals
Efficiencies	1. Developing awareness that technology has long and short pathways of workflow
	2. Thinking strategically about how to find short pathways to make learning easier
	3. Developing the attitude that finding efficient pathways is helpful for learning
	4. Finding, trying out, and practicing efficient pathways

Source: Adapted from Cassidy Puckett, "Digital Adaptability: A New Measure for Digital Inequality Research," *Social Science Computer Review* (2020), https://doi.org/10.1177/0894439320926087.

But this answer doesn't do everything. Even if all teens are taught and develop the five habits, their talent needs to be recognized and valued; it is unlikely to solve pervasive racism, classism, and sexism in technology education and occupations. It will not address how certain groups are barred from tech fields and the job market in general, given that studies show, for example, that applicants with Black- and Latinx-sounding names receive a significantly lower number of callbacks for job applications despite equal qualifications with white applicants.[23] Further, a 2018 experiment focusing on tech jobs showed that human screeners incorrectly believe that "younger black applicants have worse computer skills and worse training than younger white applicants."[24]

However, if this redefinition challenges general assumptions about technological competence, it is a good start. For example, rather than judging job applicants solely on current skill, employers might assess applicants' learning process as an indicator of how they will perform as technologies change. Thinking about habits as key to technological competence might also make it possible to identify the hidden techies, the historically marginalized students who already use these habits and have so much talent—who, when identified, can be better supported with access to opportunities and fully realize their potential.

[4]

Recognizing the Five Habits

THE DIGITAL ADAPTABILITY SCALE

In a southwestern corner of Chicago, thirteen-year-old Jasmine greets me as I enter the small front room of her grandmother's house, where she lives with her mom and younger brother. Jasmine self-identified as tech savvy and very interested in the study, but she was not identified as such by her middle-class school. School administrators admitted they were "behind the times with tech" and largely relied on students being "naturally" good with technology through socialization in a digital world, rather than offering coursework to support more and less tech-savvy students.[1] In fact, it was a challenge to identify who was who, and some teachers had no knowledge of Jasmine's "interest." Her grand-mother's house is a single story with a slanted gray roof, white aluminum siding, and windows with neat black shutters. It is surrounded by large trees, located on a corner of a quiet street a short walk from her two-story brick school building with a large grassy lawn in front. It's not what stereotypes suggest you might find on Chicago's South Side— not a neighborhood in disarray, but a calm suburban enclave, lush with trees and dotted with orderly single-family homes (almost 70 percent of them owner occupied)—and small neighborhood parks, all outlined with carefully maintained sidewalks. Highway, industry, and stretches of overgrown vacant lots are a short ride away, but here the surroundings are solidly middle class.

Jasmine's grandmother motions us to sit at a table in a room to the left of the front door. In the room next to us to the right are two large black leather couches in an *L* shape where a little boy sits watching the television I can faintly hear in the background. Jasmine smiles and quietly sits on a wooden chair to my right. I sit in the chair in front of me, with a window at my back, and pull out my computer, setting it carefully on the table. I explain I'll be asking her to learn a new technology, but I don't tell her that I'm doing this to see her technology learning habits. She nods quietly and bends slightly forward as I set up my computer and turn it to face her. From her reserved stance, I might guess she'll have a difficult time with the task I'll be asking her and other students to do: learn how to use a software program called Scratch—developed at the Massachusetts Institute of Technology (MIT) to teach basic coding, computer science concepts and activities, and computational thinking—to move a cat figure ("sprite") from one side of the screen to the other side of the screen.[2] Or, based on her demographic background (female, African American, daughter of a single parent), one might think she is unlikely to be interested in computer science. But I know better than to assume anything.

She first watches a short informational video about the software. Then, she listens intently as I tell her she has ten minutes to explore and ten to figure out the task. I also say that I'm interested in her thought process so I'd like her to "think aloud" as she works. She nods, saying nothing. Then she takes hold of the mouse I've connected to the laptop and I watch as the cursor arrow moves across the screen. What is she thinking? What does she see? She notices a block (a visual chunk of code) with text on it that says "move 10 steps" and she clicks and drags it to the center of the screen.

How did she know to do that? Why did she do that? She says she's unsure but that the words made her think the blocks could move the cat. But why move a block to the middle of the screen?

Jasmine says, "I'm not sure."

I smile. "You're not sure? Okay." I note her *willingness to try and fail* and how she's trying to decipher the *design logic* behind the blocks. She moves the cursor arrow across other blocks, reading what they say. She clicks and drags one that says "`set x to 0`" and places it above the first "`move 10 steps`" block, linking the two. She picks up another block that says "`set y to 0`" and connects it to her growing stack of blocks.

Jasmine asks, "Can you change these numbers?"

I smile again. "Can you?"

Jasmine smiles back at me, interpreting the learning process as a game (a way to *manage frustration and boredom*). She turns back to the computer, "I think you can." She changes the number of steps and the value for *x* and *y*, clicking on the set of blocks, making them flash and the cat move slightly. What is she thinking now? "It looks like when you click on the blocks, the cat moves." She could keep clicking and moving the cat to reach the other side of the box and complete the task, but she doesn't stop there. Instead, she moves her cursor across the screen, around the white box where the cat is located.

What is she looking at now? She points out there are numbers—coordinates, she thinks—in the bottom right of the white box. They change as she moves her arrow. Connecting the software to the geometry she learned in school (*use of models*) she says, "It must be a coordinate plane." She matches the *x* and *y* coordinates in the two blocks (the one that says "`set x to 0`" and the other that says "`set y to 0`") to the *x* and *y* coordinates she sees when placing the cursor on the left side of the white box. She clicks on the blocks. The cat appears on the left side of the box—now it just needs to go to the right. It's 4 minutes and 50 seconds into the task.

She drags another block to the center of the screen that moves the cat toward a "mouse-pointer." She plays with it, but she quickly realizes it moves the cat in the wrong direction (to the left, where her cursor is located). She separates that block away from the others. She also separates the "steps" block she used earlier, focusing on the coordinate blocks, now that she's read the design in a way that she under-

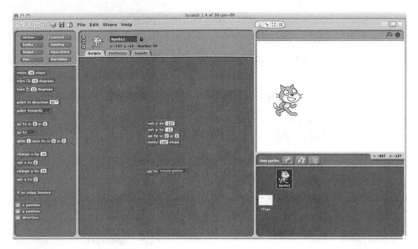

FIGURE 4.1 Jasmine's task

stands it as a coordinate plane. She picks up another block that says "go to x: 0 y: 0." She changes the numbers to match the starting blocks (–237, –13), so that it's at precisely the same level (237, –13). She clicks on the blocks and the cat moves from the left side to the right side of the box. While she found blocks earlier that moved the cat, she was looking for *efficiencies*—the fastest way to move it across the screen. It's 6 minutes and 40 seconds into the task, and she's succeeded.

"What just happened?!" I laugh.

Jasmine smiles again, "It went from one side to the other." I continue to laugh. She's solved the task in less than 7 minutes; something that took a number of the other seven students I asked to do the task much longer or they couldn't do at all. I congratulate her and decide to challenge her further because she's ready and willing. I explain the difference between a robot with a controller (something similar to what she just did) and an "autonomous" robot that moves on its own.[3] I ask if she thinks she can figure out how to make the cat move autonomously. She smiles, shrugs, and says, "Sure." (Again, showing her *willingness to try and fail*.) She sets to work, finding more programming blocks under the "control" tab and figures out three different blocks that can make the cat move more autonomously, including a block that tells the program to run when she clicks on a green flag in the top right corner of the white box and another block that tells the program to run when she clicks on the cat itself. She does both, succeeding at the challenge.

I laugh again, telling her that now she can give herself any challenge she wants, and she continues to explore. She clicks back to the motion blocks and, seeming to get more comfortable, says, "I'm thinking about this block that says 'glide' and seeing what that will do." She clicks and drags the block into the middle of the screen, types in "3 seconds" for the amount of gliding time and plugs in the same target coordinates (237, -13). She adds that to the blocks that position the cat at the starting point (left side of the white box) and clicks. The cat slides smoothly across the screen. She smiles, sheepishly. Fifteen minutes into exploring and doing the task and she's figured out five different ways of moving the cat across the screen. Has she ever done this task at school? No, they don't do that much with technology at school, but her mom is in a technology program at a nearby community college and encourages her to use it. She plans to go to a nearby award-winning technical high school next year and major in engineering.

She wants another challenge. Can she make the cat move back to its starting point after it has moved to the right side of the box? She moves the blocks so that she has her original starting blocks, the movement blocks, and then a gliding block, changing the coordinates to the starting position (-237, -13). She clicks and the cat moves to the starting point on the left side of the box, then to the right side of the box, and finally slides gracefully back to its starting point. She smiles, satisfied, ready for more.

DIGITAL NATIVE VS. DIGITAL ADAPTABILITY

Without identifying the habits Jasmine used to learn Scratch, it might seem that what she did was "natural" ability. Jasmine instead has what I call "digital adaptability." She uses the five habits in such a regular, fluid way, that they seem to come naturally to her. Digital adaptability, then, is a foundational but until now undiscovered aspect of technological competence. My redefinition of *tech competence* is: skills, literacies, *and* the technology learning habits that help individuals continually adapt and develop new or more advanced skills and literacies. In chapters 2 and 3, I described the five technology learning habits that help tech-savvy teens learn new technologies. Identifying and naming these habits in no way discounts Jasmine's and others' tech savviness—it is absolutely magical to watch. But assuming that her technological competence is a natural ability does Jasmine and others a disservice because it suggests tech savviness is something that can't be taught or learned and that those with "natural" talent will be readily identified and rewarded based on their technological merit. None of that is true.

At academic conferences, in discussion with colleagues, speaking with friends and family, or meeting new people, I am often asked what I do. When I explain I study "how teens learn new technologies," I get variations of the same response: "My three-year-old is a whiz with my iPhone. Kids these days seem to *just know* what to do. Why not study adults?"

Even when I present evidence that there are teens who struggle with technology, I still encounter the assumption of natural ability over and over again. This idea—that teens seem to "just know" what to do with technology—rests on the theory that all teens are naturally skillful, socialized to be good with technology through immersion in the technology all around them. Scholars call this notion the myth of the "digital native."[4] It's true that there are some very tech-savvy teens. I've met many. At a superficial level, it might seem like they just know what to do, in a kind of natural way.

But three parts of this assumption are incorrect. First, it's not magic; there is something tech-savvy teens do as they learn. To assume "natural" ability hides the time and effort students like Jasmine took to develop these habits. It also hides the loving encouragement of people like Jasmine's mom, the financial and emotional support of her grandmother, and her school's rigorous school mathematics curriculum (although even with less mathematical training, depending on the technology's design, students can learn new technologies—as some technologies rely more heavily on users' knowledge of mathematical concepts and procedures than others do).[5]

Second, based on stereotypes about the particular people who are "naturally" good with technology, tech savviness might not be "seen" in certain teens. Maybe an African American girl like Jasmine might not be expected to be tech-savvy. Or, as was the case at Jasmine's school, there may not be opportunities for her to share her ability with gatekeepers and potential "learning brokers" such as teachers who could point her in the direction of new learning opportunities—although her mother made up for this lack through her encouragement at home.[6] Even in schools with technology classes and other opportunities, there still may be hidden techies, as I found in my research and describe in this chapter. These kids are the "bad" kids (those who act out or perform poorly in school), whose abilities might not be recognized by teachers and therefore do not "earn" the privilege of technology learning opportunities.[7] I've met many tech-savvy teens, and they simply do not look alike.

Third, there are also teens who clearly do not "just know" what to do with technology. There are students like the ones in my web design class—Maria, Meihong, Cindy—who are perfectly capable but who need teachers who know how to support their technology learning habits. In some ways, the "intuitive design" of technologies can work against the learning process, not prompting users to think about how and why technologies are designed the way they are or learn anything about how they work. The five technology learning habits have to be taught, and they can be learned. But educators and researchers need to be able to identify their presence or absence, breadth, and strength in order to help students. So, how do we see the habits? I use two methods: qualitative and quantitative observation.

QUALITATIVE OBSERVATION: ADAPTABILITY VS. INTEREST

One way to observe digital adaptability is to ask teens to learn a new piece of technology, such as the Scratch task described at the beginning of this chapter—making sure to pose the task in as neutral a way possible and deflecting when teens ask for instruction or permission. For example, when Jasmine asked, "Can you change these numbers?" I asked her, "Can you?" Responding with questions may confuse students or make them uncomfortable if they are used to adults telling them what to do, but it allows you to see what they try without direction. Attempting this task demonstrates not only how well they do (if they are able to accomplish the task) but also *how* they do it (if they use the five habits). The task also involves asking teens to "think aloud" as they try to figure it out, since it is difficult to "observe" a thought process (which I repeatedly had to remind teens with, "Why did you do that?" "What are you looking at now?" "What are you thinking now?").[8]

In addition to the tech-savvy teens I followed to identify the five habits, I shadowed a group of eight Chicago Public Schools (CPS) eighth-grade students who varied in their technology learning habits, four in one lower-income school and four in one higher-income school. I identified these students using a quantitative measure (described later in this chapter), making sure to include students with a mix of habits, racial/ethnic and class backgrounds, and genders. I asked all of them to do the Scratch task, like the one Jasmine did, to see what differences in habits look like in person and to confirm that the quantitative measure captured differences in students' ability to learn new technologies. I also shadowed each student for two weeks (one week during the school year and one week during the summer) for a total of approximately eighty hours per student, interviewed them about their experiences in various contexts (at home, in school, among friends), talked with their parents and teachers about how they defined and taught technological competence, and had these students complete technology journals for two weeks when I was not present. Later, I did follow-up interviews with the same students in high school. I took these additional steps to investigate how students' experiences shape their habits and, ultimately, their long-term trajectories.

Teachers typically described students lower on the measure as not that "interested" in technology. One "uninterested" student was thirteen-year-old Anandi. She was small and thin with long dark hair, full of sparkling energy, frequently gesturing with her hands as she spoke. Anandi seemed skeptical that she could help me understand why some people are into technology and others are not but was intrigued by the idea of an adult following her around. She said, "I'm not that into computers," but with her family's approval, she agreed to be in the study. Anandi lived with her immediate family a few blocks from her school in a tan brick courtyard apartment building typical of Chicago. Their light-filled two-bedroom apartment had hardwood floors throughout and was sparsely furnished, with essentials including a small table in the kitchen; a futon, desk, chair, and computer in the living room; two beds in the bedroom shared with her brother; and one larger bed in her parents' bedroom to the right next to the kitchen.

Anandi explained that the furniture and computer (and its internet connection) were provided by an organization that helped them arrive in Chicago from a refugee camp in Nepal. Her family was originally from Bhutan—in fact, a large portion of her extended family lived in the building, including her grandmother, aunts and uncles, and cousins. Her mom taught elementary school at the camp in Nepal but worked at the Chicago airport at Jamba Juice, and her dad also worked in the service industry, doing maintenance in a hotel. Understanding my interest in technology, Anandi explained that the computer and internet connection at her house didn't always work well, but she said that didn't matter because she was not that into it. But what did not being "into it" mean?

At school, Anandi was highly social, and she mentioned things that happened on Facebook between her friends. But she avoided using technology even when it was available to her at school, instead writing and drawing pictures in a notebook. She attended the school's weekly computer class, but for the entire month I followed her and the three other students at her school, they primarily focused on test prep. There was only one lesson about how to use technology; it consisted of step-by-step instructions about how to insert pictures into Microsoft Word documents. She was also assigned a PowerPoint presentation about extinction that she had to complete with a classmate. She worked on the assignment with her partner during a tutoring session for other Bhutanese refugees at the school. I watched Anandi struggle and turn the computer over to her partner, a male student. After clicking briefly, she moved to a chair next to her partner and barely touched the computer, instead chatting with him and laughing while he made the PowerPoint. So perhaps she really just wasn't "interested."

But at home, Anandi admitted that she liked going on Facebook to chat with friends and leave them messages and images. She also liked to search for and watch YouTube videos of the boy band One Direction or *Ellen* talk show episodes with teen heartthrob Justin Bieber in them and videoconference with her boyfriend in Minnesota, whom she met in the refugee camp. In other words, she did use the computer for her own "interest-driven" activities. She also wanted to use technology in more "productive" ways, such as to design pictures to post on her friends' Facebook pages, which she couldn't remember how to do after her friend showed her. Also, while I shadowed Anandi in the summer, she attempted a task she had never done before: creating a fan page for One Direction and crafting images of band members holding up signs with the names of her friends. Her engagement showed a *willingness to try and fail*. However, she became disheartened after spending an hour pressing the same buttons over and over again (she did not have ways of *managing frustration and boredom*). She also made no attempt to find and *use models* to figure out how to do the task (I eventually stepped in to help after watching her struggle).

The same things happened when I gave her the Scratch task; she was nervous but expressed a *willingness to try and fail*. But she did not first explore the program as directed, which might have helped her find and *use models* (as there are examples embedded in Scratch) or connect the software to things she'd seen before. She also did not think about *efficiencies* that might help her in the task. Instead, she focused on moving the cat for the entire twenty minutes. She did try a few things, dragging blocks into the center of the screen (so, she did think about the *design logic* a bit, in terms of how elements of the software worked). But she became frustrated when the cat did not move in the ways she wanted

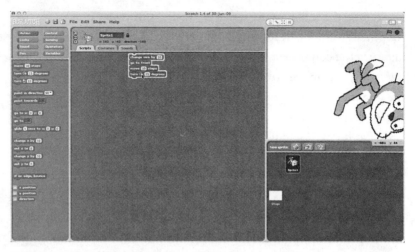

FIGURE 4.2 Anandi's task

Source: Cassidy Puckett and Jennifer L. Nelson, "The Geek Instinct: Theorizing Cultural Alignment in Disadvantaged Contexts," *Qualitative Sociology* 42, no. 1 (2019): 25–48.

(again, she did not have ways of *managing frustration and boredom*) and therefore clicked on the same commands over and over again, which made the cat spin and grow larger rather than move across the screen. This manipulation did eventually cause the cat to hit the right side of the screen, but she said she felt like she failed—a sort of confirmation that she was just not that "into" technology.

But were Anandi's challenges because of a lack of interest? Along with the assumption that young people just "know what to do," there is a related assumption that differences in technological ability are based on differences in "interest." Some kids are just more *interested* in technology (often boys) than others (often girls). Research shows that interest is indeed an important part of learning, where interest is related to positive learning behaviors (like focusing on tasks, which helps students achieve goals).[9] But there isn't evidence of what comes first—students' interest or their learning behaviors.

There's been a recent focus on designing curriculum around students' interest. In a certain way, this focus makes sense. Why wouldn't we want students to be interested in what they are learning? John Dewey, a well-known American philosopher and educational reformer, argued in 1913 that even with a mandate to be physically present at school, without interest, students' minds would be absent and little learning could occur.[10] But what many scholars call "interest-driven learning" assumes that a student's interest is already developed prior to learning.[11] This assumption skirts issues of equity. Applied to technology learning, a lack of established interest might suggest boys should be given computers and girls like Anandi, well, something else. But, what if instead interest emerges through the learning experience—and the development of a set of learning habits that help students learn?

This sequence of events was, in fact, what Dewey ultimately argued. He also said that interest happens when a person's fundamental self-expression is tied to what students are learning. Indeed, research on interest shows that it can develop *through experience.*[12] So, we should be careful not to assume that someone with less *experience* with technology has no *interest* in it. Dewey said educators can develop students' interest by "considering and aiming at the conditions that lie in back of it, and compel it."[13] He explained:

> If we can discover a child's urgent needs and powers, and if we can supply an environment of materials, appliances, and resources— physical, social, and intellectual—to direct their adequate operation, we shall not have to think about interest. It will take care of itself. For mind will have met with what it needs in order to be mind. The problem of educators, teachers, parents, and state, is to provide the environment that induces educative or developing activities, and where these are found the one thing needful in education is found.[14]

In other words, if educators craft learning experiences in an effective way and provide resources students need, they will be interested in what they are doing and learn new things. Therefore, if kids *want* to be tech savvy—something I've observed as consistently motivating across all demographics—educators should provide such an environment, including "resources . . . to direct their adequate operation." As a key intellectual resource, the habits can help them learn.

In fact, Anandi *was* interested in technological activities. She went online with her school friends and engaged in technology activities that connected her to the friends she grew up with in the refugee camp in Nepal. She was also interested in using technology for creative production, like the fan pages and images for her friends about One Direction. These activities were a part of her fundamental self-expression, and she was interested in personally meaningful technology tasks. She also did not lack digital resources; she had access to technology, even if sometimes not perfectly functional, both at home and at school. But, she was not provided the intellectual resources to help her succeed in these activities: habits that could support her while learning. So, it was difficult for her to learn new technology, and she was not very adaptable. The five technology learning habits I described in chapters 1 and 2 could help give her new ideas when the things she tried did not work (*use of models*) or techniques to buoy herself when she encountered problems (*management of frustration and boredom*).

Some observers might argue that Anandi simply didn't have strong enough interest—that was why she struggled so much with technology learning. But my research findings suggest that even when interest is high, it doesn't always translate into successful technology learning. For example, there were other students in Anandi's class who said they were *very* "into" technology. One was thirteen-year-old Rafael, a Latinx student and skateboarder who spoke with a slight California accent, even though he grew up in Chicago. Rafael was what many of his teachers called "distracted"—he spent the majority of his school time chatting with male friends, and teachers would catch him not paying attention and causing disruptions by giggling. He did not do particularly well in school. But when it came to technology, he just loved it. When we sat down in the library to do an interview, the librarian even called out from behind her desk, "Oh yeah, he's into gaming and good with technology!"

What Rafael liked most of all was playing video games. Flicking the light brown hair that hung across his eyes with a quick nod of his head, Rafael explained with a smile that his parents had recently divorced and moved into separate homes—so he had a gaming console *at both places!* It was great. He told me he'd play video games for hours and that he got into it through his older brother, cousins, and friends, who used to be better than him but now he could beat them. He also showed his parents how to find things on the internet, if they needed help. However, when I asked what he thought it meant to be good with technology, he was a bit unsure. He thought—maybe doing stuff like what he did? Playing video games, finding things on the internet. Being *into* it.

But, the Scratch task revealed that although Rafael was very much *into* technology, it didn't mean that he was adaptable. He showed many of the habits—but they were weak. After I instructed him to explore for ten minutes and then do the task of moving the cat for ten minutes, he hesitated before beginning, asking for more direction. When I shook my head, trying to encourage him to explore, he laughed. He clicked on the cat a couple times and declared, "I'm really lost." His response showed less of a *willingness to try and fail*—which he continued throughout the course of the task. "You can do whatever you want," I explained.

He did show some *design logic*. Clicking on the cat, then on the blocks of code, he said, "I think you can move the cat using these [blocks]." But he did not move the cat with the blocks, instead exploring other things. He figured out how to edit the design of the cat but worried that he might mess it up, so he said, "I don't know what I'm doing, so I'm going to exit out." (Again, he showed less of a *willingness to try and fail*.) He clicked on the Sounds tab, played the sound of a cat meowing (provided by the software), and laughed. He clicked on the Background and Paint Editor and said, "I think here you can customize the background. I'm going to see if that's what it really does." (Here he was showing *design logic* and a bit of *willingness to try and fail*.)

To change the background, he selected the brush tool and ran three red vertical lines down the white background. They appeared behind the cat. "Oh, okay," he said and played a bit more with the background, erasing the lines but then canceling that, then trying to make a checkerboard design by adding red horizontal lines to the vertical ones. But, trying to fill in the boxes he created, he selected the eyedropper tool and repeatedly clicked inside of the squares, which did nothing.

Rafael said, "I'm not sure if this is exactly the right tool . . . the eyedropper tool." He hesitated. "Is that the right tool, or no?"

I looked at him and smiled. "It's just for you to go ahead and explore."

He said, "But you gotta help me though!" We both laughed, knowing that was not the challenge.

He sighed and closed out the background, abandoning his checkerboard (showing he needed ways of *managing frustration*). He continued to click around and explore, finding a camera and taking a picture and accidentally adding it as a background. "Oh no!" he exclaimed, smiling. "I don't know what I'm doing!" Behind him watching what he was doing, I laughed along with him. He tried closing the camera, but it wouldn't close. He said to me, "I don't know how to exit this out. The camera. You maybe know how to?" This behavior did show he wanted to *use models* in the sense of asking someone else what they would do and it was one way of *managing frustration*. But asking someone to explain it to him was his *only* way of figuring things out—and it was not allowed in this task, as I explained at the beginning. He looked at me, hopeful. But I again smiled and shook my head no.

Ten minutes passed. I reminded him of the next part of the challenge to move the cat across the screen. He asked questions about how to make the cat move, "So you play it and it moves?" Realizing I wouldn't tell him he laughed and said, "I just got to figure it out myself? So mean!" Rafael right clicked (showing some sign of *efficiencies*) and accidentally clicked on a pull-down tab that said "grab screen region for new costume," dragging his cursor only across the cat's whiskers, which made the cat disappear. Rafael gasped. "I don't know what I did! How do you get the cat back?" I again didn't answer his question, and Rafael continued to click on the same set of buttons and tabs, not finding anything about the cat. He eventually clicked on a button that made the size of the white box unexpectedly shrink—also not what he'd intended—so

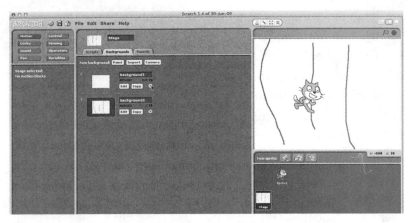

FIGURE 4.3 Rafael's task

Source: Cassidy Puckett and Jennifer L. Nelson, "The Geek Instinct: Theorizing Cultural Alignment in Disadvantaged Contexts," *Qualitative Sociology* 42, no. 1 (2019): 25–48.

he tried to click the same set of buttons to get the box back to its original size. But he couldn't figure out how to do that, either. Hesitating, he finally clicked a button with a star and question mark, just below the smaller white box, which made a new "sprite" (a little yellow figure with green feet and orange hands) appear. He played with other buttons around the white box, one of which made the yellow figure duplicate.

He now had three yellow figures—but was no closer to completing the task of moving them across the screen. I gave him a time warning at three minutes. I explained he could make the new sprites move. But he instead played with their design, seeming to give up on the task. After twenty minutes, although he did explore and showed some small signs of all five habits (*willingness to try and fail, management of frustration and boredom, use of models, efficiencies*, and *design logic*), his habits needed to be stronger to support learning a new technology. Even if he was *very interested* in technology.

One way to see the presence or absence, breadth, and strength of the five technology learning habits—and not mistake differences in habits for differences in "natural" ability or interest—is to challenge students to learn things that are new to them and think aloud as they try to figure things out. For example, a teacher or parent could give students the Scratch "performance" task I gave Jasmine, Anandi, Rafael, and others. This method is especially interesting because it shows the variety of ways teens do things like *manage frustration and boredom*. Some will simultaneously play video games if something is difficult for them to understand and they need a break; others will rest their head on a desk for a moment to take a breath. There are also multiple ways of finding and using models—for example, thinking about connections to things at school (as Jasmine did) or using the program to find examples they could emulate. In practice, the habits have many creative variations, even while fundamentally being the same set of five habits.

But giving each student a task and learning how to identify the presence or absence of any technology learning habits, which of the five habits students use, and how consistently they use each habit is tremendously time-consuming. It took me seven years, observing hundreds of teens and surveying a thousand more, to be able to see digital adaptability in this qualitative way. So, if you're a parent, teacher, or researcher who wants to understand the habits across a group in a shorter amount of time, how can you do observe their habits? A second way is to measure the habits quantitatively—which I did by using my initial observations of tech-savvy teens as information to help develop and validate a measure.

QUANTITATIVE OBSERVATION: EQUITABLY MEASURING ADAPTABILITY

We often use quantitative measures to "observe" all kinds of things—from mathematics achievement to college rankings to generational mobility.[15] They are a more efficient way of understanding broad trends and much easier than trying to observe adaptability among, for example, an entire classroom or an entire school. So, outside of asking each student to learn a new technology, as in the Scratch task, another way to "see" adaptability is to measure it. Therefore, I created and validated a quantitative scale to measure the five technology learning habits. I call it the Digital Adaptability Scale (DAS). Jasmine, Anandi, and Rafael were, in fact, part of a subset of students I studied to see what higher and lower adaptability looked like in practice and confirm that the DAS captured what it was intended to capture: those higher on the scale, like Jasmine, could accomplish the task while students lower on the scale, like Anandi, could not.

There are several benefits to quantitative measures. One is their efficiency when qualitative observation is infeasible. It's part of the reason for the use of fixed-choice exams, for example, over portfolio assessments, which can be time-consuming to evaluate.[16] Quantitative measures can provide a broader sense of student learning that can inform interventions at the individual and group level, such as which strategies students need to learn and how much practice students need to make them more habitual. They can also be useful in terms of understanding inequities in learning, as I observed in girls, who had a lower average DAS score in a sample of CPS students. And quantitative measures can help identify groups of students who are tech savvy but might not be recognized as such, which I found to be the case with lower-income and Black and Latinx students—only after I developed the measure.[17]

But quantitative measures do have some serious drawbacks, including glossing over individual nuances, like the struggles and successes I described in the qualitative accounts, into a single metric. Metrics do not capture the qualitative nature of how things occur, when complex things are boiled down to a simple number.[18] Measures are also ultimately socially produced and can contain significant biases, in part because of how they are developed. Because it is not possible to measure everyone, metrics are based on a specific sample, presenting a specific picture of what is typical. Metrics may appear to be entirely objective, but unless they are created with equity in mind, they can easily capture data wholly unrelated to what they claim to measure and as a result justify the reproduction of inequality. They might entirely exclude students like Jasmine, for example, if they measured personality instead of adaptability, as past measures did to identify potential computer scientists. As Nathan Ensmenger describes in his history of computer programming, psychologists in the 1950s and 1960s worked to create measures of personality profiles most prevalent among existing programmers and found there was only one distinguishing personality characteristic among programmers—"their disinterest in people," which "quickly became part of the lore of the computer industry."[19] Friendly Jasmine never would have passed the test.

In fact, biases in measures of learning and aptitude more broadly speaking are precisely the reason why researchers, colleges, and universities debate the usefulness of standardized tests, such as the SAT and ACT (originally known as the Scholastic Aptitude Test and American College Test) in admissions. In 2003, a retired psychologist named Roy Freedle, who worked for many years at Educational Testing Services (ETS), where the SAT is produced, found that the test was biased toward white and more affluent test takers because they scored slightly higher on the more heavily weighted "easier" verbal, mathematics, and essay questions.[20] These questions, he argued in an article in the *Harvard Educational Review*, relied on "common words" that could be interpreted in a number of ways and were biased toward white middle-class meanings of these words, such as *horse*, *snake*, *canoe*, and *golf*, which appeared in "easy" questions. Freedle found that Black and Latinx students did better on more-difficult questions that use more advanced vocabulary, with specific academic meaning, such as *vehemence*, *anathema*, *sycophant*, and *intractable*.

The response from ETS was to question the validity of Freedle's study, but the company agreed to have psychometricians at the University of California do a similar study with more recent SAT data. These researchers (Santelices and Wilson) again found similar results.[21] A number of colleges and universities have since made the SAT and ACT optional, although others continue to require their use.[22]

Although ethical issues are often discussed with qualitative research, there tends to be less discussion of ethics with quantitative analysis. Perhaps because the qualitative researcher is viewed as central to data collection and analysis, the researcher is seen as more likely to bias the data. But some scholars of measurement argue that such ethical considerations are just as central to quantitative data collection and analysis. For example, Bruce L. Brown and Dawson Hedges say that "methodological rigor is closely related to ethical vigilance: When research, statistical calculations, and data presentation can be done better and more accurately, they should be. That is, there is an ethical imperative to demand and use the highest standards of research and data presentation."[23] In some ways, ethics are even more critical of a concern with quantitative data because they might seem more "objective" in nature. Yet, the researcher is still central to quantitative data collection and analysis. Every decision—including how measures are developed, in particular—is intertwined with ethical considerations.

For these reasons, I designed the DAS to explicitly counter the hidden aspects of measurement that can work against equity. I focused on the habits of a diverse group of tech-savvy teens as the "norm" by first observing the teens in the tech programs I described in previous chapters. I did the same as I developed and validated the measure. I first translated the list of habits into a series of statements, modeled after well-established measures such as the "grit scale" that ask people to rate how much statements are "like them," and I asked about the same habits in multiple ways to make sure answers were consistent.[24] You might think *all* self-report measures introduce bias from the respondent, and some types of self-report measures are especially prone to problems, as when asking people to do self-assessments of their knowledge or skill.[25] But methodological research shows that asking students *how* they learn rather than *what* they know or can do— "Do you do X?" rather than "Can you do X?"—can yield valid and reliable data.[26]

Although I go into much greater detail in the appendix at the back of the book, suffice it to say here that to develop the DAS, I piloted the initial list of statements in a number of ways that follow standard methods for measurement development, including asking methods and content area experts to review the items, pretesting items with 25 teens through "cognitive interviews" wherein they interpreted their meaning, and piloting with 243 "average" CPS students in 2010–2011 (primarily Latinx and Black students from lower-income families).[27] Testing in this manner was a way to ensure that the DAS captured teens' learning habits regardless of their demographic background, rather than privileging particular language or knowledge more common to white middle-class students. This approach to development means that the scale may be used to more accurately understand students like the ones I taught in Oakland, without misidentifying low-income second-language learners as less capable technology learners. Then, using pilot data and a method called *confirmatory factor analysis*, I examined how items and the habits they measure clustered together to narrow the list.[28]

Next, in 2012–2013, I broadened the population of survey respondents by collecting data from a random sample of 897 CPS eighth graders drawn from twenty-seven regular neighborhood schools that serve students who live within their attendance boundaries. I included nine higher-income schools and eighteen lower-income Title I schools (a designation given when 40 percent or more students are eligible for free or reduced-price lunch). Further demographic details of the sample appear in the appendix; the sample was roughly representative of the CPS population but had an overrepresentation of white and higher-income students for comparison purposes. In my analysis, I again narrowed the number of habits and items, identifying the final five habits measured by three items each. In the survey I also included previously validated measures of technological skill (an internet skill scale), which I used to confirm that the DAS is related to but distinct from previous measures of technological competence.[29] Finally, in a study outside of Boston, I replicated the statistical characteristics of the measure with 1,285 high school students.[30]

As described earlier in this chapter, I asked a small subset of eight survey respondents—including Jasmine, Anandi, and Rafael—to do the Scratch performance task to confirm that the scale captures differences in what students actually do when they try to learn new technologies. More specifically, I showed them a brief video describing Scratch and then gave them ten minutes to explore and ten minutes to solve the problem of moving a cat figure from the left to the right side of the screen. This task is similar to the demands of entry-level computer science courses, like the Exploring Computer Science curriculum developed by the national Computer Science for All initiative (in the fourth unit, on instructional days five and six).[31] Students rated higher on the DAS completed the task, while those rated lower did not. While I conducted this task with a small strategic sample, and the students who failed the task might learn how to do it if given more time or instruction, it showed that the DAS is sensitive to differences in students' technology learning habits—and that what students do to learn new technologies can help or hinder the learning process.[32] Overall, this combination of quantitative internal and external validation as well as qualitative confirmation shows that the DAS reliably measures what I intended to measure: how a diverse group of teens learn technologies that are new to them.

Yet, although I developed and validated the measure in ways that avoid the introduction of various forms of bias and confirmed that the scale reliably measures what it claims to measure, it is critical to note that a lingering challenge remains with its use. Quantitative measures can be used in ways that do not align with their intended purpose. My purpose, like the original purpose of the intelligence quotient (IQ) test, for example, was to identify areas in which students might need additional support.[33] Using the measure to funnel or organize students into hierarchical ranks, as was subsequently done with the IQ test, is not what the DAS was designed to do. Therefore, I do not recommend using it for determining student placement in computer science courses or technology-related jobs. These types of sorting and funneling activities are not what the DAS was designed for and will do a disservice to students, educators, employers, and policy makers. But, the measure does offer an opportunity to better identify individuals who are more and less prepared for technology learning and can be used to inform teaching and school and district policy making.

THE DIGITAL ADAPTABILITY SCALE (DAS): SEEING DIFFERENCE

In sum, I developed the DAS through a rigorous process and designed it with equity and practicality in mind, to provide a tool for overburdened educators so they can understand their students' technology learning habits and "readiness" to meet new technological challenges. Research in other areas of science, technology, engineering, and mathematics (STEM) shows that students' learning habits are related to their success in these areas. For example, students who approach mathematics by memorizing procedures rather than trying to understand why to apply these procedures have more difficulty with this subject area.[34] Under-prepared students can experience high rates of failure in STEM courses, which can also determine later experiences in school, college entrance, and even earnings.[35] The DAS is therefore a crucial and practical measure; it is short and simple enough that students like the ones I taught in Oakland won't struggle to complete it. The use of this measure is also one concrete step educators can take in addressing inequities in STEM by avoiding assumptions about students' tech savviness based on race, class, and gender.

Table 4.1 shows the formatted DAS. Each item in the scale asks students to rate themselves according to the question, "How much are these statements LIKE YOU on a scale of 1 (NOT LIKE ME AT ALL) to 6 (EXACTLY LIKE ME)?"[36]

To find the overall score, items 1, 3, 5, 10, 11, and 14 should be reverse coded (rated from 6 to 1) and all items then added together. These reverse-coded items can also be used to notice if a student is rating all items similarly, because their responses to these items should be roughly the opposite of other items measuring the same habit. For the overall score, there is a total possible range of 15 to 90 points (although I've never come across any teens who scored themselves a 15).

To find the score for each habit, sum each cluster of items as follows—reverse coding items with an asterisk (*). You may notice that items measuring the same habits sound similar; that's done on purpose.

TABLE 4.1. The Digital Adaptability Scale (DAS)

How much are these statements LIKE YOU on a scale of 1 (NOT LIKE ME AT ALL) to 6 (EXACTLY LIKE ME)?						
	How much is this like you?					
(Please circle one per row)	NOT LIKE ME AT ALL					EXACTLY LIKE ME
1. When I am learning a new technology I don't think about what it was designed to do.	1	2	3	4	5	6
2. I always know how to find help if I have problems using technology.	1	2	3	4	5	6
3. If I feel frustrated when I'm learning how to use technology, I give up or let others do it for me.	1	2	3	4	5	6
4. I try to figure out faster ways of using technology (for example: using short-cuts, keyboard commands, right click menus, etc.).	1	2	3	4	5	6
5. I usually can't figure out how to use new technologies, so I don't like learning how to use them.	1	2	3	4	5	6
6. When I am learning how to use new technology, I try to connect it to other technology I have used.	1	2	3	4	5	6
7. When I am learning a new technology, I compare what I want to do with what the technology was designed to do.	1	2	3	4	5	6
8. Even if I get frustrated using technology, I never give up.	1	2	3	4	5	6
9. I am willing to learn new technology even if I fail.	1	2	3	4	5	6
10. I do not spend time learning faster ways of using technology.	1	2	3	4	5	6
11. I don't always know how to find help if I have problems using technology.	1	2	3	4	5	6
12. I think about what a technology was designed to do when I am learning how to use it.	1	2	3	4	5	6
13. Learning tricks to be faster using technology is important to me.	1	2	3	4	5	6
14. I don't like using new technology because I'm afraid I might mess up and not know what to do.	1	2	3	4	5	6
15. Even if learning how to use technology is boring, I never give up.	1	2	3	4	5	6

Note: Scale has Cronbach's alpha of $\alpha = 0.77$ in Chicago study of eighth-grade students and Cronbach's alpha of $\alpha = 0.84$ in Boston area study of ninth- through twelfth-grade students. Cronbach's alpha is a measure of internal consistency—that is, how closely related a set of items are as a group. Whereas there are debates about its meaning, I follow guidelines that categorize a reliability coefficient of 0.70 or more as "acceptable" but more than 0.90 as having item redundancy; see Jum C. Nunnally and Ira H. Bernstein, *Psychometric Theory*, 3rd ed. (New York: McGraw-Hill, 1994); David L. Streiner, "Starting at the Beginning: An Introduction to Coefficient Alpha and Internal Consistency," *Journal of Personality Assessment* 80, no. 1 (2003): 99–103.

Source: Cassidy Puckett, "CS4Some? Differences in Technology Learning Readiness," *Harvard Educational Review* 89, no. 4 (2019): 554–87, at 562.

They are designed to *triangulate* (verify with multiple data points) the measurement of each habit.

WILLINGNESS TO TRY AND FAIL (ITEMS 5*, 9, 14*)
- I usually can't figure out how to use new technologies, so I don't like learning how to use them. (5*)
- I am willing to learn new technology even if I fail. (9)
- I don't like using new technology because I'm afraid I might mess up and not know what to do. (14*)

MANAGEMENT OF FRUSTRATION AND BOREDOM (ITEMS 3*, 8, 15)
- If I feel frustrated when I'm learning how to use technology, I give up or let others do it for me. (3*)
- Even if I get frustrated using technology, I never give up. (8)
- Even if learning how to use technology is boring, I never give up. (15)

USE OF MODELS (ITEMS 2, 6, 11*)
- I always know how to find help if I have problems using technology. (2)
- When I am learning how to use new technology, I try to connect it to other technology I have used. (6)
- I don't always know how to find help if I have problems using technology. (11*)

DESIGN LOGIC (ITEMS 1*, 7, 12)
- When I am learning a new technology I don't think about what it was designed to do. (1*)
- When I am learning a new technology, I compare what I want to do with what the technology was designed to do. (7)
- I think about what a technology was designed to do when I am learning how to use it. (12)

EFFICIENCIES (ITEMS 4, 10*, 13)

- I try to figure out faster ways of using technology (for example: using shortcuts, keyboard commands, right click menus, etc.). (4)
- I do not spend time learning faster ways of using technology. (10*)
- Learning tricks to be faster using technology is important to me. (13)

The overall scale and habit subscales provide a picture of the range and strength of students' habits and help identify areas for improvement. For example, when Anandi filled out the scale, she scored lower on the *use of models*—her less-developed habit was reflected in how she approached the Scratch task, where she did not try to connect it to other things she had seen before or look for examples (which are included in the software). Students may also score similarly across each habit, like Rafael, who scored higher overall than Anandi but had room for improvement with each of the five habits. In both cases, students can be better supported with this information.

Reading these items, you might notice that I use the term *technology*. This wording might seem vague, but I tested it in two ways. First, I asked students to interpret the meaning of that word—they universally said they thought of consumer electronics (computers, game consoles, digital cameras, etc.), which is what I intended to measure, rather than the general term *technology* as meaning any type of innovation (e.g., an algorithm). Second, I tested a variety of technology-specific wording in the survey to see if students responded differently to items when I asked about hardware, software, and internet use. But I found no significant differences in their response patterns. This evidence suggests that the measure captures a generalized approach to technology learning that is helpful with a range of digital tools.[37]

What this measure allowed me to see is what digital adaptability looks like across a much wider sample of teens than I could have observed using only the qualitative Scratch task. For example, I could

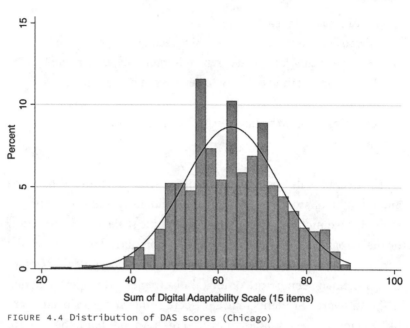

FIGURE 4.4 Distribution of DAS scores (Chicago)

Note: Mean score = 62.94; standard deviation = 10.80; minimum = 22; maximum = 90.

Source: Cassidy Puckett, "CS4Some? Differences in Technology Learning Readiness," *Harvard Educational Review* 89, no. 4 (2019): 554–87.

see what overall DAS scores looked like across the sample group in Chicago, presented in figure 4.4, which shows how students' technology learning habits vary. Scores on the scale ranged from 22 to 90, with a mean of about 63 points, in a roughly normal distribution (the curved line). What this finding means is that while a number of students had high scores with a full range and strong habits, many students could further develop their habits—those like Rafael, who scored near the mean. In a large number of cases, students' habits could be improved a great deal—those like Anandi, who scored well below the mean.

How did each of the five habits vary? In the Chicago survey, scores for the five habits (measured by three items each, as delineated earlier) ranged from 3 to 18 points. Although many scores for the habits skewed in a positive direction (to the right in the graphs presented in figures 4.5–4.9) and average scores were fairly high, particularly for the three general learning habits, they varied quite a bit. Figures 4.5–4.9

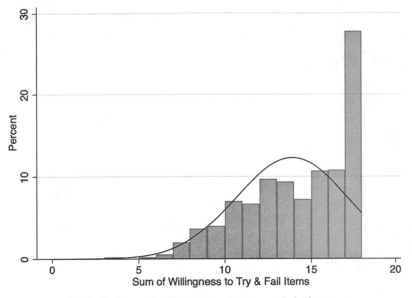

FIGURE 4.5 Distribution of willingness to try and fail scores

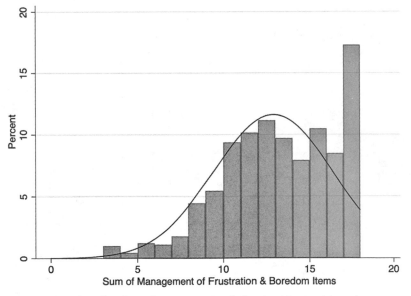

FIGURE 4.6 Distribution of management of frustration and boredom scores

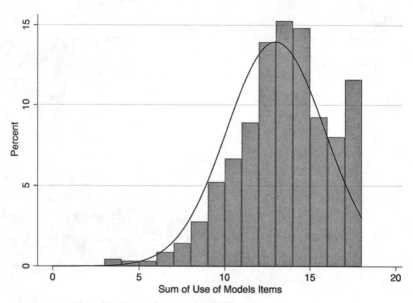

FIGURE 4.7 Distribution of use of models scores

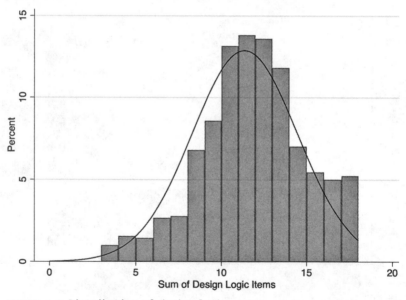

FIGURE 4.8 Distribution of design logic scores

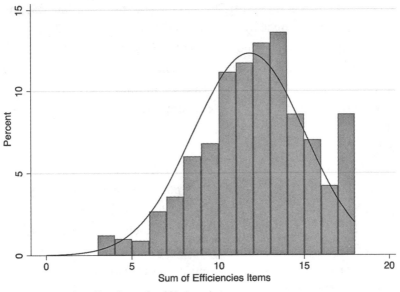

FIGURE 4.9 Distribution of efficiencies scores

show the range of scores for each of the habits. *Willingness to try and fail* had a mean of 13.90 of 15 possible points and standard deviation of 3.25 (with a normal curve, most people would fall within two standard deviations of the mean, but with skew, standard deviation is less meaningful). Similarly, *management of frustration and boredom* had a mean of 12.90 and standard deviation of 3.44 and was skewed in a positive direction. Finally, the third general learning habit, *use of models*, had a mean of 12.98 and a standard deviation of 2.86 and was also skewed in a positive direction.

In contrast, scores were lower for the two technology-specific habits and had more of a normal curve. *Design logic* had a mean of 11.36 and a standard deviation of 3.10. Similarly, *efficiencies* items had a mean score of 11.79 and a standard deviation of 3.25. These findings show that many students gave themselves a score of 3 or 4 for each of the three items on a 6-point scale—with plenty of room for development.

Overall, the scale can show us how students' technology learning habits vary, especially when it comes to the "insider" technology-specific habits. Findings from Chicago show that students are less prepared for technology learning than the idea of digital natives might suggest. Research on technological skill shows the same: that skill varies among digital natives more than you might think and can affect the ways students use technology and the benefits they derive from them.[38] These differences are especially concerning in Chicago, given the fact that starting with the graduating class of 2020 (three years after the cohort I surveyed), CPS now requires students to complete a computer science course to graduate high school.[39] Without a sense of students' readiness for these requirements, new policies trying to equalize STEM participation can create new stumbling blocks. But these findings also show that there are many students who are tech savvy—who might be ready for and benefit from new computer science courses—and, based on further analysis, that these students do not always fit existing stereotypes, as I describe in the next section.

THE DIGITAL ADAPTABILITY SCALE (DAS): EXPLAINING DIFFERENCE

Another benefit of a quantitative measure is that it can help you explore what might shape adaptability, helping to answer the question: Why do students differ in their habits? Besides the DAS items, in the survey in Chicago I also asked students questions about things that might help explain differences in their scores, including demographics (race, class, gender), personality measures, students' *orienting beliefs* (ideas about expertise in particular subject areas that can shape the learning process), level of access to financial and technological resources (computers, digital devices), and the technology practices they encounter in various social settings (including activities and how technology is taught, if at all).[40] I then ran a series of regressions, which are analyses that can take multiple factors into account at the same time. These factors included race/ethnicity, free and reduced-price lunch eligibility, gender, age, grades, whether students had a learning disability, whether students were designated as an English Learner (a person whose home language is something other than English and who receives additional support for language development), two validated measures of personality (openness and grit), and a measure of students' orienting beliefs about what it means to be good with technology ("don't know"; "can complete tasks"; "can use one piece of technology very well"; and "has strategies to learn any kind of technology"). And, yes, it was a long list, but students very kindly answered all the questions.

In terms of race, I found no significant difference between Black and white students' scores (and, in some analyses, Asian and Latinx students in the sample were significantly higher than white students). The same was true of social class; I found no differences between students eligible for free or reduced-price lunch and their higher-income peers. But with gender, I found that regardless of the other factors I included in my analysis, girls were on average consistently lower on the scale than boys. When I looked at personality measures (openness and grit), they were also consistently related to DAS scores, which makes sense: if you develop a strong set of learning habits, you are likely to persist and try new things, and vice versa. Students' orienting beliefs also correlated with DAS scores; students who had no definition for *technological competence* were significantly lower on the DAS than students who defined competence as someone who has "strategies to learn any kind of technology." So, one simple way to improve teens' technology learning is to help them define *technological competence* as including a set of learning habits. Finally, age, grades, having a learning disability, or having an English Learner designation did not seem to be related students' technology learning habits (although age did not vary that much because all students were eighth graders).

The differences by gender are worth a closer look because the average difference between boys and girls is not the full story. Indeed, there were girls who were lower on the scale, like Anandi, but there were also many girls who scored higher, like Jasmine (see figure 4.10—female students in gray, male students in white in this bar graph).

These gender differences, however, do not appear when looking more closely at the three general technology learning habits described in chapter 2. Much like the overall distribution of each of the habits,

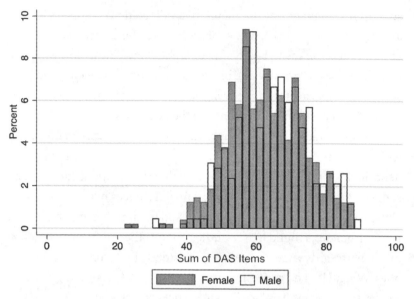

FIGURE 4.10 Distribution of DAS scores by gender

willingness to try and fail, management of frustration and boredom, and *use of models* were all fairly positive—and there were no statistical differences by gender for these habits (figures 4.11–4.13). What this finding means is that teaching girls these three general habits is unlikely to address inequalities in technology learning by gender.

However, the two technology-specific habits—the ones that are "insider" knowledge I talked about in chapter 3—tell a different story, with scores trending lower for everyone and girls scoring significantly lower than boys. Figures 4.14 and 4.15 show that boys (in white on the bar graphs) scored higher on *design logic* and *efficiencies*. But, we should be careful not to conclude that *all* girls are lower on these technology-specific habits. The figures show that there were *many* tech-savvy girls who scored as highly as tech-savvy boys on these habits. While flattening the nuance of qualitative observation with exercises like the Scratch task, with the help of the DAS it is easier to see both broader and nuanced patterns of difference among groups of students and what might explain these differences.

Beyond demographic characteristics of students, in terms of other

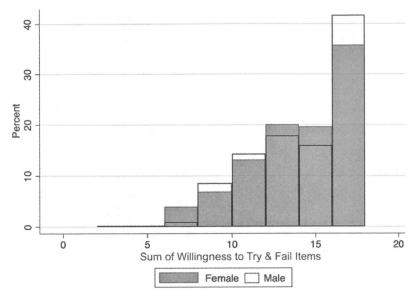

FIGURE 4.11 Distribution of willingness to try and fail scores by gender

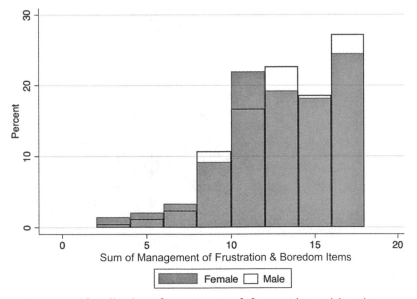

FIGURE 4.12 Distribution of management of frustration and boredom scores by gender

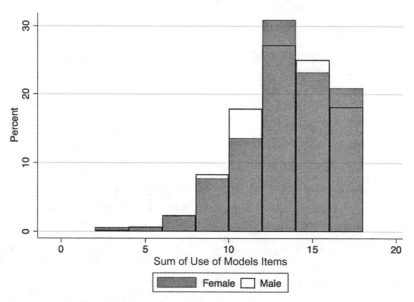

FIGURE 4.13 Distribution of use of models scores by gender

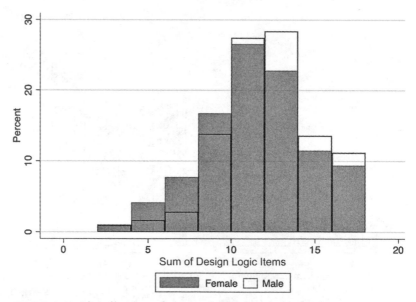

FIGURE 4.14 Distribution of design logic scores by gender

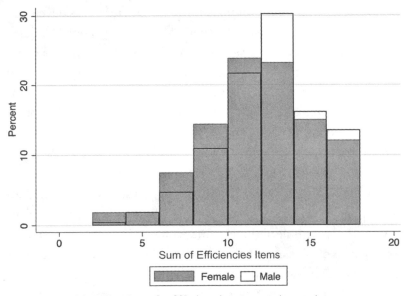

FIGURE 4.15 Distribution of efficiencies scores by gender

factors related to DAS scores, in Chicago I found that differences in most home and school resources did not seem to explain differences in students' technology learning habits. But, the technology *practices* students encountered matter quite a bit. Especially family practice. Students with families that engage in a greater number of different technological activities and explicitly teach the five habits were significantly higher on the scale than students with families that engage in fewer activities and do not explicitly teach the habits (the questions I asked in the survey about technology learning experiences in various social settings are provided in chapter 6).[41] For example, the way that Jasmine's mom encouraged her to continue learning, to try new things and keep going in the face of failure, was important to her habit development. In contrast, school technology practices did not seem to make a difference (positive or negative) once taking into account what happens at home.

Schools seem to mirror students' different experiences outside of school (although not amplify or exacerbate inequities). This similarity between school and other social contexts was the case with other students I shadowed, such as Sumalee, whose "interest" was developed at home and easily understood by her teachers. They offered Sumalee opportunities for technology learning at school that mirrored her experiences at home: adults at home and at school encouraged her to try to figure out how to use various technologies. The only school factor I found related to DAS scores was whether or not schools had comprehensive technology plans. These planning documents are no longer required by school districts, so having one likely indicates a more comprehensive and sustained effort by schools to influence their students' technology learning. Overall, findings suggest that schools could do more—and using the DAS could help schools and teachers better identify which students need support and address differences in students' experiences outside of school. I go into further detail about what educators and others can do in chapter 6.

These findings show how, on a broad scale, the measure can be a useful tool for policy makers, foundations, researchers, and educators looking to implement technology education reforms. It can inform policies and curricular design and can help document students' growth in technology learning. The measure can also be useful on a smaller scale, for classroom teachers who want to integrate technology into subject area curriculum or who teach technology classes, to understand the preparation of their students rather than, like me, wondering why some students could pick things up faster than other students. Using the DAS as a formative measure can help educators adjust their curriculum and better provide support to students who need it.

SEEING THE "GOOD" TECH-SAVVY TEENS

Besides designing the measure to be a practical tool for educators and in a way that addresses systematic bias in measurement, I also created the DAS to make the abilities of marginalized students visible. While everything described in previous chapters is intended to reimagine what it means to be tech savvy, it can be hard to see students' habits on the ground. This difficulty may especially be the case for teachers in less resourced schools, who are asked to focus on standardized tests. Or teachers who see many students every day and might not be able to observe what each student does very closely. Instead, teachers might rely on a general sense of tech savviness—something I saw in Chicago in the two schools in which I conducted observations and the twenty-seven schools where I conducted the survey.

In fact, it was often the "good kids" that teachers knew better and to whom they were more willing to open the door for "extras," such as time on the computer as a treat for finishing work earlier than other students. During my school visits, I noticed that teachers were more certain of the technology "interest" of the "good" kids—students who had good (or good enough) behavior and who did well (or well enough) in their schoolwork. Teachers would call on these students if a tech issue came up in class—a laptop that wouldn't project slides, for example. But teachers had far less of a sense of the technological abilities of "bad" students, the ones who might not listen or would act out in class. Teachers often provided extra technology time only to "good" students who expressed some "interest" in it, viewing tech use as something students earned the right to use. Students like Sumalee, another student in Anandi and Rafael's school.

"If you're looking for someone who's good with technology, I know just who you should talk to," said Mrs. Giannopoulos, a thirty-something eighth-grade social studies and English teacher with thick dark hair and a deep laugh. She smiled and pointed, "That's your girl." Standing near the front of a line of students waiting to enter a second-floor classroom, thirteen-year-old Sumalee chattered away with another student. She had dark round eyes and was a speedy and steady talker. Sumalee had lived with her grandmother in Thailand, and then the two immigrated to the United States to reunite with her mother, stepfather, and little brother. They all lived together in a small two-bedroom first-floor apartment near the school. Sumalee turned to her teacher and cocked her head. "Were you talking about me?"

She flashed a quick smile back at Mrs. Giannopoulos, then turned in my direction. "Hi, I'm Sumalee. I heard you were doing some research

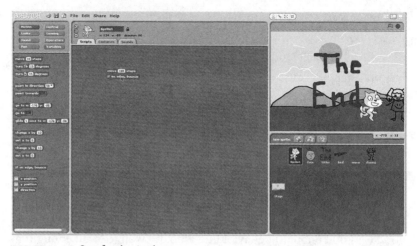

FIGURE 4.16 Sumalee's task

Source: Cassidy Puckett and Jennifer L. Nelson, "The Geek Instinct: Theorizing Cultural Alignment in Disadvantaged Contexts," *Qualitative Sociology* 42, no. 1 (2019): 25–48.

about technology. What did you want to know?" Like other students, I followed Sumalee for two weeks and was in her school for three additional weeks, following other students in her classes. She was the first student many teachers thought of when I mentioned the topic of my project; she was good with technology and they knew it. Indeed, when I asked Sumalee to do the same Scratch task as Jasmine, Anandi, Rafael, and others, she was successful like Jasmine, although she took a more exploratory, innovative approach. She spent more time clicking on various tabs to explore sounds and background designs. She edited the background of the white box to create a dirt path and grassy hills, blue sky with clouds and a sun—and changed the color of the cat from orange to aqua. She also made her own sprite—a little anime girl of her own design (figure 4.16).

How did she figure out how to design in Scratch? She explained that she connected the functionality in Scratch to a program called Paint, which she used to draw anime (using *design logic* and *use of models*). Further, while exploring, Sumalee figured out that the program could provide sample animations that could help her understand how the blocks of code worked (again through the *use of models*). She pulled command blocks to the center of the screen, first to move her anime girl, then to move the cat. After a few minutes, she successfully used the blocks to move the sprites slowly from the left to the right side of the screen, then had them bounce off the right side and move back to the left side, back and forth.

Because she was a fairly well-behaved student and was higher achieving, Sumalee's teachers "read" these abilities and often asked her to fix issues with their computers. For example, one day her math and science teacher asked Sumalee for tech help. Sumalee did not have to explain that she was good with technology—and she did not even need to be told the password for her teacher's laptop. She was asked so often to help that she knew the computer password by heart. But Sumalee was not the only student in her class who was good with technology.

In fact, unbeknownst to their teachers, some students were doing advanced technological activities outside of school. One day during my monthlong observation, Rafael and a couple other boys mentioned that a friend of theirs—Tomás—was "coding in C." Standing in line in the hallway one day, I was surprised when they pointed to a boy I'd seen repeatedly coming to school or class late, missing school, coming unprepared (without books, paper, things to write with), or crafting ways to avoid schoolwork. Hearing his name, he turned and smiled. What was he doing with computers? He'd been working on understanding how to program operating systems. Leaning in to tell me his secret, he bragged, "My computer has the Blue Screen of Death right now!" clearly seeing this as a badge of honor. I gave him an impressed look. He spun in a circle flicking his head around, pretending to play air drums, and was quickly reprimanded by a teacher to get back in line. Still nodding his head to the beat of his own drum, he followed his peers into class.

I then paid attention to dynamics like Sumalee and Tomás's contrasting access to school technology learning experiences while visiting the twenty-seven Chicago schools to survey students. Teachers routinely picked the students who completed the survey earlier than other students to use classroom computers, a treat earned by the "good" students who they knew were "interested" in technology. Although well intentioned, this practice is problematic for two reasons. First, it does not allow the "bad" kids, like Tomás, to be recognized for their ability and receive academic benefits for their skill. Research shows that teachers view tech-savvy students as "smarter" and therefore more academically capable.[42] Therefore, if "bad" students (lower achievers, students who pay less attention or act out in class) could be recognized and rewarded for their technological ability, it might balance teachers' view of their capabilities in general and they might have a better experience of school. Second, it leaves behind the "bad" students who are interested in technology but less adaptable, like Rafael, who would benefit from more technology learning experiences at school.

This practice of providing additional learning experience to only "good" and "interested" students excludes students who might need help (like Rafael) and students who are equally or more tech savvy but viewed as "troublemakers" (like Tomás). This exclusion can have profound implications, with teachers acting as gatekeepers, shutting off possible future educational and occupational pathways. We misidentify who is good in tech if we only observe savviness among the academically and technologically advantaged, privileging those in relatively more advantaged positions. My hope is that the quantitative measure may also help in seeing the "bad" students as capable and providing them the support they need. The DAS makes recognizing hidden techies possible—it can help push back against bias. Having a measure that helps teachers see beyond the "good" and tech-savvy kids can also help "bad" students see themselves and their futures in new ways.

Within and beyond schools, the DAS can also identify when differences in adaptability *do not* explain inequalities in access to things like advanced computing courses, high-skill high-wage jobs, and healthcare technologies—when biases in social contexts better explain unequal outcomes. The measure can be used, for example, to empirically test when technology learning potential is underestimated, in the same way research shows academic skills are underestimated in lower-income schools and among high-achieving Black and Latinx students.[43] For example, the measure could be used to identify cases where workers with high adaptability are assumed to be incapable of acquiring new technological skills.

Research studies suggest that there are many tech-savvy marginalized students, but most current studies of this kind are qualitative in nature. They show that discriminatory beliefs and practices—rather than differences in ability—can block female and minoritized groups' unequal representation in tech.[44] The DAS allows for broader national and international quantitative investigation of these qualitative findings. Further, the DAS may be used as an intervention to identify adaptability among groups whom gatekeepers (teachers, employers) might assume are less capable, to counter the race-, class-, and gender-biased stereotypes about technological competence that also shape self-selection into tech fields.[45] Of course, the measure is not a panacea, but it's one concrete tool that educators, policy makers, and researchers can use to help address inequality in these fields—and perhaps use to rethink inclusion in tech as a whole.

CONCLUSION: SEEING HABITS QUALITATIVELY AND QUANTITATIVELY

Chapters 2 and 3 identified the technology learning habits of a diverse group of tech-savvy teens. This chapter described how to observe these habits in both qualitative and quantitative ways, including what differences look like when handing a teen a new piece of technology and saying, "Try to learn this." Or, if closely observing students is not feasible, giving them the Digital Adaptability Scale to understand the habits they use, the breadth and strength of their use, where they could use a bit of help, and where they might surprisingly excel—rather than assuming we know what teens can do. These habits are important because they signal a readiness for learning a wide range of digital activities, from designing visual images to programming. Further, as I describe in chapter 5, these habits also are essential for preparing students for new computer science requirements for high school graduation and for their future educational plans and aspirations.

Whereas some discussions of the "leaky" STEM pipeline assume a lack of skill on the part of women and historically marginalized groups, the picture painted by the DAS is more complex. Certainly, some students need better preparation for technology learning. However, there are also many groups currently marginalized in technology fields who are more adaptable than stereotypes might lead us to believe. These prejudices can serve as a barrier to further develop digital competencies. I offer the DAS as a tool for measuring teens' digital adaptability developed with a diverse group of students to combat the potential reproduction of inequality in quantitative measures (standardized tests) and qualitative measures (teacher evaluation).

Indeed, many hidden techies already exist, characters like Shuri from the movie *Black Panther*, hidden except for those who recognize her talent in Wakanda. Or, real people like Katherine Johnson, an African American mathematician and early computer scientist at NASA. *Dominant groups refuse to see them.* Measures can be powerful sorting tools that can justify exclusion. But the measure I presented in this chapter is intended to be a tool for equity; a way to identify the students who need support as well as to see students who we might not know are good with technology, like Jasmine or especially Tomás, students who are ready for the next challenge. They might not even truly believe they're good with technology or acknowledge their potential until they see it confirmed by others. But, I've seen them everywhere. They are in Chicago, plugging away in the recording studio at YOUmedia. They are in New York City, spending time indoors on a beautiful summer day to put computers back together again and again. They are in the San Francisco Bay Area learning how to design video games. They are our answer to the problem of a "leaky" STEM pipeline—if only we would notice and support them. The DAS, perhaps, can help.

[5]

The Five Habits, Teens' Futures, and Digital Inequality

The previous chapters described the five technology learning habits—*willingness to try and fail, management of frustration and boredom, use of models, design logic* (thinking about why technology is designed the way it is and decoding that logic to accomplish particular goals), and *efficiencies* (finding quicker ways of using technologies). But these technology learning habits are only consequential if they influence students' futures, helping them step confidently into future roles wherein continual technology learning is necessary. This chapter makes this link; it demonstrates that the habits are connected to two things research shows are critical for teens' educational and occupational futures: their plans and their aspirations.

How are plans and aspirations pivotal for teens' futures, in general? Research shows they can be highly predictive of what teens actually do—acting as a prerequisite for the completion of a college degree within science, technology, engineering, and mathematics (STEM).[1] Beyond shaping the trajectories of individual lives, teens' plans and aspirations matter for income inequality, given the unequal demographics of higher-earning STEM fields and occupations. Encouragement can help support plans and aspirations, but it does not provide students with concrete ways to accomplish what they hope to achieve.[2] In contrast, learning the five habits can be a more tangible method for success in technology learning. Therefore, teaching the habits may be a crucial leverage point for addressing digital inequality.

Yet teaching the five habits is not enough. It is equally crucial to confront the role that educational and occupational gatekeepers play in digital inequality. If gatekeepers' understanding of technological competence is reoriented to see learning habits as an indicator of true future potential, this new definition can work to counter the race-, class-, and gender-based biases that shape digital inequality. I note the importance of gatekeeping in this chapter and then address it in greater length in chapter 6, where I provide specific recommendations to address it. But before doing that, I first show how the five habits connect to the technology-related plans and aspirations that can shape teens' technological futures.

STRONGER HABITS, CLEARER FUTURES

Recall from the beginning of chapter 4 the strong technology learning habits of thirteen-year-old African American student Jasmine—and how she solved the Scratch coding task faster than any other teen who took on the challenge. How might Jasmine's habits relate to her future trajectory? When I first met her in the eighth grade, she told me she planned to go to the Chicago High School for Agricultural Sciences. She explained that the school had a good track record at getting students into college and offered technology and engineering-related training to help her with her future educational and occupational aspirations. Looking into the school once Jasmine enrolled, I found out that more than 81 percent of its graduates enroll in college, compared to roughly 67 percent of all students in the Chicago Public Schools system. When I checked back with her after her first year of high school, I asked how school was going and whether her aspirations in technology and engineering had changed. They had not. What were her goals for the future? She replied:

> I plan on going to go to a technical college and maybe becoming a technical engineer. That's what I want to do. . . . [My high school is] a good school and there's different pathways into different careers. . . . They have mechanics and technology, but you can't join until your junior year; that's what I'm going to do.

These goals had not changed since grammar school, inspired by her mom's own background in technology-related fields and encouragement of Jasmine's interest in technology. Jasmine explained that her mom had "gone to college for technology" and, at one point, worked "making TVs and computers." Jasmine said she primarily picked up her technology learning habits "from my mom because she's always used technology and I've always watched her using it." Based on her mom's modeling and encouragement, Jasmine's habits became second nature, and a career in technology seemed a reasonable goal.

This relationship between Jasmine's aspirations and the development of her strong technology learning habits may not be causal. Instead of habits fueling her aspirations, she may have had these goals and therefore developed habits to achieve her goals, or habits and aspirations may have been mutually reinforcing. Either way, the habits did help her learn. Further, I noticed a clear pattern among the teens I interviewed: those with better-developed technology learning habits had stronger aspirations for technology-related careers and took clearer steps toward their goals.

Compare Jasmine's well-established habits, course taking, and future educational and occupational aspirations to Rafael's. Remember from chapter 4 that despite his strong interest, Rafael's habits were less developed, and he struggled with the Scratch challenge, ultimately failing to move the cat figure from the left side of the screen to the right side of the screen. How might his habits be related to his future? When

I met him as an eighth grader, Rafael told me that he'd like to be able to be able to "fix computers, remove viruses," activities similar to what his dad did as an electrician; fix electrical things. He said, "My computer at my Dad's house got a virus because my cousins were using it— my dad forgot about it [being broken], so [I'd like to know] how to do that, fix it. Because I don't want to do anything dumb and mess up the computer even more." He seemed very worried about breaking things— something he said his parents emphasized. Did he have any aspirations beyond fixing his computer? Well, his parents told him he's going to see technology everywhere in his life, so he has to "get used to that." How well did he think he should be able to use technology?

> RAFAEL: I guess, for jobs, [because] most jobs use computers,
> so [I'll] have to do that. [My mom] talked about how I need
> a job and get used to the technology they have [at the job]. . . .
> [Her expectations are] mostly about me just working. That
> was like the one thing she said about tech—some might be
> good and some bad, some out of date and some brand new.
> [At her job], the technology they have, I guess she's like, [it's]
> really old.
> CASSIDY: And you just have to deal with whatever?
> RAFAEL: Yeah.

In other words, Rafael thought he should be good enough to get by, whatever that might mean. In contrast to Jasmine, Rafael's vague goals for technology learning reflected his vague notion of what it meant to be good with technology and his underdeveloped technology learning habits. He had potential, given his strong interest in video gaming and technology in general, but it wasn't enough to help him succeed when taking on new challenges and feel like he had future beyond "get[ting] used to the technology they have" in jobs.

When I followed up with Rafael at the end of his freshman year in high school, he said his new school had some technology classes. One was a medical class in which students could "learn about medical technologies." Another was a dance class wherein students "use computers for music." Had he considered taking these classes? Had his future goals changed at all?

> RAFAEL: I don't know. I've been focusing on work and football. . . .
>
> CASSIDY: Do you think you'll learn about and use technology in college or in jobs?
>
> RAFAEL: Yeah, in my future job because if you see a business place, restaurants, they have it, like for searching things. Like AutoZone, searching things up, what you're going to get. Banks, they search things.
>
> CASSIDY: What would you like to do in the future?
>
> RAFAEL: I guess it'd be in college playing football, just getting a, like, decent job where they pay me really good, that's basically my goal right there. Cause I need a job, so I could just buy my own stuff; I don't like asking for things [from my parents], it makes me feel weird. Sometimes I don't really do nothing for it, I don't know.
>
> CASSIDY: What are decent jobs?
>
> RAFAEL: My uncle works at a bank. . . . I see that there's decent money where he can buy things. My dad works at [an electric company] that pays him well. How I think of a decent job is getting you what you need and a little [of] what you want. That's basically how I think of it. Not a job that makes you do a whole bunch of work. Like, when you leave you feel a little tired, but not that tired. Like that.

Rafael's goal was different from Jasmine's: to get a job where the pay could get "what you need and a little [of] what you want" and "when you leave you feel a little tired, but not that tired." It left out any notion of what the librarian said about him: "Oh yeah, he's into gaming and good at technology!" Why hadn't his love of technology translated into course taking and future educational and occupational aspirations?

Certainly, family technology practices played a role in shaping Rafael's technology use and his aspirations in the future, as his parents were mostly worrying that he might "mess up the computer" rather than encouraging exploration for a future tech career. This experience was also something I found in the Chicago survey: students with families who encouraged a range of technological activities and explicitly supported students' technology learning had stronger habits, which—as I will explain in the next section—are related to stronger aspirations.[3]

Both at home and at school, Rafael didn't have adults who showed him how he might pursue his passion for video gaming with more advanced computing, nor did they help him develop habits to support his learning. I could see how his budding interest in technology might not reach its full potential in witnessing his frustration during the Scratch task. Rafael might have been better supported by educators like the librarian, who was already enthusiastic about his interests. These habits—and more concrete direction for where they might lead—might have helped him be more successful with technology learning, build his skill, and encourage his pursuit of further technology education in high school and beyond. But little is known about the link between technology learning habits and tech-related educational and occupational futures.

THE IMPORTANCE OF ASPIRATIONS

However, we do know in general that plans and aspirations are key to students' futures. When a person says they plan to take classes or expresses career-related goals or choices, it shapes what they actually do to accomplish those goals.[4] Even if what a teen expresses as a career goal might seem unlikely to reflect their future, extensive research shows adolescent aspirations can be essential to future achievements. Aspirations influence how students behave as they move forward in the paths they pursue. Indeed, a large and long-established body of research on aspirations shows that they are an early indicator of later educational attainment and future occupations.[5] For example, in a British cohort study in 2001 that followed 7,649 people from ages sixteen to thirty-three, 51 percent of health professionals matched their teenage aspirations in terms of their actual occupational attainment.[6]

Research in STEM more specifically shows that aspirations for careers in these fields are strongly predictive of educational outcomes.[7] In a 2006 study using the 1988 US National Educational Longitudinal Study data, Robert H. Tai and colleagues found that aspirations held in high school are strong predictors of college major and earning a bachelor's degree in STEM; thirteen-year-olds who aspired to careers in science were 3.4 times more likely to graduate with a degree in the physical sciences or engineering than students without such aspirations.[8] Likewise, Stephen L. Morgan, Dafna Gelbgiser, and Kim Weeden found that the occupational plans of high school seniors are strong predictors of initial college major selection in STEM.[9] In other words, aspirations have real consequences for students' lives.

These consequential plans and aspirations form in early adolescence.[10] In childhood, ideas about future occupations may be largely based on fantasy, but aspirations shift and become more tangible with age.[11] Although there is some debate about precisely when this change occurs, the general consensus is that in early adolescence people think more concretely about their future possibilities and that these ideas influence subsequent actions in preparing for chosen career paths.[12] Adolescence is also a time when the structure of schooling allows students to make decisions (to the extent that they can) about curricular and extracurricular activities that support the pursuit of certain fields, which can shape subsequent educational and occupational attainment.[13]

So, where do the five habits fit in?

THE ROLE OF HABIT

Research on learning in general shows that students' learning habits shape their enjoyment and efficacy *as they learn*; their immediate experience of success or failure.[14] So, because habits shape the learning process, they also might shape students' longer trajectories, but research has not investigated this connection. My qualitative research—like the conversations with Jasmine and Rafael presented at the beginning of this chapter—suggested such a link. For example, Rafael was interested in technology, but he didn't know how to effectively respond in the face of failure because he had not been given the tools to do so. It therefore made sense that he might not aspire to and pursue technology-related fields and occupations. Instead, he'd shoot for jobs where he'd adjust to whatever the job required and rather than pursing his initial interests in technology, even if in the eighth grade he had said he was "really into" gaming.

This shift in Rafael's aspirations is reflective of a process sociologists call "cooling out," whereby historically marginalized students with higher aspirations are taught to aim for more "realistic" goals. They are taught to pursue jobs matched to their social position (e.g., vocational work for lower-income students), even if it's now more likely that lower-income students will aspire to go to college.[15] Even higher-achieving lower-income students—including valedictorians of their graduating classes—often end up in less prestigious colleges.[16] This situation can be the result of structural issues, such as lack of access to resources. Lower-funded schools, for example, might not offer students access to advanced technology classes (which was not the case with Rafael). But it can also be the result of cultural processes such as explicit coaching from counselors and placement in lower-tracked courses. Or, as it seemed to me with the case of Rafael, it can be the result of no one helping the student develop stronger learning habits to be more efficacious learning new things (like Scratch) and (perhaps as a result) develop stronger aspirations in STEM.

Yet, while my qualitative observations suggested such a link, they might be considered too "anecdotal" to support the claim of a connection between technology learning habits and students' futures. Certainly, watching students trying to figure out how to use Scratch and listening to their plans whether or not to take future tech courses, major in technology-related fields, or go into future tech careers made it seem likely I would see the same patterns with a larger number of teens, across broader samples. So, to test this hypothesis, I included questions about students' future plans and aspirations my surveys—first in Chicago with 897 eighth-grade students and then in a replication study in a school district in the Boston area with 1,285 high school students in grades nine through twelve.

In both studies, I found a consistent relationship between students' technology learning habits and their technology-related educational plans and future occupational aspirations. More specifically, about their educational plans, I asked if students could see themselves taking a technology course in the future or majoring in computer science. I also asked about their aspirations—if in the future they might start a technology business or become a computer programmer, web designer, network specialist, or technology teacher. I asked students to rate each possibility on a scale from 1 = "Definitely NO" to 6 = "Definitely YES." In Boston, I also added questions about engineering (an additional STEM field, likely associated with technology learning habits) and plumbing (less related to digital technologies, less likely associated with technology learning habits) to see whether students' responses would follow expected patterns.

Figure 5.1 shows the correlations between aspirations and Digital Adaptability Scale (DAS) scores in both studies. As presented in the bar graph, I found statistically significant positive relationships between students' technology learning habits and all plans and aspirations ($***p \leq 0.001$) in both studies, with the expected exception of becoming a plumber. What the numbers mean is that there is a small to moderate positive relationship between the DAS and future plans and aspirations. The higher a student is on the DAS, the more likely they are to plan to pursue further technology education and aspire to technology-related career paths.

While these data are not longitudinal, what the correlations in the two studies show is that the five technology learning habits are positively associated with how students see their technological futures at two pivotal stages of their education (middle grades and high school).

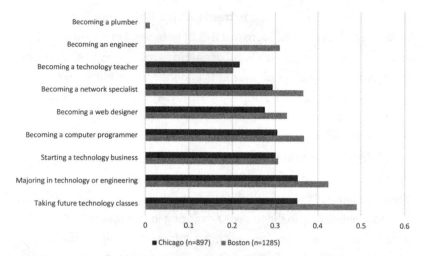

FIGURE 5.1 Correlations between DAS and STEM educational plans and career aspirations, Chicago and Boston

Note: Pearson's correlation coefficients, which range from 0 to 1 (for positive relationship). Correlations 0.1 to 0.29 are small; those between 0.30 and 0.49 are moderate. See Jacob Cohen, *Statistical Power Analyses for the Behavioral Sciences*, 2nd ed. (Hillsdale, NJ: Erlbaum, 1988).

This finding confirms with quantitative data what I saw when I observed and interviewed Jasmine, Rafael, and other students. What struck me in a qualitative way was there in the quantitative data: technology learning habits are connected to students' educational plans, as well as how they see their futures in a range of technology-related fields and occupations—including creative, entrepreneurial, and purely technical ones.

There are two reasons why this finding is important. First, given that educational experiences, plans, and aspirations shape actual trajectories, this consistent relationship between the habits and students' plans and aspirations suggests a link between the habits and where they will likely end up in their lives. Second, developing habits is more immediately achievable than supporting longer-term aspirations. Helping students realize their aspirations is a longer, more complex process—and involves a range of factors outside schools and out-of-school programs, particularly the influence of families.[17] As Jill Bystydzienski, Margaret Eisenhart, and Monica Bruning describe of an after-school intervention designed to encourage girls to pursue STEM pathways, "It is not enough to spark interest. [Students] need substantial financial resources, as well as ongoing social and educational support, to make the transition from an interest . . . to a college major and a career."[18] But defining *techno-logical competence* in a way that includes learning habits and developing students' habits so they are successful in their learning process can help support students' futures.

By helping teens develop strong habits, schools may be better able to encourage groups otherwise disinclined to pursue careers in tech-related fields and occupations. While these correlations still do not demonstrate a causal relationship between the five habits and plans and aspirations—better technology learning habits may encourage aspirations and vice versa—habits can be a more concrete objective for educators and parents to teach their children than trying to encourage their aspirations. Therefore, building students' habits may be an achievable way of helping shape students' futures and addressing equity. Moreover, so is showing educational and occupational gatekeepers that habits are critical indicators of students' talent—and of course, providing access to educational and occupational opportunities.

HABITS, ASPIRATIONS, AND LEARNING OPPORTUNITIES

Back when Jasmine was in eighth grade, I met and followed another middle-class student in her school named William. Similar to Jasmine in many ways, William was an African American student who lived with his grandmother, aunt, and mother in a single-family home, a bit farther from their school. Quiet and polite, he did not immediately brag about any technological ability despite knowing the focus of my study. He simply explained, like Rafael, that he was "really into video games." His aunt, who sat with us at the round kitchen table as William and I talked, teased him, "Are you?" He smiled back at her. When I handed him the Scratch task, just like Jasmine, William had a *willingness to try and fail* and read the *design logic* of the program as a coordinate plane. He very quickly and easily solved the challenge of moving a cat figure from the left to the right side of the screen. We both laughed at how quickly he solved the challenge. What was he planning to do in the future? Baseball. He loved baseball. But, also definitely technology in the future—in high school and beyond.

When I talked to his mom, who worked for the Chicago Transit Authority attending switches along the railroad tracks, she reiterated what William said about his love of technology. She said that he "hook[ed] up everything in the house" and was "more tech savvy" than she was. What were her expectations for William's technology learning? And, where should he learn it?

> I want him to be great with technology. [If it's] this important now, only imagine in the next twenty to forty years, so I want him to get as good as possible. William only being thirteen now, the computer—it's his era. He's always had access. So, he should take well to the computer. It would bother me if he didn't. . . . [He should] definitely learn [about computers] at school, maybe from me but I don't have computer knowledge. I only go online and shop, just learned how to email. So, not from me, but I prefer from school. I don't care what he picks up from friends as long as it's not negative. I [encourage him by] ask[ing] about everything pertaining to the computer.

In fact, William's elementary school (kindergarten through eighth grade) had very limited technology teaching, although at the time of our interview when William was in eighth grade he said that in one of his classes he was doing research where he had to "use computers to complete the project." When I visited the school that both he and Jasmine attended and described the focus of my study, the principal apologized for their lack of technology use. She said they were "behind the times," but I was more than welcome to do research at the school. William said that he'd transferred into the school, and in his prior school, his fifth-grade teacher taught him how to put a computer together.

William was clear on his mom's general expectations that he should be "as good as possible" with technology and able to answer any questions she might have when it came to computers. But the majority of his knowledge of technology came from his friends. How did he describe his friends? William said, "All my friends, they know [technology] way better than me." How did he know they were good with technology? They spent a lot of time at it—and taught him specific tricks (*efficiencies*) he previously didn't know how to do:

> Well, some have numerous social network pages like Facebook, Twitter, MySpace. One has three computers [to tinker with]. They play Xbox a lot during weekdays and weekends. I can only play on weekends. When we're playing [video games], they teach [me] how to do special moves and use codes to get you to the next level, to put you on different places like on top of a building.

Through his friends, mom, and past teachers, William understood that being good with technology was key and that what it took to be good was a willingness to try, to practice and keep learning, to use others to help the learning process, to understand the design, and to learn tricks embedded within that design. In other words, William practiced all five of the technology learning habits.

Where was William after his first year in high school? He was fortunate to enroll in a high-achieving public high school with ties to the University of Chicago and ample technology learning opportunities. In ninth grade, he took two semesters of robotics and loved it. In the class, they did online assignments and challenges through Code.org. He signed up for the elective because he "wanted to try something new, see what I could stretch my mind to do." In the rest of his classes, they didn't use technology that much, but they did have lots of technology available that he could use, such as iPads and laptops. Students could also use their cell phones during some classes, depending on the teacher. At home, he still played a lot of Xbox—he had a new one "with better graphics and connects you right to the internet, has Wi-Fi." But his mom still restricted his use to only on the weekends, after chores were finished, and only if he kept his grades up and was well behaved at home. Other changes included his mom getting a new phone, his grandmother getting a new laptop, and his own switch to Instagram rather than Facebook. He was also friends with new people in his new high school—who were just as techie as his elementary-school friends.

Of robotics, William said that it "showed me a different way to think and express myself, like new ways of thinking outside the box to solve things and brainstorm." So, that changed the way he thought about how technology could be used—and the ways he thought about using technology in the future. He said:

> [I plan] to take more [tech] classes in high school and in college. I learned I could use technology in a job, in creative ways like using technology for designing. [In the future], I want to have four years of college and a master's degree. I haven't changed my goals since grammar school. But I have changed the way I think about technology [in terms of how you can use it]. But not my larger goal [to go to college and beyond].

Just like Jasmine, William's well-developed technology learning habits supported his goals in early adolescence, and he followed what he said he'd do in elementary school, taking the robotics classes that he was fortunate to have available to him in high school. His experiences in high school were positive as well, and they exposed him to more creative technology uses, encouraging his continued interest in technology. He was fortunate to have a combination of strong learning habits and access to engaging educational opportunities—and high school course offerings and educational gatekeepers (counselors, teachers) supporting his access and leading him toward his future goals. A combination of all three—habits, aspirations, and access to opportunity—positively shaped William's trajectory.

HABITS, ASPIRATIONS, AND INEQUALITY

Given that habits and aspirations seem to be connected, and habits are more tangible and therefore may be easier to teach than aspirations, will developing students' habits easily address inequalities in STEM? The short answer is no. It can help, particularly for students like Rafael who could benefit from developing stronger habits, but it likely will not be enough. Like William and Jasmine, students also need learning opportunities and gatekeepers who recognize their potential and open doors for them—in school, outside school, and in the working world. Yet, habits are an essential piece of the puzzle, particularly given their relationship with aspirations, which in turn are critical to students' futures.[19]

Currently, efforts to diversify STEM and address income inequality in the United States focus heavily on increasing historically marginalized groups' aspirations in scientific and technical work.[20] These efforts may be bolstered by encouraging students to understand *technological competence* to include a set of habits that help continual learning and to develop these habits as practical tools students can draw on during the learning process. The notion of technology learning habits may also help open doors for students by reframing how gatekeepers (educators, employers) understand competence—as well as through increased educational opportunities both inside and outside school. But, exactly how understanding and developing habits can be used to address the specific dynamics of gender-, class-, and race-based inequities is a bit more complicated. Although a more detailed analysis of the complex factors that shape the relationship between students' learning habits and aspirations is beyond the scope of this book, other work provides clues and shows that race, class, and gender dynamics each pose particular challenges.

Of the three, gender inequality in STEM might seem the most straightforward: findings in this book and other research show clear disparities by gender in terms of both technology learning habits and STEM-related aspirations.[21] Research has long documented lower aspirations in STEM among girls.[22] Whereas some research shows equal interest and aptitude of boys and girls up to age ten, gender differences emerge in early adolescence when future aspirations solidify.[23] For example, in a study of a national sample of high school seniors, Yu Xie and

Kimberlee Shauman found gender disparities in the intent to declare a STEM major, such that the probability of reporting an intended STEM major was 60 percent less for females than for males.[24]

What might explain these differences in plans and aspirations? One possibility is achievement; if girls do worse academically in STEM, they might not want to pursue these fields. Yet research shows that achievement does not explain most gender differences in STEM educational and occupational plans and aspirations. Before high school, achievement differences between male and female students are small.[25] By high school and in college, gender gaps in test scores largely disappear, and remaining differences are too small to explain gender disparities in major and degree attainment and employment.[26] Another possibility is girls' lower confidence in their abilities (lower "self-perceptions") and less enjoyment of their learning in STEM, which research shows can lead them to pursue other fields.[27] For example, in a nationally representative study, researchers found that female high school seniors' lower self-perceptions in math explained differences in declaring a STEM major.[28] Given these findings, teaching girls the five learning habits—particularly the technology-specific habits of *design logic* and *efficiencies*—might help. Teaching girls these habits and to understand them as indicative of their ability should make the learning process easier and more enjoyable and improve their self-perception.

However, there is a complication to note with girls' aspirations—studies show that context matters. In more affluent contexts (countries, districts, schools) there are larger gender disparities in aspirations and achievement in STEM than in less affluent contexts.[29] In my own work, I continue to investigate gender gaps in aspirations in more and less affluent schools. Although beyond the scope of this book, my initial investigations suggest that gender gaps in tech-related aspirations may be smaller in less affluent schools.[30] But, more work is necessary to unravel these complex dynamics. Some scholars argue that gender construction within more affluent contexts is the problem because more affluent boys are framed as "geniuses" in STEM and there is an overall more conservative view of gender roles in more affluent contexts.[31]

Broader gendered stereotypes about the nature of STEM work and workers can also powerfully influence gender disparities in achievement and aspirations in these fields.[32] So, an essential part of the effort to reduce gender inequality in STEM must focus on countering stereotypes of technological work with an explicit redefinition of what it means to be good with technology that moves away from the assumption of "natural" gifts.

Class- and race-related inequalities in STEM fields are also complicated. For both class and race, in my survey of 897 Chicago Public Schools eighth graders, I found no significant differences in the technology learning habits of lower- and higher-income students or between racial and ethnic groups. Given that research shows lower-income students and marginalized students have lower access to in-depth technology learning opportunities in schools, this finding suggests that support beyond schools is key to current patterns.[33] In my survey, I found that out-of-school supports (such as the family practices and programs described in this book) were related to students' learning habits, but not most things that happen in school.[34] However, schools *can* play an important role in terms of providing access to advanced learning opportunities. Significantly, they can help convert a student's potential into educational and occupational rewards by certifying students' technological competence.

Indeed, there are both structural and cultural reasons why historically marginalized students' potential is unrealized. Research shows that students from lower-income families have significantly less access to formalized pathways into STEM educational and occupational fields. They attend schools with less experienced teachers and have less supportive academic environments.[35] Less access and support seems to dampen lower-income students' aspirations in these fields, which are significantly lower than the aspirations of higher-income students; as a consequence, so is their attainment in STEM.[36] Lower-income students report feeling significant constraints when making choices about education; unsurprisingly, those who perceive higher barriers and lower support have lower aspirations for the future.[37]

Even though lower-income families are more constrained in terms of financial resources and time, many of them do support engagement in STEM.[38] My research shows that lower-income families (and not just parents, but also grandparents and extended family) help students by encouraging their learning habits, as I will describe further in the next chapter. In fact, based on both the survey and my qualitative observation, it seems that students' experiences outside school are currently the major factor shaping students' learning habits—all the more reason it is vital to recognize students' potential and provide greater access to formal technology learning opportunities.[39]

Finally, racial disparities in STEM are interrelated with class given that historically marginalized racial groups are overrepresented among low-income families, so all the lessons for social class apply. In terms of formal learning opportunities, research shows that the racial segregation of K-12 schools goes hand in hand with the concentration of marginalized students in poorly funded, underperforming, and understaffed schools with fewer qualified teachers, fewer advanced courses, larger class sizes, and less up-to-date educational materials. Yet, numerous studies show that after taking into account all the things that limit students based on their social class, a large portion of the racial achievement gaps and aspirations in STEM are eliminated.[40]

So, how does this research all fit together? These findings suggest that gatekeepers are a central piece of the puzzle. Schools administrators and teachers as well as more affluent white parents, in effect, often bar minoritized and lower-income students from educational opportunities.[41] Black and Brown students are more likely to be placed in lower-tracked courses, even when accounting for class background; that is, they are placed in classes lower than their actual achievement might suggest, where their teachers have lower expectations for learning.[42] Taken together, the combined effects of class- and race-based disparities lead historically marginalized students to drop out of STEM.[43] Beyond providing more learning opportunities for these students, we must ensure that educational (and occupational) gatekeepers do not create roadblocks for them in STEM. In other words, the answer to race-, class-, and gender-based disparities in STEM is more about fixing access and gatekeeping than about fixing kids.

ADDRESSING INEQUALITIES

Research in STEM shows that learning experiences at school, at home, and with friends can influence student achievement and interest in STEM subject areas—which then shape students' future aspirations.[44] While most of this work focuses on mathematics and science, the same findings are likely true for technology learning as well. Therefore, the two major impediments to equitable plans and aspirations in technology-related fields and occupations are (1) lower "self-concept" among girls (i.e., not believing they "fit" in STEM fields), and (2) lower access to high-quality learning opportunities (shaped by both structural and cultural barriers) for female, lower-income, and minoritized students. These problems are ultimately issues of gatekeeping, where inaccurate ideas about what it means to be good with technology (that it is a natural gift) and resource gatekeeping push otherwise talented people away from learning opportunities and out of tech fields.

How this inequality can be addressed remains a concern. Efforts to increase marginalized students' self-concept and enjoyment of STEM could help. But, as Catherine Riegle-Crumb, Chelsea Moore, and Aida Ramos-Wada argue, such efforts can be challenging in the context of No Child Left Behind because high-stakes testing makes it more difficult to "promote a love of science," which makes it all the more critical for teachers to use pedagogical approaches that make learning enjoyable, such as "active and cooperative learning."[45] Informal learning contexts, where testing does not constrain curriculum and educators are free to be more creative in their approach, may more easily provide transformative learning experiences.[46] Research shows that extracurricular activities play a central role in shaping gender differences in plans to major in STEM fields.[47] Given that so much of a student's life is spent outside school and the fact that what students do during this time plays a pivotal role in learning, the social supports provided by the out-of-school programs where I found so many tech-savvy teens are essential to addressing inequality in STEM.[48]

Access to high-quality learning opportunities, high-quality curriculum, and knowledgeable and experienced teachers, both inside and especially outside schools, is therefore fundamental to more equitable technological futures. To increase such access, it can be helpful to involve industry professionals, like the instructors in many of the programs I observed. But no educator (or parent) has to be an expert—simply knowing and supporting the five technology learning habits I have outlined is a start.[49] In terms of formal educational pathways, students who have access to high-quality technology courses have a huge advantage; research shows that aspirations can weaken when opportunities are blocked within institutions—whether through a lack of school resources, biased gatekeeping measures, or outright discrimination, these negative experiences in school tend to dampen students' aspirations.[50] So, one major way to address digital inequality is to end the gatekeeping that perpetuates it and help students realize their full potential.

CONCLUSION: TECHNOLOGICAL FUTURES

Plans and aspirations play a central role in students' futures. Students' learning experiences in courses, in extracurricular activities, in out-of-school programs, at home, and among friends—if they are fun and rigorous and help build confidence—can enhance these plans and aspirations. Learning habits play a vital role in success or failure in the learning process; stronger habits can help students like Rafael know what to do when they encounter new challenges. The five technology learning habits I have presented can provide a new leverage point for developing students' plans and aspirations in tech-related fields and occupations. Although more research is needed to understand causal links, it is promising to see how consistently the five technology learning habits connect with students' goals for the future. The five habits offer educators and parents a concrete way to help to support students' pathways. Further, when we redefine *technological competence* with a focus on learning habits, students can benefit by seeing themselves as more capable than they might initially might have imagined.

This redefinition may also convince gatekeepers to open opportunities for students who might otherwise be assumed less capable—and equitable access to learning opportunities is key to equitable futures. For example, in a study of the Digital Youth Network (DYN)—one of the programs included in this study and described in further detail in the next chapter, Brigid Barron and colleagues compared lower-income and historically marginalized students in Chicago to a group of more advantaged middle-school students in California's Silicon Valley. Whereas the DYN students began sixth grade with fewer technology learning experiences than the Silicon Valley students, by the end of eighth grade, the DYN students had more learning experiences and significantly higher aspirations in tech entrepreneurship, design, engineering, and technology teaching than the Silicon Valley students did.[51]

But stereotypes about what "tech-savvy" people look and act like need to shift. The ability for individuals to live up to their aspirations is shaped by influential gatekeepers—parents, teachers, and employers.[52] How these gatekeepers define *technological competence* and mark boundaries between those who do and do not belong can shape aspirations along the career path as well as the amount of time learners persist in STEM fields. The indicators of belonging should be technology learning habits rather than the irrelevant social cues driven by stereotypes about who is "naturally" gifted that currently shape our views of who belongs in tech.

How can necessary changes happen? I provide practical steps in the next chapter.

[6]

Tackling Digital Inequality

GATEKEEPERS

> Justice requires not only recognition but redistribution;
> neither alone is sufficient.
>
> Christina Dunbar-Hester, *Hacking Diversity: The Politics of
> Inclusion in Open Technology Cultures*

So how do we make technology learning and use more equitable? This chapter offers the concrete, practical tools and advice I wanted as a teacher—but it also goes further to understand and address broader forces shaping digital inequality.

The first step in addressing digital inequality is to observe students' learning habits qualitatively or quantitatively, including the three general habits (*willingness to try and fail, management of frustration and boredom, use of models*) and the two technology-specific habits (*design logic, efficiencies*). Once we understand students' strengths and where they need support, the second step is to help students further develop the habits that are vital to their technological futures. How can educators and parents do this? In this chapter I describe in detail how the programs and families I observed taught each of the five habits.

But beyond observing and developing students' habits, another issue that must be addressed is how gatekeeping shapes students' technological futures. So, I explain how technological gatekeeping works, why it is problematic, and why it has been so durable over time. How might educators, parents, and policy makers address this aspect of digital inequality? Again, the answer is to first observe it. The tools I developed in my research, including the Digital Adaptability Scale (DAS), can be used as indicators of how students experience gatekeeping. Scores on the DAS not only show which habits students have developed and which ones need more support, but they also indicate the extent to which students have or have not been prepared for technology learning, which is itself a form of gatekeeping. In addition to the DAS, I developed a set of measures that can identify *where* students experience gatekeeping in their technology "learning ecology": in school, at home, and among friends.[1] With this information, we can avoid advantaging some and disadvantaging others. We can target teens lower on the DAS who might be lacking support, and we can ensure that students higher on the scale have adequate access and support to deepen their skill.[2] But first, it is important to understand the problem.

THE PROBLEM OF GATEKEEPING

You may remember that in my very early research with my web design students, I asked them to draw a "computer type" of person—to imagine who is tech savvy. This activity was based on the Draw-a-Computer-User Test, which researchers have used to understand students' ideas about who is good with computers and their own self-perception as skillful "computer-types."[3] Research shows that stereotypes about role characteristics emerge in any field. In computer science, the stereotype is typically male, white, or Asian. Although students' self-perception is not governed by these stereotypes (it does not necessarily undermine students' perception of their own skillfulness), it can influence who chooses to participate in these fields.[4] Most of this research on stereotypes focuses on students' perceptions of stereotypes and how the ideas they hold can shape their trajectories. But what about the stereotypes that policy makers, educators, parents, employers, and other gatekeepers might hold?

How gatekeepers understand who is well matched to activities in science, technology, engineering, and mathematics (STEM) based on perceived "talent" also shapes who is included and who is excluded in educational and occupational pathways.[5] For example, teachers and parents often believe boys have greater natural talent in math than girls do, which creates advantage for boys in math-related educational pathways.[6] In STEM occupations, both men and women believe scientists are typically male, and men in male-dominated fields such as computer science hold a particularly strong belief that men are better in math and science than women are.[7] These views have persisted over generations and are consistent across gender and racial groups in the United States.[8]

Stereotypes can have tangible negative consequences for those who do not fit them. For example, research shows that at the national level, the more people implicitly associate men with science and women with the liberal arts, the greater the gender gap in science achievement in that nation.[9] Gender and racial stereotypes promote prejudice and discrimination, resulting in exclusion or exit from these educational and occupational fields.[10] If gatekeepers view technological competence as a "natural" ability found among those currently dominating tech fields (white, Asian, male), it leaves little space for recognizing the talent of less stereotypical groups. It also makes it hard for those who do not fit the stereotypes, such as Asian males who might need more support with their technological learning.[11] In other words, stereotypes keep all kinds of people out of fully participating in our digital world.

Given the persistence of stereotypes, reimagining who is good with technology might seem difficult, but local organizations can be powerful contexts within which such ideas can be addressed.[12] At Urban Promise Academy, when Principal Montes suggested to a male student that he join my web design class, the student said, "Isn't that a *girl thing*?" as if it was utterly obvious a boy didn't belong in a tech class. The girls-only class did defy stereotypes in radical ways; in fact, all my students drew female "computer types." This shift demonstrates what gender scholar Barrie Thorne argued decades ago: that the "dynamics of power, like those of gender, are fluid and contextual" and that "this sense of a play of possibilities has concrete implications for social change."[13] If local context can shape these ideas in powerful ways, it suggests that these contexts can help change ideas about who is good with technology and stop technological gatekeeping. But how? The first step is to observe it.

MEASURING GATEKEEPING

How do students experience gatekeeping? It turns out that it varies greatly but usually occurs in one of two ways. Gatekeeping may prevent students from developing basic *technological competence* by not being encouraged to develop the five technology learning habits (which was the case for Rafael from chapter 4, who was known as a "bad" kid so did not get opportunities for technology learning in school the way "good" kid Sumalee did, despite strong interest). Or, students may be barred from advanced technology learning opportunities because their technological competence and readiness for future challenges go unrecognized or opportunities are not available to them. For example, there might be no computing courses offered at their school, which was the case for Imani in Mouse/Geek Squad Summer Academy whom we met playing Guitar Hero in chapter 2, who said she'd only had typing class in school. These latter experiences (nonrecognition, lack of advanced opportunities) might help explain why in my research I found no significant differences in the five habits by racial or ethnic background or socioeconomic status, yet these groups continue to be marginalized in tech.[14]

So, how do we observe technological gatekeeping? As noted at the beginning of this chapter, the first step is to identify students who have experienced gatekeeping by measuring students' habits using the DAS. Students lower on the scale have experienced some form of technological gatekeeping, through a lack of access to fundamental technological training. In other words, the DAS can show who has been adequately prepared for tech learning and who has not. This DAS-based identification process helps thwart the categorization of some students as more "naturally gifted" with technology than others, instead replacing that notion with the idea of preparation or "readiness" for technology learning.[15] The measure also offers information about how students have been prepared: What is it that students do as they learn—and which habits need more nurturing? This information would simultaneously identify students who experience gatekeeping in their technology learning, allow for more targeted intervention, and help identify students with well-established learning habits who are ready for more advanced challenges. (They might otherwise be overlooked, which is a different form of gatekeeping.)

The information derived from the DAS is especially useful in school districts implementing new computing curriculum, to ensure that students are equitably prepared for technology classes and activities, such as new Computer Science for All (CS4All) initiatives. In Chicago, the school district went so far as to introduce a computer science graduation requirement. But without gathering information about student preparation, the requirement is likely to further disadvantage those inadequately prepared. Using the measure to identify and target these students will avoid doubly disadvantaging them.

The second step is to get a sense of how students experience gatekeeping in their learning ecology—at home, at school, among friends—by asking about students' technology learning experiences in these contexts. I formalized this step in the series of survey questions presented in tables 6.1–6.4. In schools, it might be tempting to assume that if students have a technology class, they must be learning about technology. I've even seen teachers in schools with mandatory technology classes make this assumption. For example, I watched as Anandi, whom we met in chapter 4, struggled when her science teacher assigned a PowerPoint presentation to the class based on the assumption that all students would know how to use PowerPoint because they were enrolled in a technology class. But few of them had experience with the program, and some, like Anandi, let better-prepared classmates do the assignment.[16] For the same reasons, simply having a tech teacher—which was the case in most Chicago schools I visited (although certainly not all schools within the district, or across the country)—might suggest that students are learning about technology. But the technology teachers I met in Chicago lamented that they rarely were able to use their expertise and well-developed technology curriculum because of the time taken up by standardized testing and test prep.[17] Additionally, as with the comparison of Rafael and Sumalee, students can have highly contrasting experiences of tech learning in the same school and the same classes. Instead of reaching all students, computer use may be allocated to the "good" (well-behaved, higher-achieving) students and not the "bad" (distracted, lower-achieving) students.[18]

To understand students' unique experiences, I asked a set of five questions about the extent students are taught the five habits at school (see table 6.1). These questions allowed students to report individual experiences within schools and classrooms, rather than assuming stu-

TABLE 6.1. School technology teaching scale

How much do you agree with the following statements ABOUT SCHOOL, with 1 being "strongly disagree" and 6 being "strongly agree"?						
	How much do you agree?					
(Please circle one number per row)	Strongly disagree					Strongly agree
At school we are taught that it's okay if we fail when using technology, just as long as we try.	1	2	3	4	5	6
We are taught at school to never give up, even if we get frustrated or bored using technology.	1	2	3	4	5	6
At school we are taught how to find help if we have problems using technology.	1	2	3	4	5	6
At school we are taught to think about why technology was designed the way it was.	1	2	3	4	5	6
At school we are taught tricks to be faster using technology (like shortcuts, keyboard commands, right-click menus).	1	2	3	4	5	6

Note: Overall scale has Cronbach's alpha of $\alpha = 0.84$.

Source: Cassidy Puckett, "CS4Some? Differences in Technology Learning Readiness," *Harvard Educational Review* 89, no. 4 (2019): 554–87, at 568.

dents experiences were uniform, even if they were all required to take a tech course.

Again, you might note that I used the word *technology*, rather than *computers* or names of specific devices. I did so to include the range of devices students might encounter (computers, video game consoles, cell phones, etc.).[19] The responses to these questions can reveal whether schools support groups' habits—in other words, the extent that gatekeeping happens at school.

But other social contexts can be equally consequential for gatekeeping and should be considered as well. For example, my research in Chicago revealed that what happens at home currently plays a central role in shaping students' habits—and although schools might respond to these habits, they don't currently tend to develop them. This finding was reflected in Sumalee's experiences, presented in chapter 4. At home her "Granny" encouraged her habits (described in greater detail later in this chapter), and, based on teachers noticing her habits (like Mrs. Giannopoulos knowing she was techie), she was similarly encouraged at school.[20] I measured home tech practices with a set of five questions designed to parallel those at school (see table 6.2).

Home practices also play a central role in gatekeeping, as research shows home is often where differences emerge in STEM.[21] For example, who at home has access to a computer, and where is it located? Early PC advertising encouraged the purchase of personal computers for boys, who more commonly had them in their bedrooms and spent more time overall on the computer, playing video games and learning how to use a range of devices.[22] This practice was observed some decades ago, of course, but these are still critical questions to ask children and teens. Who is given a tech toy (robotics set, video game console, etc.) to tinker with? Whose social media use is monitored more closely? It is not a given that family dynamics are equalizing for everyone.

Finally, friends can be highly influential for a range of outcomes— and although we may not think of peers as "gatekeepers," research on peers suggests they can shape what and how students learn. For example, a 2012 study found that friendship groups that valued and sup-

TABLE 6.2. Home technology teaching scale

How much do you agree with the following statements ABOUT YOUR FAMILY, with 1 being "strongly disagree" and 6 being "strongly agree"?						
	How much do you agree?					
(Please circle one number per row)	Strongly disagree					Strongly agree
My family teaches me that it's okay if I fail when using technology, just as long as I try.	1	2	3	4	5	6
My family teaches me to never give up, even if I get frustrated or bored using technology.	1	2	3	4	5	6
My family shows me how to find help if I have problems using technology	1	2	3	4	5	6
My family teaches me to think about why technology was designed the way it was.	1	2	3	4	5	6
My family shows me tricks to be faster using technology (like shortcuts, keyboard commands, right-click menus).	1	2	3	4	5	6

Note: Overall scale has Cronbach's alpha of α = 0.85.

Source: Puckett, "CS4Some? Differences in Technology Learning Readiness," *Harvard Educational Review* 89, no. 4 (2019): 554–87, at 566.

ported STEM learning could be protective for girls and help strengthen their interest in these fields.[23] To ask students about the extent to which friends helped support their technology learning habits, I posed a set of five questions designed to parallel those at school and home (see table 6.3).

Following past research, I was unsurprised to find that friends' practices also influenced the development of the technology learning habits. For example, the majority of support that Rafael received was not from school nor his parents but from his friends. Friends were likewise influential to Sumalee's habits (specifically, the friends with whom she'd play online games), although her family and teachers encouraged her as well.

It also matters how these various social spheres align. For Jasmine (whose experiences were detailed in chapters 4 and 5), her habits were supported largely at home and among friends and a bit at school (although they lamented not offering more technology teaching). Overall, this reinforcement made Jasmine's habits much stronger than

TABLE 6.3. Friends technology teaching scale

How much do you agree with the following statements ABOUT YOUR FRIENDS, with 1 being "strongly disagree" and 6 being "strongly agree"?						
	How much do you agree?					
(Please circle one number per row)	Strongly disagree					Strongly agree
My friends tell me that it's okay if I fail when using technology, just as long as I try.	1	2	3	4	5	6
My friends tell me to never give up, even if I get frustrated or bored using technology.	1	2	3	4	5	6
My friends show me how to find help if I have problems using technology.	1	2	3	4	5	6
My friends help me think about why technology was designed the way it was.	1	2	3	4	5	6
My friends show me tricks to be faster using technology (like shortcuts, keyboard commands, right-click menus).	1	2	3	4	5	6

Note: Overall scale has Cronbach's alpha of $\alpha = 0.79$.

Source: Cassidy Puckett, "Technological Change, Digital Adaptability, and Social Inequality" (PhD diss., Northwestern University, 2015), 162.

Rafael's and helped her move in a more certain way toward a technological future. Sumalee similarly received support in all three places (although she received more support at school than Jasmine did). So, a full picture of students' experiences includes understanding each social setting (in school, at home, among friends) as well as their experiences across these contexts.[24]

But note that these measures do not capture all contexts where students might learn about technology. We could also collect quantitative data about places like the award-winning programs where I initially observed tech-savvy teens.[25] To ask students about the extent to which such places helped support their technology learning habits, I posed a set of five questions about after-school and summer programs, designed to parallel those asked regarding school, home, and friends (see table 6.4).

The DAS, combined with these measures, can show where and how students experience technological gatekeeping and help identify students who would benefit from particular types of intervention pro-

TABLE 6.4. Out-of-school technology teaching scale

How much do you agree with the following statements about AFTER-SCHOOL OR SUMMER PROGRAMS, with 1 being "strongly disagree" and 6 being "strongly agree"?						
	How much do you agree?					
(Please circle one number per row)	Strongly disagree					Strongly agree
In after-school or summer programs, they teach me that it's okay if I fail when using technology, just as long as I try.	1	2	3	4	5	6
In after-school or summer programs, they teach me to never give up, even if I get frustrated or bored using technology.	1	2	3	4	5	6
In after-school or summer programs, they teach me how to find help if I have problems using technology.	1	2	3	4	5	6
In after-school or summer programs, they teach me to think about why technology was designed the way it was.	1	2	3	4	5	6
In after-school or summer programs, they teach me tricks to be faster using technology (like shortcuts, keyboard commands, right-click menus).	1	2	3	4	5	6

grams. For example, if students experience little technology learning at home, there may be effective ways to engage families and help them encourage their children to develop strong habits—for example, the Family Creative Learning program developed at the Massachusetts Institute of Technology (MIT).[26] In the program, families use tools such as Scratch to create interactive stories, games, and animations—and both parents and students develop their technological skills. Or, if students experience little out-of-school technology learning, it would be helpful to provide access to programs through networks such as Hive NYC Learning Network or Chicago Learning Exchange.[27]

ADDRESSING GATEKEEPING: WHAT PARENTS AND EDUCATORS CAN DO

While gatekeeping is a problem and these measures can help identify where students experience it and where intervention might be needed, what next? How do we create more inclusion within these spaces? For that, parents and educators can draw on lessons from the families and programs that supported the many tech-savvy teens I describe in this book. Within each of these contexts, teens experienced the exact opposite of gatekeeping—the programs systematically cultivated the five habits: *a willingness to try and fail, management of frustration and boredom, use of models, design logic, and efficiencies*. Rather than assuming technological ability is a natural, fixed characteristic, families of tech-savvy teens and the technology programs they attended explicitly taught or demonstrated these habits. They took this approach so teens could shape our technological futures—like William's mom (from chapter 5), who said, "[If it's] this important now, only imagine in the next twenty to forty years, so I want him to get as good as possible." In the following sections, I describe how families and programs cultivated each habit and summarize key takeaway points for teaching the habits and undoing the harm of gatekeeping.

Teaching *Willingness to Try and Fail*

When I visited Sumalee at home in the small two-bedroom apartment that housed her mother, stepfather, brother, and grandmother, one of the things that stood out was how her "Granny" interacted with Sumalee around technology. Granny had been Sumalee's caretaker for three years prior to their immigration to the United States to follow her mother and stepfather, who had already moved. In her family, Granny was the biggest supporter of Sumalee's tech habits and argued with her parents to give her more time on the computer. Granny also encouraged the specific development of Sumalee's *willingness to try and fail* by subtly communicating the expectation that Sumalee could solve any technological issue—and so, she should try.

In one of the many interactions between Sumalee and Granny, I watched as Sumalee clicked away on a laptop playing an online game and was briefly interrupted by Granny. In my notes I wrote:

> Granny came into the living room where Sumalee and I were sitting, and, without any verbal directions, handed Sumalee a camera.

Sumalee put the camera on picture viewer mode and zoomed in and handed it back to her Granny, so that Granny could look at pictures from the wedding they'd gone to this morning.[28]

I asked if Sumalee had ever done this task before (helped with the zoom on the camera) and if so, if Granny knew she could do it. To both questions Sumalee responded no. This interaction was a typical thing Granny did: handed her things, expecting her to go ahead and try, even if she failed. This encouragement did not require an adult technology expert. In fact, it helped that Granny and Sumalee's parents were not very tech savvy (though they provided ample technology). Sumalee was confident she could figure things out based on her experiences with online gaming, where she was coached by her *guild* (group of online gamers) how to learn new tricks and had worked her way up to guild master. She also knew how to find help if she needed it (through the *use of models*).

In all the technology-related programs I observed, instructors similarly monitored students' willingness to try and fail and encouraged it over and over again. Dan, one of the instructors at the Bay Area Video Coalition (BAVC) Bay Unity Music Project (BUMP) Records whom we met in chapter 3, said that the program's overall goals are for students to gain a basic understanding of recording and mixing; the equipment; and the general workflow of recording, producing, and promoting music. Putting all that new knowledge together, students should get a good first recording. About his teaching approach, he said:

> [I start by] getting a gauge of where students are at, what they're *willing to learn*. It's good to be triple-threat—they can make beats, write lyrics, and produce. . . . So, to start we plug them in, show them how to set up the studio, the importance of sound proofing. Then, it's being familiar with all of the main buttons (*points to buttons in Digidesign Digi 003 which can be used to manipulate Pro Tools using the recording studio's boards*). The curriculum is trying to get in the right amount of info to condense in a certain amount within a month.

To get students through their packed curriculum, BUMP explicitly taught the same habit Sumalee's Granny did when handing her a camera: communicate (through action or explicitly stating) the expectation that students will be able to solve anything and celebrate any attempt as a success to help students try again. Getting things perfect was decidedly *not* the goal—the goal was to get students to try things out and learn from what they did. This approach reduces gatekeeping by creating an environment where students are encouraged to try, celebrate what they try, and learn from what happens, rather than be afraid and discouraged from future technology learning.

STRATEGIES TO TEACH *WILLINGNESS TO TRY AND FAIL*:
- Communicate the expectation that students can figure things out.
- Celebrate students' attempts as successes.
- Ask students to try learning a range of technologies (practice through repetition).

Teaching *Management of Frustration and Boredom*

As discussed in earlier chapters, *management of frustration and boredom* involves drawing on a repertoire of techniques to manage the challenges students face when learning new technologies. A repertoire is helpful because if one approach does not work, learners have a number of others at their disposal. Typical techniques include *framing technology learning as a process* and *practicing imperfection*, together with the ongoing addition of many other creative approaches (such as those described in chapter 2: *pivoting, breaking down tasks, blocking out distractions*, and *enlisting others to help manage frustration*). Together, this array of techniques can help when frustration and boredom inevitably arise during the learning process.

How can this habit be taught? Developing a repertoire to manage frustration and boredom was an explicit part of most programs, with instructors coaching teens. They would first explain that students should *expect* frustration and boredom—in other words, they would normalize it. Then, they would offer ways to work through challenges. Instructors said when teens tried multiple techniques to manage frustration and boredom, it was a major marker of student development and helped them get better at what they were doing. Dan at BUMP Records said:

> Tech-savvy students focus on the project at hand . . . they get in the zone, focus on things like writing a song. They are a little more focused in what they're doing, not wanting to take breaks. For example, Christine, her first verse in an earlier song, the intro was the last thing she recorded, enunciation wasn't great. You see the growth in the first verse of a later song and it's much fuller, more polished. As long as everyone stays humble and remembers *it's a learning process*, you'll see major change and the most learning.

Explaining to teens that trying to learn new technologies is a "process" and repeatedly reminding them of this idea helped teens use this framing to get through difficulties. And, programs encouraged students to practice imperfection.

Instructors in Digital Youth Network (DYN) workshops at YOUmedia Chicago coached students so they understood that the challenges they faced were part of the learning process. In music production, African American instructor and professional musician Simeon (whom we first met in chapter 3) helped a Black female student named Aria who came to the workshop wanting to create a song with sounds she'd gathered on her phone. Simeon said some encouraging words and helped her import the sounds from her cell phone into GarageBand, then had her take over. But, even though she was at first *willing to try and fail*, she got stuck. Noting her frustration—with her hands off her keyboard, perhaps on the edge of giving up—Simeon stepped in to coach her by framing difficulties as something needing a technical fix:

Simeon returns to where Aria sits, hands on lap. He asks for her headphones, turns the computer slightly toward him, and listens.

> SIMEON: [The sounds] are kind of tweaky. Did you designate tempo?
>
> ARIA: No.
>
> SIMEON: I like the sounds you're using, but you gotta find the sequence. So, you go to Control>Tempo (*demonstrates on her computer*).

Simeon looks at Aria. She sighs and looks down, like she's ready to give up.

He shifts the computer back toward her, with a nod, encouraging her to try again. She takes a breath, pauses, and then puts her hands to the keyboard and mimics the steps Simeon just demonstrated. Simeon touches the table beside her as a quick gesture of recognition and moves on to help another student.

Quickly, Aria refocuses on her work.

Not long after, everyone in the workshop shared the first draft of their songs. Aria explained that her piece was based on the *House on Mango Street* chapter "My Name." She described the struggles she'd had with the song, then she played it for the room. Other students and instructors commented on her progress, affirming that song creation was a learning process. A Black male student named Charles, his hair pulled back in a bundle of short dreadlocks, said, "I like it, it's got a lot of potential." Simeon agreed, adding, "I like your sound choices. It's got a mood." Simeon also commented that all the students' "first beats" were better than his first beat—telling them they, too, could become highly skilled professionals.

Programs also encouraged students to look for and add to their repertoire of management techniques. Instructors coached students to shift purposefully to something else, such as playing a video game if they got frustrated in BAVC game design (*pivoting*); providing students with a list of smaller steps involved in a technology project to make learning more manageable, such as the steps to put a computer together in Mouse/Geek Squad (*breaking down tasks*); and suggesting students use headphones to maintain focus in Youth Movement Records, or YMR (*blocking out distractions*). Finally, programs encouraged teens to continually develop their management repertoire by watching what others would do and asking for help (especially from instructors). In short, programs taught *management of frustration and boredom* through normalization, explanation, repetition, recognition, and ongoing development. Overall, this habit lessened gatekeeping by making frustration and boredom an expected and ordinary experience in the technology learning process and equipped students with a few key approaches and ways to find new management strategies.

STRATEGIES TO TEACH *MANAGEMENT OF FRUSTRATION AND BOREDOM*:

- Set the expectation that learners will encounter frustration and boredom when learning new technologies.
- Explicitly help learners frame technology learning as a process.
- Remind learners of techniques for managing frustration and boredom.
- Celebrate learners' failures during the learning process as successes.
- Advise learners to continually develop new approaches to manage their frustration and boredom.

Teaching *Use of Models*

Many programs encouraged the *use of models*, telling students to use people (instructors, peers) and objects (other technology products, online searches) to understand what they could do with technology and how they could accomplish their goals. One way programs supported the *use of models*—common in many out-of-school programs— was through apprenticeship with industry professionals (filmmakers, musicians, videographers, technical experts) who were trained in youth development methods.[29] Instruction by professionals was the case at all BAVC programs, YMR, Mouse/Geek Squad Summer Academy, and DYN. In addition, YMR and DYN engaged students with other working professional artists in their community and beyond.[30] In their book *The Digital Youth Network: Cultivating Digital Media Citizenship in Urban Communities*, Brigid Barron and colleagues describe it this way:

> From the engineers who directed the robotics and game design pods [groups] to the spoken-word artists who led the digital queendom and spoken-word pods to connections with artists outside of school, students in DYN encountered a range of professionals enacting roles that they were learning to take on themselves. These adults not only shared their work and knowledge with students but also encouraged the students to create and sustain their own good work. For many students, this link to the professional world was a source of inspiration for creativity and took the production process out of the narrow boundaries of a single assignment or class and into the real world.[31]

Programs structured a form of digital apprenticeship that invited students into the professional world, to engage in "authentic" technological work, as in the chapter 3 account of Gisela at Radio Arte creating a *radionovela* that "sounded like NPR."

BUMP director and instructor Robert Collins, a bespectacled Black man with a welcoming low-key California vibe, explained that the program was designed with industry standards in mind. This approach was largely because he and other instructors came from industry. His experience as an artist manager and in marketing informed this approach. The program was rigorous in holding students up to industry standards—in the same way YMR executive director Ryan Nicole Peters, a Black woman and Grammy-nominated MC and poet, described that program:

> I don't dumb things down. . . . I consistently teach [program participants] the vernacular of music; how to talk the language of the industry. They don't know they're getting that. We have intelligent con-

versations about music, using the language of the industry. . . . It's really through practice that kids will pick things up. You have to know the structure first, then you can blow that up. [I teach them to] keep track of the steps you take, write it down. A lot of this is sort of project management—defining your concept, improving, tweaking. In the program, students have real-world deadlines, like performances—at some point they have to stop tweaking and recording and go perform.

Through these practices, teens learned how to become fluent community members who understood the norms, values, and appropriate ways of contributing within what scholars call a "community of practice."[32] Instructors also shared with students the multiple sources they draw on in their work, demonstrating that being an expert meant using a range of models. For example, BUMP instructor Dan explained:

[Students] hear from an artist how this works, you can be as good [as] or better than the people that influence you. If you never fully feel like you're better, then your work will get better. So, I'll say things [to students] like "Take your favorite album and make the same album. See if yours can go toe to toe with that." We encourage and build that into the program. Listen to those who influence you—there's often a formula.

Collins likewise explained that BUMP helped students identify models by encouraging them to listen to a range of music to inform their work, breaking down harmonies in songs to "open them up to other ideas." The BUMP curriculum was conceptually organized around a model of how songs are constructed: first laying down beats, then putting together song elements (sounds, vocals) that "go together sonically," and then exposing students to new models for how songs can be put together. In other words, all programs taught students that being a professional meant looking for and using models.

Instructors encouraged students to seek out multiple models so that they could continue to learn and improve even if one particular model failed to help. In many programs, activities and structures inherently encouraged students to identify and use multiple models, and not just instructors but also peers. For example as described in chapter 2, at Radio Arte, the program was structured so that students worked in teams and shared work with other teams through ongoing formal peer critique sessions, which encouraged students to use other teens in the program and the work they produced as models.

This use of peers as models was also the case across other programs where teens worked in groups, watching what their peers did as they learned new technologies. For example, Raul at Campbell Middle School Mouse Squad California (MSCA) said, humbly, that all his friends were "pretty tech savvy" and use one another as models. He said they instant message each other advice and subscribe to YouTube channels for the latest tech information to stay on top of ever-changing technologies and to find new models for learning. He explained, "I ask for help if I don't know. Like, friends who are good at certain things, I can figure out who has used the same program before." How did MSCA encourage this interaction? He said his program leader and teacher Carrie Tibbs told students not to worry and encouraged them to ask someone else for help. The best way to get help, Raul said, was to explain what you understand and "what part you don't get." All programs encouraged students to *use models* to help them learn, whether people or objects/information online or within software programs, and to understand that anyone or anything could be a potential model at some point in the learning process. Overall, these approaches helped create a more social and inclusive experience for students.

STRATEGIES TO TEACH *USE OF MODELS*:
- To the extent possible, embed technology learning in communities of practice (with professionals and peers).
- Explicitly encourage learners to identify multiple models (people, technologies, and technological products) from which they can learn.
- Structure the use of multiple models into learning experiences.

Teaching *Design Logic*

You'll recall from earlier chapters that *design logic* is thinking about why technologies are designed the way they are and decoding that logic to accomplish particular goals. Coaching students' *use of models* can also help students use *design logic* by encouraging them to notice similarities between the design and function of two technologies and to try to transfer the logic of one system to another. But *design logic* should be an explicit part of the learning experience, given that it may not otherwise be clear to students that comparing designs of various technologies is not only something you do but also a way of thinking (thinking about *why* a technology is designed, how it was designed, and what its functions might be). And because the logic of one technology may not readily transfer to another or a new technology might be entirely novel, *design logic* must be explicitly taught.

Program instructors in all programs plainly explained the logic behind design features. For example, at YMR, African American instructor Tony helped students understand the *design logic* behind technologies unfamiliar to them, such as software designed to visually represent a "rack" of studio equipment (this type of design is known as "skeuomorphic design," like a calculator app on a smartphone or computer).[33] In one interaction between Tony and white teen Kyle (a pair we first encountered in chapter 2), Tony helped Kyle understand the logic behind Reason, an audio production software. When Kyle asked for feedback on the first draft of his song, Tony listened and suggested that Kyle could add instruments. To help Kyle with this task, Tony explained how to understand the visual design of Reason.

> TONY: Maybe [add] synth instruments. It's the same process. Go to the folder, could go to Reason Factory Sound Bank, same place as the drums.
>
> KYLE (*holding one headphone to his right ear*): It's not playing them.
>
> TONY: Did you make a mixer?

KYLE: No.

TONY: Okay, hit Create, then drag it to the back [of the "rack,"
what looks like the back of a stereo, where wires connect].
You need the mixer to control everything. *Like in a real studio,*
say you have a bunch of mics, they're plugged into a mixer.

In this case, Tony tried to help Kyle understand the design by explaining how it mirrors real-world objects. The software itself helped in this instance because its visual design mirrored tangible technologies' physical design, thereby making the logic of its function more explicit. As Andrew Eisele points out in the instructional book *Sound Design and Mixing in Reason*:

One of the most fascinating and exhilarating aspects of Reason is the reverse side of the rack. As a teaching tool, it offers a glimpse at how to wire up a physical rack and connect analog synthesizers and sequencers. . . . Other programs offer similar types of control, but you need a degree in computer science to be able to program them.[34]

Regardless of the design of the software, instructors emphasized the importance of understanding the logic of the technology's design in learning how to use it—and students said this habit helped them learn.

Other instructors taught *design logic* within and across software programs. In another class at YMR, the white male instructor Chris (who appeared in chapters 2 and 3) led his Pro Tools class through the logic of how hardware and software work together. I noted:

Chris writes the words "MIDI" and "AUDIO" across a large white board at the front of the room. He points at the word MIDI and turns to the class and says, "That stands for something. What is that?"

A few students guess (music, instrument).

Chris says, "Musical Instrument Digital Interface. Now, why is that important? (*not waiting for a response*) Because in this course we mainly focus on audio, but all keyboards communicate through MIDI—you're not recording audio, you're recording MIDI. It's like a brain and your body's movement. You're just recording instruction, not the actual music."

Chris pauses, then continues: "Some people ask, why start there? I think it's good to understand conceptually how things work. . . . Pro Tools is the industry standard. Any studio worth its salt has Pro Tools. So, it's important to know how things work."

Chris also told the class to explicitly connect the logic of other software that they are familiar with to the program they are learning—that they might be similar, combining *design logic* with *use of models*. I wrote:

> Chris explains how the Edit window functions. He asks the class, "What if I wanted to move it around?"
>
> Multiple students call out, "Click and drag!"
>
> He asks, "If I drag it, what tool do I use?"
>
> Students again chime in, "The hand!"
>
> Chris nods and says, "It's like a Word document, dragging words around."

By quizzing students on Pro Tools features, Chris coached them to think about the logic of the program and how it might function like other programs.

In subsequent classes, students asked Chris about what particular software was designed to do in terms of the overall music production process, proactively trying to understand a software's *design logic*:

> MICHAEL (a Black male wearing a white polo shirt): Is Pro Tools how you finalize the project, like master it?
>
> CHRIS: Well, there's another program I use, but it's 50K [$50,000] to get that. Mastering is a different art. You might be a good track artist, but that's different from mixing. And

mastering is different. You could do all three, but typically you pick one and spend your time there.

MICHAEL: What [software] is good to know for mixing?

CHRIS: Important to know and use Logic, you put it into Pro Tools, put in vocals, send it to a mastering person.

MICHAEL: In Pro Tools, everything has to be separated [by me]?

CHRIS: Forget about automatic. "Will Pro Tools do that for me?" No. "Can I do that?" *Yes*. We'll talk about that, especially in beats class. We'll come together with beats class to bring it together. Between now and then, use the practice sessions. Push buttons, make mistakes. That's how we learn.

Chris emphasized the limits of the software—it was not made to automatically do things for a user. He also tied the process of coming to understand the software's *design logic* to a *willingness to try and fail*—pushing buttons and making mistakes is how to learn what a technology is and is not designed to do.

Finally, across all programs—as seen in the foregoing examples—programs explicitly connected teaching *design logic* to the specific goals teens were trying to achieve, such as Michael's goal of mastering his album. This connection, too, helped create an inclusive learning experience by inviting students to think about their own goals in the learning process—and explicitly teaching *design logic* was helpful in developing teens' technological competence.

STRATEGIES TO TEACH *DESIGN LOGIC*:

- Explain that trying to understand the design of a technology can help in the learning process.
- Encourage learners to think about why a technology was designed the way it was (e.g., by asking questions, encouraging comparison, explicitly interpreting its design).
- Help learners think about their goals relative to their emerging understanding of a technology's design to help in the learning process.

Teaching *Efficiencies*

Finally, to include students in their "tech-savvy" community, all programs I studied taught faster ways of accomplishing technology tasks (*efficiencies*). This learning happened through both teacher-student instruction and peer interaction. Instructors repeatedly explained shortcuts and encouraged students to look for and use them. They taught keyboard commands for computer use in general (such as Apple/Command+C or Crtl+C for copying) and commands specific to particular pieces of software students were learning. Instructors explained that these "tricks" could help students be more proficient. They also described how *efficiencies* might be transferred from one type of technology to another, combining the *use of models* and *design logic* with *efficiencies*. They further communicated, by emphasizing *efficiencies*, that a central feature of technological competence and a way of signaling membership as a tech insider is knowing tricks. Using *efficiencies* could identify you as tech savvy.

For example, in DYN workshops at YOUmedia Chicago, instructors explained and repeated keyboard commands. During a music production workshop, a Black male student named Aaron who brought his younger brother to the class asked instructor Brother Mike how to make a new track in GarageBand. Brother Mike—a charismatic Black mentor and professional poet who would lovingly guide students through any challenge— responded by calling out a keyboard command. Aaron tried the command, with Brother Mike looking on, waiting to see whether he'd gotten it. But for some reason—whether he didn't understand what Brother Mike said, pressed the wrong buttons, or did not press them at the same time—Aaron couldn't figure out the command. Brother Mike moved closer to Aaron's computer and demonstrated the command on the keyboard as Aaron looked on. Then, Aaron mimicked Brother Mike's actions as Brother Mike looked on and nodded as Aaron successfully created a new track. Brother Mike then showed him how to extend the track. Aaron smiled and said, "Okay!" and proceeded to work on his song. "Word," said Brother Mike, touching Aaron's shoulder and moving on to help other students.

Programs also encouraged students to help each other, to show shortcuts and tricks to one another. For example, in many programs more experienced students formally worked as teaching assistants, or students who had been in the programs in prior years helped newer students with the insider tricks they'd learned. For example, in an interview at YOUmedia, a tall Black male student named Jacob who wore rectangular metal-rimmed glasses said he liked that instructors and other students would "physically show him how to do something" and then he'd "try it [and] repeat that [process of showing and trying] multiple times" to finally get the trick down. By teaching students insider tricks, over and over again, programs showed that shortcuts existed, communicated that they were essential to the learning process, explained them both verbally and physically, repeated them, and encouraged everyone to share their tricks—all so that students would become part of their tech-savvy community.

STRATEGIES TO TEACH *EFFICIENCIES*:

- Explain that all technologies have short and long pathways to accomplish tasks and tell students it is helpful to look for shortcuts in the learning process.
- Describe or demonstrate shortcuts that may be used across technologies and within specific technologies.
- Encourage learners to seek out hidden shortcuts through the *use of models* (observing and asking what others do and seeking out other types of resources to help identify shortcuts).

ADDRESSING GATEKEEPING: WHAT ORGANIZATIONS CAN DO

Beyond teaching the five technology learning habits and helping students define *technological competence* to include these habits as a central feature, organizations that function as gatekeepers can take other steps to address digital inequality and build more-inclusive environments. Why are organizations so important? Many scholars argue that it is within organizations—particularly organizations representing central social institutions such as schools and workplaces—where inequalities are produced, exacerbated, or addressed.[35] Individual gatekeepers, such as teachers or parents, can support students' habits. But, historically inequitable structures and practices within organizations—called "inequality regimes" by inequality scholar Joan Acker—are key to gatekeeping. In organizations, groups and resources are sorted and matched, shaping the nature and extent of (in)equity.[36] For example, some students are categorized as "good" students (like Sumalee), who could earn "extra" technology learning experiences, while "bad" students (like Rafael) could not. Following this research, I explain in the remainder of this chapter how organizations can take steps to address the systematic exclusion of women, Black and Brown students and workers, and people from lower socioeconomic backgrounds in tech-related educational pathways and occupational fields.

In Education: Designing "Responsive" Contexts

In terms of how schools can create more-inclusive technology learning experiences by race, class, and gender, research shows that it is critical to create what Spencer Foundation president and UC Berkeley professor Na'ilah Suad Nasir calls "responsive" learning contexts. To be more efficacious for marginalized students, Nasir argues that schools should engage in explicit racial socialization and other identity work because these processes are already happening implicitly within schools and classrooms. Nasir sets forth five principles for identity building with regard to race, to which I add class and gender.[37] These principles are as follows:

1. Caring relationships among members of the (school) community
2. Spaces where students are cared about as whole people
3. Access to material resources for all students

4. Culturally relevant practices
5. Explicit conversations about race, class, and gender and managing discrimination and bias

With regard to material resources and managing discrimination and bias, Barrie Thorne recommends promoting cooperative relations among students by (1) using criteria other than gender or race to group students; (2) affirming and reinforcing the values of cooperation among all kids regardless of social categories; (3) organizing students into small, heterogenous, and cooperative work groups; (4) facilitating kids' access to all activities (including equal access to computers); and (5) actively intervening to challenge the dynamics of stereotyping and power.[38]

Although not all the technology programs I describe in this book explicitly addressed every one of these points, all emphasized the first four of Nasir's principles in such a way that students developed the five technology learning habits. More concretely, one of the ways programs helped build caring relationships, made students feel cared about as whole people, were given access to material resources, and engaged in culturally relevant practices was to design learning experiences that focused on things students cared about. At Radio Arte, teens developed radio segments based on their interests, like Gisela's radio segment on the experience of being bilingual (described in chapter 3). In all BAVC programs and at YMR, teens worked on projects explicitly related to developing their interests in music, video production, and video games. In DYN workshops at YOUmedia Chicago, students worked on creative projects seeded by their interests in a community context in which they could develop meaningful goals.[39] Some families provide support as well. But based on my research findings, schools could do much more to design learning experiences around these principles and develop students' technology learning habits.[40]

The structures of formal educational programs and their organizational culture can indeed be changed for the better. In an effort to expand women's participation in computer science in higher education, for example, social scientist Jane Margolis worked with Allan Fisher, former associate dean for undergraduate education in the School of Computer Science at Carnegie Mellon University, to address gender inequality at the university. They increased outreach to local high schools and changed admissions requirements so that prior experience and standardized test scores were no longer barriers to entry. They redesigned introductory courses to combine discovery-based real-world problem solving together with programming basics to give students a broader sense of what they could do with programming and to address preparation gaps. They shifted more experienced and effective teachers to lead introductory courses and introduced gender equity training for teaching assistants. They also adapted other courses to focus on real-world problems, such engaging with local community nonprofits.

Finally, they worked to change organizational culture, especially around the computer scientist stereotype of a "boy hacker." To create change, they worked with faculty on ways to promote a different notion of the ideal computer scientist, similar to how this book redefines *technological competence* and ideas about who is tech savvy. Based on these changes, Carnegie Mellon successfully increased the percentage of women in computer science from 7 percent in 1995 to 42 percent in 2000, and it had climbed to 48 percent in 2016.[41] This result shows that shifting organizational policies and practices can create change, as long as equity is the central goal.

In the Workplace: Recognizing Expertise, Making Jobs More Equitable

The research findings in this book are also relevant for jobs, for teens entering the workforce as well as for workers of all ages who must develop and continually maintain technological competence as technologies change. In this context of change, expertise can be difficult to identify and develop. Research shows that in a changing environment, people often resort to stereotypes. Ambiguity is often resolved when we "rely on irrelevant cues such as gender to identify who has the necessary skills to achieve specific goals or tasks," thereby amplifying existing inequities by race, class, and gender.[42] Culturally shared beliefs about the appropriate roles and abilities of categorical groups (race, class, gender) have widespread effects in the workplace.[43] Indeed, workplace inequality is produced by gatekeeping, where categories of people are matched to categories of jobs and activities. This gatekeeping happens first in the hiring process when employers hire people who are "categorically similar" to them, a process justified by educational credentialing, which is also subject to gatekeeping.[44] Within jobs, gatekeeping also occurs for "upskilling" (training) current employees; opportunities are often given to those already advantaged. Or, if access to training is provided to everyone, training may not translate into equitable promotions. These gatekeeping processes keep women, lower-income, and historically marginalized racial and ethnic groups in lower-status positions.[45]

All this gatekeeping consolidates power, prestige, and wealth within advantaged groups. It is a loss for workplaces, as well as the greater good, when so much human potential goes untapped. For example, male students from lower-income backgrounds are often placed into lower-tier vocational tracks—not completely isolated from technological pathways, but not included in higher-status forms of technical work, either. Some observers argue that the very idea of tiers within technical work, whereby some forms of this work are paid more than others, is the result of the social construction of the idea of "job skills." Activities done by more advantaged groups (college-educated white males) are typically viewed as requiring more "skill" and paid a higher wage, despite mixed evidence that other forms of technical work take less "skill."[46] Often, educational credentials validate the categorization of jobs as higher- or lower-skill ones, and gatekeeping occurs among these tiers. For example, in the 1960s, more than seven hundred programming trade schools were established for those without college degrees, but employers preferred job candidates with college degrees, even if they had less programming experience.[47]

This stratification of jobs and sorting of people can occur even if activities across jobs are strikingly similar. For example, Clive Thompson's 2019 book *Coders* describes the story of a rural tech start-up called

Bit Source, created by unemployed miners in Kentucky. Of its founder, Rusty Justice, Thompson writes:

> [Justice] knew that mining workers were intelligent, trainable, and frankly already steeped in technology. "We're perceived by people that we're not smart, that we're hillbillies," he tells me. But coal miners already work like programmers: They sit in one place all day long, patiently running high-tech equipment and solving problems. "It's a highly technological business," he says. "You have this image of a guy who has a pickax and lunch bucket. But they use robotics, they understand fluid dynamics and hydraulics."[48]

In other words, although stereotypes might suggest that lower-income workers are a poor fit for "high-skill" jobs, differences in educational credentials may not actually represent differences in learning or skill.[49] Rusty and Bit Source successfully pushed back on these classist assumptions in technological work, reframing it in more equitable ways.

In fact, gatekeeping and opportunity hoarding are not inevitable. Ideas about categories of people and who is best suited to use certain forms of technology have changed over time and can continue to change. For example, early in computing history, women played a large role. They were the majority of the first programmers during World War II, and their participation was steady even after the war relative to other STEM fields—more than one in four programmers were women by 1960.[50] As computing developed, science and technology scholar Janet Abbate observes, masculinity and femininity "were part of the cultural vocabulary that was used to define what a computer was and who was best qualified to use one."[51] If used for calculation, computers were best matched with women doing administrative work. Or, if used for management, computers were best matched to the men in charge.

Gender categories also shifted as a result of technology use. Women's early engagement in technological work helped redefine gender. As Abbate explains, "female programmers and computer scientists leveraged their status as professionals to fashion new personal identities that united femininity with technical expertise."[52] These debates over the meaning of technology use stagnated when marketers sold the personal computer as a masculine activity and women's participation began to decline in the 1980s. Little has changed since. But the lessons from this book can counter long-standing biases by redefining *technological competence* to include technology learning habits. This redefinition and ways of measuring the habits can help better identify who is technologically competent and who needs more support. It can also break open the technological "clubhouse" where membership is defined by stereotypes rather than actual competence.[53]

Being barred from valued occupations is a well-established explanation for the perpetuation of inequality.[54] But even if access to these jobs becomes more equitable, there is a further risk that "high-skill" jobs will decline in pay, power, and prestige—a process called *devaluation*.[55] Such is often the case within and beyond technology-related fields, particularly for women.[56] As jobs transition in terms of their demographics, those who increasingly occupy "nontraditional" roles tend to be undervalued in their pay, and their skill is underestimated by coworkers.[57] For example, in male-dominated fields, women are considered less skilled regardless of actual expertise.[58] As a result, as more "nontraditional" groups fill jobs and fields become more equitable in composition, these jobs are often devalued.

So we need to change not only the biased perceptions about technological competence but also the unequal value given to technological tasks.[59] Research shows that many tasks are already "typed" by race, class, or gender and valued in inequitable ways. For example, in terms of gender, sociologist Cecilia Ridgeway argues that stereotypically feminine tasks such as caregiving "must come to be valued more like agentic, stereotypically masculine tasks."[60] Similarly, in tech-related fields, without efforts to address inequality, emerging technological activities can also be typed by race, class, and gender and valued in biased ways. For example, during the first dot-com boom in the 1990s, web design jobs started out in a more gender-neutral way. But, as web design advanced, the field segregated tasks by gender. Companies categorized "front-end development" and "design" tasks as "softer" and "feminine" jobs appropriate for women. In contrast, they categorized "back-end" coding tasks as the "harder" more "masculine" domain— and value was distributed accordingly.[61] How can this inequality be addressed? One way is for higher-status groups to take on currently "lower-status" tasks, to make activities more status ambiguous and help increase perceived value. And groups must work on the same tasks in the same jobs, rather than in task-segregated positions. When tech employers and policy makers work to ensure that the composition of the workforce is balanced, rather than dominated by a particular group, they are helping us reach digital equality.

Now, you might ask, why would employers and other technology-related organizations want to change? Because inequality does not help—and can even hurt—organizations. Research shows that when work is valued unequally within for-profit businesses, it does not bene-fit companies. It instead only benefits advantaged groups within those organizations. For example, research shows that when women's work is devalued within for-profit businesses, neither do profits go up nor does the total cost of production drop. Instead, male coworkers are the only ones who benefit.[62] In contrast, research suggests that greater diver-sity benefits organizations. For example, in a study using a national sample of for-profit businesses, Cedric Herring found that greater racial diversity is related to increased sales revenue, more customers, greater market share, and greater relative profits. He also found that greater gender diversity is related to increased sales revenue, more customers, and greater relative profits.[63] So, companies should want to attract and retain a more diverse workforce with equitable pay.

So why, then, are these inequality regimes so difficult to change? One reason, says Joan Acker, is because the interests of the ruling class "outweigh the class, gender, and race interests of those who suffer inequality."[64] Those in power don't want to share. Even though eco-nomic interests might not be at stake, inequalities can be perpetuated for other reasons, notably perceived status threats. For example, the pay of Black and white workers in similar jobs could be made more equitable by increasing Black workers' pay. Doing so does not change the white workers' pay, but the white workers might nonetheless perceive it as a threat. Acker and others argue that more-successful equity projects, such as affirmative action, have three similar characteristics: (1) they are narrowly targeted to specific inequality-producing mechanisms; (2) they have "combined social movement and legislative support outside the organization with active support from insiders"; and (3) they involve "coercion or threat of loss."[65] As a result, it will likely take both internal actions and external pressures for such change to occur. It's difficult, but it can be done.

ADDRESSING GATEKEEPING: WHAT EVERYONE CAN DO

Given how stereotypes work to exclude groups from computing, a final and crucial step in addressing digital inequality is for people in general to redefine what it means to be good with technology and whom that includes. This step is especially critical for teachers, to help learners push past stereotypes and ambient cues about who belongs in tech-related fields and occupations to reorient their learning. So, everyone should understand that technological competence is a process rather an end point. As discussed in chapter 4, such a framing can influence learners' "orienting beliefs," or ideas about the nature of expertise in particular subject areas that can shape the learning process.[66] These ideas influence students' thoughts, actions, and feelings as they learn. A redefinition of *technological competence* can help learners push against the idea that technological ability is fixed (something you have or do not have), as well as whom that includes.

Research shows that orienting beliefs are strongly related to the skills students develop. For example, as noted in chapter 4, students with lower mathematics achievement often believe being good in mathematics is defined by the ability to memorize procedures rather than understanding why and under what circumstances to use particular procedures.[67] Learners then behave in ways that match their orienting beliefs, such as memorizing instead of strategizing, which can shape what they learn. In my research in Chicago, I found that orienting beliefs had the greatest single association with the development of the five technology learning habits.[68] Given this finding, one direct way to influence students' technological competence is to explicitly define *technological competence* as a set of habits—something all the programs I studied did, which helped create more-inclusive technology learning communities. This redefinition can be encouraged by families as well. These redefined orienting beliefs upend the stereotypes that can dissuade girls, lower-income students, and historically marginalized racial and ethnic groups from pursuing technology learning.

How can others help? One way is a collective reimagining of a "computer type" of person in a way that is more equitable, which can help address gatekeeping. Often, there is a default to tech entrepreneurs like Steve Jobs, which I've seen time and time again used by computer science teachers and in the media as the ideal tech type. But these images could just as easily be replaced with the teens in the pages of this book—Jasmine, Sumalee, Gisela, William, Miguel, and many others. Or, by imagining the adults they could become—people like Christine Darden, a pioneering Black female mathematician and aeronautical engineer who eventually became head of a directorate at NASA and was interviewed for Margot Lee Shetterly's book-turned-movie *Hidden Figures*.[69] Or other pioneers like Evelyn Boyd Granville, Grace Murray Hopper, Winifred Asprey, and so many more.[70] Or contemporary technology leaders, like Joy Buolamwini and Timnit Gebru, whose work uncovers the intersectional biases embedded into the design of artificial intelligence.[71] Of course, this task can be difficult given the erasure of the history of African Americans and other historically disenfranchised groups in computing.[72] It is worth the effort, however, because amplifying voices currently involved in technology-related programs as well as uncovering those hidden from dominant historical accounts can help call into question entrenched ideas about "computer-types" in radical ways.[73]

To address stereotypes, the diverse group of tech-savvy teens I describe in this book provide a counterpoint for reorienting ideas about technological competence based on race, class, and gender. Imagining Jasmine or Gisela, for example, pushes against the idea that only affluent white or Asian males are good with technology. A redefinition of technological competence as a set of learning habits also opens the black box of "natural ability" that gives stereotypes their power. The Digital Adaptability Scale makes that redefinition concrete and observable, allowing parents, educators, employers, and other gatekeepers to see the technological potential they might otherwise miss. The DAS and the technology teaching scales derived from it can provide insights into how to better support the ongoing process of technology learning. The recommendations I have provided about how to teach each of the habits and how to create more inclusive organizations can also help address gatekeeping mechanisms. Ultimately, stopping gatekeeping is the only way to fully address digital inequality. Yet there's more to consider in this radical reimagining—as I explain in the conclusion that follows.

Conclusion

ENVISIONING AN EQUITABLE FUTURE

> What the best and wisest parent wants for his own child,
> that must the community want for all of its children. Any
> other ideal for [education] is narrow and unlovely; acted
> upon, it destroys our democracy.
>
> John Dewey, *The School and Society* (1907)

A LETTER TO MY STUDENTS

During the celebrations for the first graduating class of Urban Promise Academy (UPA) in Oakland, I presented a letter as a gift to my web designers—to Amairani, Maria, Meihong, Cindy, and all the other girls in the class. From my initial investigation with my students, I knew I had barely scratched the surface in terms of understanding what it means to be good with technology. While I had much further to go to answer this question, there were some things that were already clear about the individual and collective strengths of my students. I told them:

June 2004

To My Web Designers,

There are people who are shocked when I tell them I am teaching a group of girls web design.[1] A lot of people think girls aren't interested in computers, that they can't use them and don't want to. But that's not true; you've proven them wrong.

This year, you've shown me what working with computers *really* means:

1. Working with computers means **working together**. You are so good at working together, making decisions as a large group and working in small groups. Not many people can do that, even as adults. You've shown me how a group works together to make a project happen!

2. Working with computers means **trusting yourself and each other**. You are very honest in your critique of what good websites look like and what bad websites look like. You share your designs and stories with the class. You ask great questions. You rely on one another to remember to take pictures, do surveys of students and teachers, and work hard together on making web pages and sharing what you find on the internet with others. You impress me with how you are highly skilled at trusting others and being trustworthy.

3. Working with computers means **having fun**. You guys are so good at having fun. You're ready to play silly games and run around on fieldtrips. I appreciate your willingness to take risks and have some fun, to be so silly on BART [Bay Area Rapid Transit] that you can't stop laughing even after we sat for hours in traffic on our way back from the Tech Museum. You are great to be around because you're so much fun, and that's why other people will want to work with you in your future.

4. Working with computers means **being persistent**. When you make mistakes you keep going, figure out what's wrong (either by yourself or with friends), and make it even better. You keep working even outside of class. You write emails, search the internet, make web pages, write online journals, listen to music, and make designs—inside

and outside of class. You come in to work on our website even when it's not during our regular class time. You keep going, keep working on computers and showing everyone who might doubt that girls can be experts at computers that they're wrong to doubt you!

I appreciate every moment this year that you've inspired me. I appreciate how you work together, trust yourself and each other, have fun, and are persistent. I hope you continue to work with computers and disprove people who think girls aren't good at computers. You are fantastic and you can only get better from here!

Thank you for a wonderful year!

Sincerely,

Miss Cassidy

The last point in the letter—about persistence—was the one that kept me up at night, wondering about what Cindy described as "not giving up." It sent me all across the country to find the answer, given that no existing research—until now—could tell me: What would help my students learn? How could I better teach them how to not give up?

These questions led to everything contained in this book, which is so much more than their answer: an evidence-based redefinition of *technological competence*, a stronger appreciation for why this redefinition is important for equity, and a clearer understanding of the dynamics of gatekeeping and what can be done to address it. Initially, my motivation was to better define goals for teaching. But that redefinition also helps upend a belief in "natural" technological ability that makes it difficult to address educational and occupational inequities in STEM and stifles a more innovative, equitable democracy. When we replace existing and historically misinformed definitions of *competence* with Chicago eighth grader Sumalee's definition—*habits that help you continue to learn*—we can help children focus on the learning process, acquire new skills, and innovate for an unknown future; reorient how educators, parents, and employers see technological competence and potential futures; and reformulate how we collectively understand the problem of the *digital divide* between which students need help and which students have been barred from educational and occupational opportunities but are already prepared for new technological challenges.

It might seem naïve to suggest that focusing on habits can do all these things. Yet, many well-known social theorists, from Thorstein Veblen to Max Weber to W. E. B. Du Bois to Pierre Bourdieu, argued that habits can reveal key insights—not just about how and why people behave the way they do but also *about the social order*.[2] For example, in his classic 1903 book *The Souls of Black Folk*, Du Bois famously argued that Black people's actions are viewed through a racialized lens—a "veil of color"—that structures how they are understood and valued by white people. As the present-day education scholar Antar Tichavakunda explains, despite similarities between students of different races who "earned the same high grade on a business exam," for example, talent is not universally recognized. Rather than viewing all students as strong, "non-Black students, faculty, and staff might view the Black student through a racialized lens," simply "as a Black student."[3] Further, although certainly the failure to recognize their full humanity does these students harm, as Du Bois argues, the deeper pathology lies in a society that fails to recognize its own assets.[4]

When we observe the technological prowess of diverse, tech-savvy teens like Jasmine, Gisela, and Sumalee—teens who visibly enjoy the challenges of technology learning—the narrower vision of tech as solely comprised of "computer boys" who have a magical natural ability makes little sense.[5] In fact, my research suggests there are many "hidden techies": groups who are historically marginalized in tech, whose talents go unrecognized and uncultivated outside of innovative programs such as Radio Arte, Digital Youth Network (DYN), Mouse, Youth Movement Records (YMR), Global Kids, and so many others—programs that serve diverse populations, where tech skills are initially developed.[6]

Looking back on my letter, although I did not yet fully understand technological competence, I could easily understand the strengths of my students, particularly in terms of the "soft skills" (ability to work in teams, communicate, plan) at the core of technological work.[7] But even these strengths can be reinterpreted by gatekeepers in ways that undermine them. In fact, research shows that employers can differentially value such soft skills depending on the context and who's being evaluated. For example, although employers might express a desire for tech workers with soft skills, in practice women are stereotyped as "naturally gifted" in this area and funneled into lower-wage non-technical-track jobs (management, marketing, public relations), limiting their advancement in technical positions.[8] Following Du Bois, this biased treatment suggests that the deeper problem is a society that fails to cultivate, recognize, and value its own talent; in other words, the problem is a society where gatekeeping exists at all.

THE ENGINES OF (DIGITAL) INEQUALITY

For decades, public policies and education reformers have tried to address digital inequality by increasing technological infrastructure for schools and broadening access to technology education.[9] Yet inequities continue. In chapter 6, I noted that gatekeeping plays a central role in perpetuating these problems, and I offered some tools to measure and address gatekeeping. But, you might wonder, why does this gatekeeping continue? As I argued in chapter 1, what fuels gatekeeping is the use of overlapping and competing logics of technology education *for society*, *to serve markets*, and *for individual advantage*. The latter two march toward an unequal society. *Serving markets* means that technology education should efficiently sort individuals into roles best suited to their "nature." It means assuming there are "naturally" tech-savvy individuals and using whatever means to identify them—including stereotypes and biased measures—to determine (and justify) social and economic hierarchies in the digital age. Helping cultivate *individual advantage* means that technology education should produce winners and losers in a "meritocratic" competition for technological skill and using this biased process to similarly justify social and economic hierarchies.

These three competing logics move education and society in two directions, and although the first logic *for an equitable society* might be advocated in some educational policy rhetoric, the logic of *individual advantage* dominates policy and practice. The latter logic can be seen in technology education policies since the 1980s, which emphasize how technology can help individuals get ahead. These policies, particularly concerning issues of internet connectivity at the end of the twentieth century, did result in increased technological access.[10] However, it also created a context wherein the competing logics of democratic equality, social efficiency, and particularly individual advantage became intimately intertwined so as to make them almost indistinguishable, despite moving toward different ends. As Rosemary Sutton explains:

> So the argument went, for the country to remain competitive and retain the quality of life enjoyed by the predominately white middle class, the education system had to be reformed, and this reform had to focus on technological skills for all students. *Thus, for reasons of self-interest, attention had to be paid to the school computer use of poor, minority, and female students.* A concern for equity can be argued as part of any democratic system, but rarely was this moral argument made in discussions about technology, because during the 1980s this was not believed to be persuasive.[11]

Since that time, policy and practice have functioned as a winner-takes-all competition, cloaked under the rhetoric of an equity perspective—leaving unquestioned the contradiction that competition and sorting, which fuel gatekeeping and opportunity hoarding in education, could somehow produce equity.

The long-term result has been sustained and dramatically unequal technological fields and occupations, where advantaged groups have only increased their representation. A 2016 US Equal Employment Opportunity Commission report entitled *Diversity in High Tech* stated that compared to all other private sector industries, whites, Asian Americans, and men participated and held leadership positions at disproportionately higher rates in tech, especially in Silicon Valley.[12] At a public meeting presenting the report, several executives discussed these problems. Kweilin Ellingrud, a partner at consulting firm McKinsey & Company, said, "We will not harness the power of technology to tackle a broader set of societal challenges unless the technology workforce better reflects society."[13] Another report in 2017 by the National Coalition for Women and Girls in Education, citing National Science Foundation data, lamented the low number of women in engineering, mathematics, and computer science:

> The proportion of women working in engineering is still extremely low. Women made up 15% of engineers in 2015, up from 6% in 1983 but only a slight gain over the 2006 figure of 12%. In mathematics and computer science, the proportion of women in the workforce continues to decline, from 31% in 1983 to 27% in 2006 and less than 25% in 2015. It is unlikely that women's ability in these fields has deteriorated, so this decline more likely reflects working conditions or other factors that impede female participation.[14]

These figures, and particularly the declines since the 1980s, suggest what Jane Margolis and Allan Fisher so aptly argued in their 2002 book *Unlocking the Clubhouse: Women in Computing*—that the goal of reforms should not be to "fit women into computer science but rather *change* computer science."[15] How can this change happen? I provided part of the answer in chapter 6, in terms of how to address gatekeeping, but even attempting these changes still leaves the *engines* of inequality firmly in place. The larger issue that must be addressed is how to move technology education (and education in general) away from the logic of *individual advantage* and *serving the needs of markets* and toward *democratic equality*.

ADDRESSING (DIGITAL) INEQUALITY

So, what can be done to address the deeper roots of digital inequality and the gatekeeping mechanisms that push marginalized groups out of technological fields and occupations? It will require two simultaneous efforts—to focus on technology education as crucial *for a democratic society* and to resist the lure of the logics of *serving the needs of markets* and *pursuing individual advantage* that promote gatekeeping. In fact, the lessons of this book could easily be misapplied toward the latter two aims, unwittingly contributing to the perpetuation of inequality—but this unwitting perpetuation of inequity is not inevitable. Beyond the specific steps described in chapter 6 that parents, educators, and organizations can take to develop teens' habits and support their recognition, there are four additional ways to ensure greater equity in technology fields and occupations.

1. We can advocate for *all children* to learn these habits, as a necessity for *democratic equality*. While more advantaged families might use the lessons of this book to coach their children, they could instead push for such an education for *all* children by encouraging schools to orient curriculum and pedagogy around adaptability and advocating for a more robust funding base for technology education programs like the ones described in this book. In fact, many of these types of programs exist in economic precarity, based on securing grant funding rather than being treated as a fundamental part of educational infrastructure—despite the fact that research shows in-school and out-of-school extracurricular experiences are critical to learning, particularly in STEM fields.[16] As a result, some of the programs I observed, such as Radio Arte, no longer exist. So, a clear step would be to advocate and vote to support funding these programs to acknowledge their necessity and support their continuance and expansion.

There may be a temptation to use this book to help particular children get ahead. I described this concern in my undergraduate Digital Inequality course in which I'd shared early book chapters. One student named Josué posed a particularly pointed question in response: "Well, what would *you* do?" In other words, what would I do as a well-educated middle-class white person, if I were a parent? In all honesty, I told him, I would probably want to use the lessons in the book to help my children. Who wouldn't? This thinking is, alas, the same way that so much racial and socioeconomic inequality is produced.[17] Over the life course, inequality at a young age can lead to what is known as the "Matthew Effect," whereby students with early advantage reap greater advantage over time, widening gaps between more advantaged and less advantaged students.[18] Such processes continue throughout schooling, encouraged by an emphasis in the US educational system on individual advantage and competition and through the intensive parenting styles of middle-class and affluent white families.[19]

But, helping *your* child or *your* students doesn't necessarily have to translate into perpetuating inequality if you take action to ensure that *all* children experience an equally engaging technology education curriculum. Such action would help close the gap between advantaged and disadvantaged students and avoid a situation where the habits of advantaged children might be more closely cultivated and recognized as technological competence. As I argued in chapter 1, when a minority of the country exerts power over the social, economic, and political tools on which our democracy now functions, it does all of us a disservice. So, a first step is to understand and advocate for technological competence and full digital inclusion as *a fundamental necessity for our modern democracy—something everyone needs to develop.*

In fact, the students and programs I introduced in this book already take this approach. Rather than making programs fiercely competitive to shut people out, they work collectively to everyone's benefit. For example, in I Dig Zambia at Global Kids in New York, students would notify instructors if they saw peers having difficulties and, with good-natured joking, help solve problems. In an instance while everyone was working to put fossils together in Second Life, Caleb, a Black male with silver-framed glasses and a gentle approach to helping others, checked on Keisha, whose extended family I later learned was originally from Guyana. This moment was not the first time Caleb or others checked on one another. Caleb turned and said to instructor Shawna, "She's getting frustrated." Israel, a Latinx teen with curly hair tucked in a ponytail, also turned from his computer to help Keisha (he was on her team and checked in with her and others throughout the program). He asked, "Did you go behind the tent [in Second Life] and get stuck?" She smiled and admitted, "Yeah." Keisha nudged Caleb, teasing him for telling others about her struggle but also seeming pleased he helped her. Caleb smiled back. Israel showed her how to move out from behind the virtual tent. There seemed to be no bashfulness in learning from and helping others; I Dig Zambia, like all other programs, was structured so that teens were encouraged to ask for and offer help, in a collective effort. If teens can take responsibility for the welfare of others in small and big ways, it seems adults can do the same.

2. Along these lines, a second step we can take is to resist framing technology learning as a means to *serve market needs* or *for individual advantage*, as these ideas motivate gatekeeping. Social mobility (the perspective of *individual advantage*) was precisely what I'd wanted for my students and how I talked about technology learning with them. But, I now understand that this way of viewing technology education leaves many others behind because it requires that someone fail.[20] In fact, research shows that early efforts to make tech more inclusive were largely unsuccessful because politically powerful actors pursued an agenda that kept gatekeeping intact, rather than pushing for systemic change. This pattern continues in more recent efforts. As science and technology scholar Janet Abbate explains, "examples from the 1960s to the 2010s suggest that authentically empowering practices must be informed by situated critiques of the dominant computer culture that recognize and challenge its systematic racial and gender biases."[21]

To take this second step, we need to ask critical questions about the purpose of technology education and help students be critical users of digital technologies. Teaching the habits will help increase students' adaptability, but without a critical lens, teaching the habits may simply prepare students for changing markets without being able to combat possible negative implications of emerging technologies. For example, stronger technology learning habits may help students become more efficient in their consumption of new technologies and therefore contribute to environmental degradation and public health problems.[22] Or, it may make them be more adaptable to the needs of the "gig economy," supporting companies that rely on contingent and precarious labor.[23] So, any educational efforts to address race, class, and gender-based exclusion in tech must continually ask fundamental questions about its larger purpose ("to what end?") and how to achieve these goals.[24]

3. We must question the origin story of computing as individual ambition and retell it as a collective endeavor. The often repeated but largely unsubstantiated rendering of Silicon Valley as birthplace of social computing and innovation suggests that meritocratic competition led to the rise of technological winners. In contrast, technology historian Joy Lisi Rankin shows in her book *A People's History of Computing in the United States* that early networked computing efforts involved collaborative work. This work happened among not just the governmental agencies and corporations typically understood as central to networked computing but also teachers and students. These "unsung pioneers" helped shape the digital world in ways unrecognized by the myth of the "computer boys" and the rise of Silicon Valley. Instead, these pioneers worked together on academic computing systems—activities that were the precursors to today's social computing.

Based on this retold origin story, Rankin argues that we can reimagine computing designed *for democracy*—for example, to view social computing as a public good, created by the people for the people. Translated to the technology learning habits described in this book, this view furthers the idea that we do not need to advantage our own children or our own students but instead participate in cooperative work for future social and technological innovation. Doing so would help strengthen the idea that technological competence is foundational to our democracy, that it should be taught in all schools to all students, rather than through sorting and competition where already more-advantaged groups typically win.

4. Finally, we can ensure that the lessons from this book do not perpetuate inequality by advocating for the stronger regulation of gatekeeping practices. We can push for a greater focus on equity in tech education and occupations, where laws are already in place to regulate gatekeeping but need stronger implementation. For example, in terms of gender and education, Title IX regulations require that educational institutions receiving federal funding evaluate policies and practices and adopt and publish grievance procedures and policies against sex discrimination. Whereas in the past Title IX has primarily been applied to sports, advocates argue for its application to STEM education. In a 2010 report by the American Association for University Women entitled *Why So Few? Women in Science, Technology, Engineering, and Mathematics*, authors Catherine Hill, Christianne Corbett, and Andresse St. Rose noted that the law "could be used to improve the climate for and representation of women in STEM fields."[25] The authors argue that greater enforcement of Title IX through more widespread, frequent, and consistently administered compliance reviews could help identify when educational opportunities are systematically denied to otherwise well-prepared students. The same could be done with other laws prohibiting discrimination in education (by race, color, national origin, age, and ability).[26]

This enforcement of antidiscrimination laws could be helped with the use of the DAS, identifying students who need further support as well as those barred from more advanced technology training despite their preparation. However, care would need to be taken to ensure that the measure is not used to justify exclusionary practices, in ways similar to the historical use of the SAT.[27] For example, the fact that girls are on average lower on the DAS could be used to justify their exclusion in tech education—rather than interpreting this finding as a need for *greater* educational opportunity for some girls and ignoring the fact that many girls have technology learning habits that are as well developed as those of boys. Instead, the DAS can help in the examination of how equitably educational organizations provide access and train students in technology. Audits of organizational equity, from schools to employers, can help to address these issues systematically.[28]

So how do we combat the deeper roots of gatekeeping and digital inequality? Overall I advocate a comprehensive approach that includes seeing technological competence as fundamental to democracy and advocating equitable access to technology education, resisting the idea that using technology education for private benefit (for markets and individuals) can serve a public need, retelling the origin story of innovation as fundamentally collective rather than individualistic and competitive, and increasing regulation of equity in tech.

SEEING THE HIDDEN TECHIES

Gatekeeping dynamics and logics that fuel them are not unique to technology education; they are just one instantiation of the mechanisms of inequality deeply embedded in the grammar of schooling and in the function of other social institutions and broader US society. They are sustained by deeply entrenched beliefs that the United States functions as a meritocracy—that societal success simply reflects talent, ambition, and hard work.[29] In fact, research shows that the more unequal a society, the more likely citizens will view success in meritocratic terms, clinging to the idea that a person's talent alone creates their success, rather than acknowledging the role of racist, classist, and sexist gate-keeping in how successful people get ahead.[30] This finding might make it seem as though change is impossible, but there have been historical moments of substantial change and progress—for example, dramatic progress in gender equality from the 1970s to the present. But, there is continued cause for concern as such progress has slowed or stalled in recent years.[31]

The broader question is: How do we see our future? As the case of technology education shows, competition and individualism have created a dynamic wherein those in dominant positions fail to fully cultivate, see, and make use of a broad swath of existing talent. This failure hurts our collective well-being—we miss out on all the new and creative ideas that could help our ability to respond to the challenges we face as a country and as a world. To instead see people for their incredible capabilities—to persevere, to innovate, to see things in a completely new light—can make us collectively stronger.

In May 2001, I sat in a large auditorium on an old wooden theater seat in the now closed Calvin Simmons Middle School—one of the many large schools in Oakland that did not meet the needs of its students and prompted the creation of a community of small schools, including UPA. Around me was an excited group of students in Urban Arts Academy, an after-school arts and youth leadership development program. I was barely out of college and not yet teaching technology classes at UPA, as the school would not open until September 2001. At the front of the auditorium, Montes, then a teacher at Calvin and founder of Urban Arts, stood onstage and asked everyone in the room to close their eyes. He told the students the story of what their performance would be like the next night—they would be onstage, peering out into a sea of faces, and yes, it might be scary. But then, in front their friends and family, they would perform and show everyone all that they had practiced throughout the year and how much they were capable of. *And they would be recognized for their talents.* Everyone would be impressed with all their hard work—even the haters, who might make comments but would still understand the gifts they saw before them. It was a story to help students imagine a world where their talents would shine and they would be seen and celebrated.

When I first started teaching technology classes at UPA, through word of mouth I was aware of many technology learning spaces that, like Urban Arts Academy, respected teens and recognized all they have to offer the world. These programs and the teens within them helped me understand what it truly means to be good with technology—and how much we've missed in terms of their contribution to society. These tech-savvy teens exist, all across the country, practicing habits many gate-keepers most certainly do not see. They are constantly at risk of being erased through institutional myths about their lack of skill to explain their marginalization in technology-related fields. Yes, many students need help in developing their technology learning habits, skills, and literacies—but those in need of support do not precisely match up with the demographics of those excluded from tech fields. Instead, we need to better see the talent we have and to help students see the talent they have within themselves. Indeed, a crucial step in addressing gate-keeping and the engines that fuel it is a collective reimagining of "the geek instinct." The ideas that help us make sense of the world and take action—our "social imaginary"—about who is capable of effectively using the powerful technological tools of the digital age needs to shift to something more equitable.[32]

In Ruha Benjamin's 2019 book *Captivating Technology: Race, Carceral Technoscience, and Liberatory Imagination in Everyday Life,* she describes the "purportedly unbiased" technologies that "extend prison spaces in the public sphere" as well as "deepen racial hierarchies" and serve as a form of social control. Drawing on the work of anthropologist Arjun Appadurai and historian Robin D. G. Kelley, Benjamin quotes Kelley to note that "without new visions we don't know what to build, only what to knock down. We not only end up confused, rudderless, and cynical but we forget that making a revolution is not a series of clever maneuvers and tactics but a process that can and must transform us."[33] Benjamin argues that a "radical imagination is central to refusing discriminatory design and building a just and habitable world" and that imagination "is now central to all forms of agency, is itself a social fact, and is the key component of the new global order."[34] Benjamin explains:

> The task, then, is to challenge not only forms of discriminatory design in our inner and outer lives, but to work with others to imagine and create alternatives to the *techno quo*—business as usual when it comes to technoscience—as part of a larger struggle to materialize collective freedoms and flourishing. . . . [A] liberatory imagination opens up possibilities and pathways, creates new templates, and builds on a black radical tradition that has continually developed insights and strategies grounded in justice.[35]

In this book, I have followed this idea—that to shape the future in more democratic and equitable ways, we must be able to imagine a different future. I have provided some concrete and perhaps deceptively simple ways to redefine who is fully capable of not just participating in but leading our technological world—far from the victim image on which so much of digital inequality scholarship currently rests.

What it takes to see the hidden techies—or everyone's true competencies—then, is a reimagining of a possible world. One where the assumption is that marginalized groups are capable and, when given the support, can innovate for a more fully realized democracy. A world where people see these groups as qualified leaders, not as the *Black Panther* character M'Baku saw Shuri—"a child" incapable of overseeing technological advancements. In an interview about her character in *Black Panther*, actress Leticia Wright, who played Shuri, said filmmaker Ryan Coogler encouraged her to avoid playing to the stereotype of a "serious" technologist and instead told her to shine and let the rest of the world catch up:

> I came in with an approach to be very serious and very strong, but Ryan [Coogler] let me know that Shuri needed to be the love and the

light of the film. He was like, "Hey Tish, smile, be happy, encourage your brother and the people around you." . . . People can easily underestimate Shuri. When she opens her mouth about technology, it's like, "Oh, whoa, okay. You're really smart!" And I've had to just embrace that.[36]

I take this reflection to mean that teens should be who they are and, if adults are willing and looking for the right things, they will easily find all the hidden talent right there in front of them. *Seeing*—understanding teens' abilities—and developing teens' technological competence has happened and continues to happen in spaces like the Digital Youth Network, YOUmedia, Radio Arte, Youth Movement Records, BAVC, the Field Museum, Global Kids, Mouse, and in many other organizations and programs. But, these programs can only do so much on their own. The task ahead, then, is to support and amplify these efforts—and to take concrete steps toward a more equitable future.

Acknowledgments

This book would not have been possible without a tremendous amount of support, throughout my academic and professional journey, and in the research and book writing process. In terms of early advisors and unflagging advocates, I am thankful for my undergraduate advisor at Brown University, Susan Smulyan. Susan helped me see that I could make a contribution simply with my ideas—and took the time to help me to become a better researcher and writer. I am also grateful for Dean Carol Cohen, who told an overwhelmed, fish-out-of-water low-income freshman that she did, in fact, belong at a place like Brown.

At Stanford, Brigid Barron and Dan Schwartz have both been unshakable, long-term supporters. Brigid advised my very first efforts to understand my students at Urban Promise Academy, shared survey tools, wrote letters for graduate school applications and fellowships, read my dissertation proposal and papers, connected me to the Digital Youth Network when I arrived in Chicago, and has been generally excited and encouraging of my work for many years. I also want to thank Denise Pope, whose qualitative methods class left me ready for so much more, and who helped me see beauty in my writing. I also benefited from friends and colleagues who fed my curiosity in technology and education, especially Angela Booker, Tamecia Jones, Pui Ling Tam, Lori Takeuchi, Eric Bailey, Peter Worth, Kihyun Ryoo, Hillary Milks, Susie Wise, and Sandy Johnson. The Learning Design and Technology program helped start this project, and it was a privilege to be there with all of you. After Stanford, I was fortunate for the mentorship of Saul Rockman, Beverly Farr, and to work with my wonderful colleagues at the educational research firm Rockman et al. There, I was supported in my continued teaching at Urban Promise Academy. A special thanks to Kristin Bass, who later facilitated my entry into research sites.

At Northwestern University, the research described in this book would not have been possible without the careful guidance of my "lifetime appointment" advisor, Jeremy Freese. I was also lucky to have a dissertation committee comprised of Leslie McCall and Brian Powell (at Indiana), who closely read my proposal, gave feedback on the Digital Adaptability Scale (DAS), and helped me refine dissertation chapters, from which this book draws. All three were generous with their time, thoughtful with their feedback, and unflagging in their encouragement of what I understand now was a naively ambitious project. Jeremy, of course, deserves the most thanks for convincing me to attend Northwestern in the first place and for his advice throughout my doctoral studies and since. I couldn't have asked for a better mentor in my corner.

But the Northwestern bench runs deep. The broader scholarly community helped buoy my research, including the support of Wendy Espeland, Christine Percheski, Jeannette Colyvas, Chas Camic, Laura Beth Nielsen, Eszter Hargittai, and Elizabeth Lewis Pardoe. I also benefited from the keen eyes of Wendy Griswold and the Culture Workshop, colleagues in the Multidisciplinary Program in Education Sciences in the School of Education and Social Policy, and so many brilliant graduate student colleagues and friends, including Theo Greene, Nicole Gonzalez Van Cleve, Corey Fields, Stacy Lom, Daphne Demetry, Gemma Mangione, Jean Beaman, Yuli Patrick Hsieh, Brian Keegan, Kelly Iwanaga Becker, Mecca Zabriskie, Arend Kuyper,

Spencer Headworth, Jordan Conwell, Jess Meyer, Amelia Branigan, Russell Malbrough, Ricardo Sánchez, Amy Myrick, Anthony Johnson, Katie Day Good, Alejandro Morales, Courtney Patterson-Faye, Caroline Vial, Cheryl Berriman, Kiyona Brewster, Marina Zaloznaya, Elizabeth Onasch, Dawna Goens Leggett, and so many others whose paths I was fortunate to cross and who helped me in big ways and small.

While a PhD student, I was part of the MacArthur Foundation-funded Digital Media and Learning (DML) community, and I benefited from the collegiality of an exciting group of scholars. In particular I'd like to thank James Paul Gee, who brought together the Emerging Scholars Group (or "Gee Unit") of early career scholars, and who believed in this project, helped me find funding, and wrote letters of support. I'm grateful for the group and everyone I met through DML, especially Ugochi Jones, Ricarose Roque, Meryl Alper, Caitlin Kennedy Martin, Sinem Siyahhan, Adam Ingram-Goble, Peter Wardrip, Padraig Nash, Osvaldo Jiménez, Nathan Holbert, Robb Lindgren, Mark Chen, Matt Gaydos, Dylan Arena, Shannon Harris, Danielle Herro, Maritza Lozano, Dennis Ramirez, Maria Solomou, Jacob McWilliams, Amanda Wortman, Benjamin Stokes, Christo Sims, Ben Shapiro, Amanda Ochsner, and so many others involved in the DML-funded programs described in this book, especially Brother Mike Hawkins. I learned so much from each of you and was so lucky to be in your midst!

In terms of research field sites, I am indebted to the various programs and schools that graciously allowed me to collect data, in the Bay Area, Chicago, New York, and Boston. This list includes programs where I observed the incredible talents of tech-savvy teens who defy stereotypes. It also includes the Chicago Public School District, where many district and school administrators, teachers, parents, and students let me chase down my research questions in their schools, year after year, including during the 2012–2013 school year that included a teacher strike and massive school closings. I'd also like to recognize the school district just outside of Boston where I was able to further test the DAS. This research was also made possible with data collection help from students, friends, research assistants, and collaborators in Chicago

(Nathan Knize, Will Garza, and Kimberly Singletary) and high school assistants in Boston, who did the nitpicky things required to make a large research project run smoothly (transcribed interviews, lugged iPads, collected surveys, etc.)—all with a good sense of humor intact.

Various grant-making organizations made data collection, analysis, and dissertation writing possible (including the training necessary to complete a mixed-methods study). The project was funded in part by the Institute of Education Sciences/US Department of Education through Grant R305B080027 to Northwestern University, a Clogg Scholarship to attend an Inter-university Consortium for Political and Social Research Summer Program, a Northwestern Sociology MacArthur Research Grant, a Northwestern Graduate Research Grant, a Technology Grant from Northwestern IT Group, a National Science Foundation (NSF) Dissertation Improvement Grant, the *Emerging Scholars' Group* at the University of Arizona, a Mellon/American Council of Learned Societies Dissertation Completion Fellowship, and an NSF-funded postdoctoral fellowship (Award IIS-1450985) at the Tufts Center for Engineering Education Outreach. Every word expressed in this manuscript is mine alone and does not represent views of these supporting parties—but without their generous backing, this book would not have been possible.

At Emory University, I've been blessed with helpful mentors and colleagues, especially the astute advice of Rick Rubinson and Tim Dowd. I've also benefited from the assistance of the Center for Faculty Development and Excellence, through scholarly publishing funds and faculty writing groups, orchestrated by the outstanding Allison Adams, and supported by the directorships of Pamela Scully and Eric Weeks. Words cannot express my gratitude for the sharp eyes of writing group members Arun Jones, Rosemary Hines, Tanine Allison, Tony Healy, Dilek Huseyinzadegan, Gerard Vong, Michael Berger, and Richard Hermes. In the year of the pandemic, it was a joy to write alongside a wonderful group of fun-loving French historians, thanks to an invitation from Judith Miller. It was at Emory that I participated in the National Center for Faculty Development and Diversity (NCFDD) Faculty Success Program and met my wonderful writing accountability partner, Michelle Troberg, whose kind words helped me persist in challenging times. Also key to the book were the thoughtful observations of my students at Emory, including Michaela Jenkins, Amari Sutton, Sara Feinstein, Josué Rodriguez, Chloe Gaynor, Alexis Palmer, Hannah Chong, Grace Cole, and my undergraduate Digital Inequality and Culture & Society classes. I am also grateful for funding support from the Laney Graduate School and Emory College of Arts and Sciences.

Outside Emory, Jan Half read the entire draft manuscript and provided rich feedback—thank you so much for that, and for welcoming me to Mouse CA. I am also grateful for an impeccable developmental editor, Jane Joanne Jones, who read every word, helped me find clarity in my argument, and cheered me on. All writers should have someone like you! At the University of Chicago Press, Elizabeth Branch Dyson has been the most enthusiastic and encouraging editor anyone could ask for, especially important for a first-time book author. Elizabeth saw the book even before I ever did, calling it "inevitable." You have truly been a blessing! I also want to acknowledge the editorial team, faculty board, and anonymous reviewers who helped me craft a better book, even during a global pandemic.

Writing a book is hard work. I could not have done it without my cheering squad: Atul Varma (who also provided critical data collection support and the lovely map in the appendix), Jess Klein, Dixie Ching, Ariam Mogos, Rafi Santo, Yoon Jeon Kim, Kimberly Austin, Kimberly Rivas, Marcus Lumpkin, JoVia Armstrong, Brian Gravel, Freeden Blume Oeur, Jennifer Nelson, S. Marshall Perry, Julie Winter, Deb Sandweiss, Abby Paske, Colleen Kuusinen, Judith Liao, Abja Midha, Jason Li, Marisa Murgatroyd, Eric Tucker, Zoe Sullivan, Zembaba Ayalew, Kate Pousont Scarborough, Meghan Foley, Sarah Chandler, Carson Converse, Matt Rafalow, and Dawna Goens Leggett. You provided much-needed support and encouragement, gave valuable feedback on ideas, and/or read responses to reviewers and pieces of the book—some of you read every last word of it! Thank you all so much!

My all-female web design class at Urban Promise Academy was

where this research all began, and I am incredibly grateful for the strong school community of parents, educators, and especially amazing students, who were the first to indulge my inquiries. In particular, I want to recognize Cindy Marlene Chavez, who over the years has been my student, teaching assistant, research assistant (including during the research for this book), friend, and family. It's been such an honor to watch you grow and learn from you.

Finally, I'd like to thank Dinah, Dosa, and Azuki for their companionship and the unwavering support of my East and West Coast family. Especially my Grandma Rae and Grandpa Ben; Aunt Josy and Uncle David; cousins Mike, Suling, Natalie, and Russell; Jamie, Rich, Miles, and Maya; my brother Tad and nephews Lucien and Finn; my dad and Robin; and Daniel and my mom. All of you encouraged me to be creative, curious, silly, persistent, and adaptable. I love you.

Appendix

I used a mixed-methods approach to define and operationalize the technology learning habits that help tech-savvy teens, to examine how they vary and what supports their development, and to understand how they are connected to broader forms of inequality.[1] In the social sciences, there has been a long history of debate about the value of qualitative versus quantitative approaches.[2] While such debate persists, a growing body of scholarship recognizes the importance of mixed-methods research that employs both approaches.[3] Scholars doing mixed-methods work range on a conceptual and methodological spectrum from treating qualitative and quantitative work as distinct but complementary to treating these methods in a way where they are fully integrated.[4]

On one end are studies in which methods are distinct, where quantitative methodologists might partner with qualitative researchers to provide both types of data in a single study, such as Paula England and Kathryn Edin's *Unmarried Couples with Children*.[5] Or, the same researcher might use each approach within the same study, such as Mario Small's use of surveys plus interviews with a subsample of survey respondents in his *Unanticipated Gains: Origins of Network Inequality in Everyday Life*.[6] On the other end are studies wherein qualitative and quantitative methods are overlapping and mutually constitutive, such as narrative analysis that moves into formal modeling methods, or techniques such as "fuzzy sets" that combine qualitative and quantitative assessment in the same instrument to "enrich the dialogue between ideas and evidence."[7] The majority of my own study treads a middle ground—at times distinct but always intertwined. More specifically, I used an approach known as an *exploratory sequential design* wherein qualitative data inform quantitative data (in this case, the development of the Digital Adaptability Scale, or DAS) and then an *explanatory sequential design* to examine and explain DAS response patterns using quantitative then qualitative data.[8]

My approach was inspired by psychologists Donald T. Campbell and Donald W. Fiske's "multitrait-multimethod matrix" (or MTMM) paper, published in 1959, which argues that the best way to operationalize a construct is to measure multiple traits (e.g., openness, contentiousness) using multiple sources (e.g., self-report, teacher report).[9] Reading Campbell and Fiske's paper in a graduate course on causal inference, I thought, perhaps naively, "I can do that!" Thus, the MTMM idea organized how I thought about each step involved in the project, from identifying, defining, and operationalizing a construct (i.e., digital adaptability) to validating its measurement and description. This framework parallels the general influence of the principle of multimethod confirmation on mixed-methods research.[10]

Often, I encountered confusion when discussing this project, particularly when I tried to present methods together—but it was the most appropriate approach to answering my research questions about how to define and observe a new construct. Although doing a mixed-methods study posed some challenges to forming a scholarly community, methodologists I encountered reassured me the approach was necessary for the project.[11] Those methodologists included my dissertation chair, Jeremy Freese, who started out as a qualitative researcher and then helped write a book on regression. (Grad students, take note—you never know where your work will take you!)

In the following sections, I describe the methodological steps of my study. Overall, the study adds to the growing number of social science researchers who argue that the field can be improved by greater use of mixed-methods research and advocate expanding publication venues, increasing the availability of high-quality mixed-methods training, and creating professional communities.[12] To this end, this reflection offers an in-depth example of how conduct to such a study—in particular, what is involved when defining, operationalizing, and examining a new concept.[13]

CONSTRUCT DEVELOPMENT: PERSISTENCE TO ADAPTABILITY

When I first started this project, I kept using the word *persistence*. "Persistence?" advisors and peers would ask me, "What is that? What does that mean?" What they were asking was how to define the construct. Typically, researchers do this work by reading research literature to see how something is defined and operationalized (i.e., measured, whether through survey, historical records, observations, interviews). However, the research on persistence did not focus on learning but rather completion. Finishing grade levels. Graduating high school and especially college. Of course that is important, but it was not what I was interested in.

So, I had to use another way of defining what I meant by students "not giving up" in their technological learning. To do so, methodologists recommend observing and interviewing the "target population" (the group for which you would like to later use a measure to observe the construct), using qualitative data to develop a quantitative measure.[14] This approach helps ground the concept and measure with empirical data. Drawing from research on cognition and learning that studies what people do as they learn, my target group was tech-savvy teens. But not just any teens—I targeted teens who do not fit the race-, class-, and gender-based stereotypes of tech because I knew such students existed, there was much to learn from them, and defining tech savviness based on their habits was a first step toward countering stereotypes.

Finding a Diverse Group of Tech-Savvy Teens

Observing and interviewing tech-savvy teens was just the first step of my overall research project, but it was foundational to the rest of the study and the majority of this book, so I describe it here in greater depth. I identified my sample through their participation in exemplary technology programs. In total, I observed just a handful of the numerous programs across the country providing STEAM education (science, technology, engineering, arts, and mathematics).[15] This observation group included ten programs—five in the San Francisco Bay Area, three in Chicago, and two in New York City. Understanding that learning can be context-specific, I included programs occurring in school, after school, in the summer, or a combination, as listed in table A.1.

Programs served teens from upper elementary through high school and varied in their structure (most had formal projects or attendance policies, others provided drop-in experiences). In all, technology learning was a primary focus (e.g., building computers) or a secondary focus (e.g., learning Second Life software to simulate an archaeological dig). Programs delivered curriculum through in-person and online components across a range of technologies. Many were connected to the MacArthur Foundation's Digital Media and Learning (DML) Initiative from 2004 to 2017—including the Bay Area Video Coalition (BAVC, pronounced "Bay-Vac") programs, Mouse programs, Global Kids (GK), the Field Museum, and Digital Youth Network (DYN) at YOUmedia Chicago. The DML initiative "supported research and design experiments to better understand how digital media are changing the way young people learn, play, socialize, and participate civically and how those insights could be used to improve education."[16] All programs were free; three offered stipends.

I targeted programs serving a range of racial, socioeconomic, and

TABLE A.1: Overview of programs

Program name and location	Observation context	Number observed/ interviewed	Primary focus
Digital Youth Network at YOUmedia (Chicago)	After school	9	Audio and video production
WhyReef at the Field Museum (Chicago)	After school	10	Biology and ecology
BAVC Digital Pathways video production (San Francisco Bay Area)	After school	9	Video production
BAVC Digital Pathways game design (Bay Area)	After school	10	Game production
BAVC BUMP Records (Bay Area)	After school	9	Audio production
Youth Movement Records (Bay Area)	Summer	11	Audio and video production
Radio Arte (Chicago)	Summer	11	Audio production
I Dig Zambia at Field Museum (Chicago) and Global Kids (New York City)	Summer	19	Archaeology, global leadership, civic engagement
Mouse/Geek Squad Summer Academy (NYC)	Summer	12	Technology skills
Mouse Squad CA (Bay Area)	During and after school	11	Technology skills

gender groups to avoid conflating "successful" technology learning strategies with race-, class-, and gender-based approaches to learning. To collect information about demographics before my visits, I asked program directors about the teens who attended. Based on directors' estimates, the sample was gender balanced, with about 40 percent Latinx, 30 percent African American/Black, 18 percent white, 10 percent Asian, and 2 percent Native American. I also oversampled students whose home language was something other than English (about 35 percent) to examine how language development might influence technology learning.

In total, I observed or interviewed 111 teens. Nine of the ten programs served a small number of students per session. Mouse/Geek Squad Summer Academy was larger (about 100 teens) and organized into smaller cohorts of 10–15 that met together in the morning, lunch, afternoon break, and end of the program. There, I followed a cohort identified by program directors and excluded other participants from my overall count of study participants (about 90). In seven programs, I conducted more than two hundred hours of observation (one week in each) and did five-minute informal interviews with all teens I followed, posing questions during and between activities. I also did longer ten- to twenty-minute interviews with a third of the participants (3 or 4 per program; 22 total) in longer breaks, sampling to reflect program demographics. Based on logistical considerations, in the three BAVC programs I did shorter observations and longer interviews that included all participants.

During observations, I looked for moments when students were asked to learn new technologies or engage with them in new ways, instances when students encountered difficulties and how they responded, and times when they expressed how they felt about the learning process. Wherever possible, I videotaped activities and in short interviews asked questions about program activities. In longer interviews, I asked for more detailed information about what helped students in their learning process in the programs and other contexts. I shall describe each program in detail in the sections that follow.

DIGITAL YOUTH NETWORK (DYN) AND CHICAGO PUBLIC
LIBRARY (CPL) AT YOUMEDIA

At the very beginning of my study in 2008, I asked experts in technology and education to guide my choice of programs in which to observe tech-savvy teens. One expert I asked was Dr. Brigid Barron at Stanford, who recommended I reach out to DYN, a youth development organization in Chicago she collaborated with through MacArthur's DML Initiative. DYN is a digital technology-based youth development program started in 2006 by Dr. Nichole Pinkard that includes in-school, out-of-school, and online components. The program was designed to create a compelling reason for students to develop the digital literacies valued across the communities where they spent their time.[17] DYN was embarking on a new project with the Chicago Public Library (CPL) to create a teen technology space called YOUmedia. There, I began my study in January 2009 and, after visits to the Bay Area, New York City, and other parts of Chicago, I returned and remained for the next few years.[18]

While there are now twenty-three locations, the original YOUmedia was housed at the main CPL branch, the Harold Washington Library Center, a hulking brick building the size of an entire city block, with huge green metal owls (symbolic of wisdom) perched high on the building's pediment watching passersby far below. Today, if you enter the main entrance and follow a sign with an arrow pointing down a corridor to the right, you'll find a brightly colored teen space bursting with books, sewing and art projects, video game paraphernalia, audio production tools and a recording studio bustling with activity.[19] This teen space was where artists Chance the Rapper and Noname hung out after school as teens.[20] But that was a little while later. When I first visited in January 2009, construction was still under way, so DYN's workshops at YOUmedia met in small classrooms and music practice rooms on the eighth floor.

During those initial sessions, I observed a video production workshop and a music production workshop, led by veteran DYN mentors Brother Mike, Simeon, and Raphael, and I met many tech-savvy high school students, some of whom had already been involved in DYN in elementary school.[21] Other teens heard about the program from local librarians or peers involved in DYN. For example, a regular attendee at music production named Jacob, a tall Black male with rectangular metal-rimmed glasses, said he heard about it from a friend through a mass Facebook post. He decided to attend because he was into poetry and writing lyrics and wanted to create his own "beats" (songs) but didn't have the skills (yet). He had received his own computer in seventh grade (three years prior) and learned to use Movie Maker video editing software to do "a couple history projects" for school. For music production, he and other students were making songs to reflect chapters from Sandra Cisneros's book *The House on Mango Street*. He was excited to learn how to "interpret things to create original music" and how to use the audio editing software GarageBand. What was the best thing about the class? He said it was how the instructors taught things through demonstration and then let students try again and again until they got it right. In other words, it was a safe space to make mistakes and get support.

After observing DYN's workshops at YOUmedia once a week from January through March 2009, the new teen space opened up downstairs and I continued to observe and visit other branches doing YOUmedia activities through 2012. A 2013 report by the Consortium on Chicago School Research on the first three years of the center described demographics of teens at YOUmedia as attracting "an estimated 350 to 500 teens" per week, and their largest single demographic group was African American males, like Jacob or Maurice, another teen heavily invested in video production with DYN who went on to study film in college.[22]

WHYREEF AT THE FIELD MUSEUM

Also in Chicago, I connected with the Field Museum of Natural History through the DML network. I first met with Dr. Audrey Aronowsky, at the time scientific program manager in the Biodiversity Synthesis Center, in late spring 2009 to hear more about the multiple technology-related programs the museum offered. One, called WhyReef, was a new marine biology and ecology program for younger teens that would meet Tuesdays and Thursdays after school in fall 2009. It would be a chance to see younger teens and compare their habits.

Program activities included meeting Field Museum scientists; visiting the nearby Shedd Aquarium; doing virtual "dives" to understand coral reef ecology, conservation, and restoration in a simulated coral reef (called "WhyReef") housed on the popular website Whyville.net

and earning "clams" to spend in Whyville; and producing digital artifacts related to marine ecology, such as public service announcements
about ocean and lake ecology.[23] The Field Museum advertised to
Chicago-area teachers, who nominated the diverse participating students who received certificates for being part of an effort to understand and advocate for aquatic ecosystem conservation and restoration.
I observed program sessions and a family celebration at the end.

BAVC NEXT GEN: VIDEO PRODUCTION, GAME DESIGN,
BUMP RECORDS

Before I visited WhyReef in the fall, I ventured out to California to
visit three after-school programs just ending and one summer program starting up. The after school programs were run by BAVC, as
part of its Next Gen youth programming curriculum.[24] BAVC was
established as a nonprofit in 1976 with the goal of making media technology more accessible to marginalized communities and nonprofit
organizations. In 1997, BAVC started providing two workforce development training programs—one for adults (JobLink) and the other for
youth (YouthLink)—to train "disadvantaged" groups in media technology skills. In 2006, BAVC combined YouthLink with another audio
and video production program called YouthSounds and renamed the
expanded programming Next Gen.[25] These programs were also award-
winning, recognized and supported through technology or workforce
training grants from the US Department of Labor, California State
Workforce Investment Board, San Francisco Mayor's Office of Economic and Workforce Development, California Emerging Technology
Fund, the MacArthur Foundation, and the National Science Foundation, among many others.[26]

Dr. Kristin Bass, senior researcher at the educational research and
evaluation company Rockman et al (where I also worked prior to pursuing a PhD), introduced me to the Next Gen programs. In total, I visited
three of their programs occurring after school—each of which had a distinct history as well as a connected trajectory. At the time, BAVC's Next
Gen included an array of introductory and advanced programs: Digital

Pathways (introductory video, audio, animation, and game design), an advanced audio production program called Bay Unity Music Project (BUMP) Records (which earlier merged with YouthSounds, then joined BAVC with YouthSounds), an advanced video production program called The Factory, and a series of in-school programs. I began with visits to two Digital Pathways programs (video production and game design). These were ten-month programs for students grades 9–12 that engaged students in long-term media projects. I first visited video production and was connected to game design by BAVC staff.

BAVC Video Production. Video production was a long-standing part of BAVC, established with the YouthLink program in 1997. When I visited, associate director of Next Gen programs Naomi Kawamura was guest leading a video production class. The small class comprised Asian, Black, Latinx, white, and multiracial teens. They discussed audio production for filmmaking, shared work for critique, and edited their work—content and activities incorporated throughout the video production curriculum.[27] Several students attended "Bal" in the Excelsior District (a high school serving primarily lower-income Latinx and Asian students) and were involved not only in video production but in other BAVC programs as well.

BAVC Game Design. At the end of my visit to video production, Naomi—an Asian woman who brought a seriousness and kindness in her engagement with students and others—recommended I visit game design, a new BAVC program. Game design had striking diversity by race and gender, given the gaming industry. For example, a 2017 survey by the International Game Developers Association reported that 21 percent of 963 gamers in the national survey were female.[28] In contrast, BAVC's game design program was much more inclusive than the game design industry, with 40 percent female, 93 percent students of color, and 93 percent from low income backgrounds.[29] Instructors in game design, as in many other programs I visited, were industry professionals with an interest in teaching, trained by program staff in youth leadership development and ways to create safe spaces for community building.

Game design's first-ever graduating cohort had an upcoming celebration at 410 Townsend, near the downtown Caltrain Station. At the time, this area was more industrial, but it now houses the headquarters of businesses including Pinterest and Airbnb. The celebration took place in a small converted warehouse that served as an office building, although it looked as though the building was mostly empty at the time. Teens presented their games in labs with rows of computers where caretakers, siblings, friends, and BAVC staff and supporters sat listening. Students stood at the front of the room with their game projected on the wall behind them and proudly talked about their projects, their experiences in the program, and how their interests and life experiences were reflected in their games. At the conclusion of each presentation, students received awards for successfully completing the sequence of workshops and creating a video game.

BAVC BUMP Records. The third Next Gen program I visited was BUMP Records, again based on BAVC staff recommendations, at one of their after-school locations on Sixteenth and Telegraph in Oakland. Looking at its website before the visit, I could tell BUMP was a place I would find tech-savvy teens. It said:

> Bay Unity Music Project (BUMP) Records is a music performance and production program for Bay Area youth ages 14–19. With the help of professional instructors, young people learn to compose music and lyrics, DJ, and produce and record original music using industry-standard technology. BUMP producers also get hands-on entrepreneurship training and experience in producing, branding and promoting albums. Participants have use of music production software and a professional-caliber rehearsal and recording space, free of charge.
>
> Since its founding in 2003, BUMP Records has become the Bay Area's leading production and performance program focused on urban music, with participants representing twelve middle schools, high schools and community centers, six albums produced to date, tracks licensed to companies like Mercedes Benz and independent film producers, and sales agreements with top online retailers iTunes, eMusic, and Rhapsody.[30]

BUMP started at McClymonds High School, where it merged with media production program YouthSounds. Then, in 2006, the programs joined BAVC as part of its Next Gen programs.

BUMP Director Robert Collins said in an interview that the most important goal of the program was for students to "express themselves." Collins explained that there were several tiers to the program—school-based, advanced artist, advanced tech. BUMP offered a school-based program at McClymonds, where the instructors started teaching the audio software programs Reason and GarageBand, and later added Fruity Loops. The Telegraph location was advanced artist—a performance and audio production program that Collins said was "mostly audition based." Participants spanned an age range from fourteen through nineteen years old, including high schoolers and some young adults in college—anyone "motivated" to participate. Students often came through the McClymonds program, so they were already well versed with software; the advanced program helped them refine their skills. There were about fifteen students per semester, and at the end of the program, students performed in a community celebration and distributed their work on iTunes.

Collins also explained that because BUMP's advanced tech tier was part of Digital Pathways, it overlapped with video production and game design at advanced levels. In that tier, students worked on real-world film production "on the street" and interned with record labels, animation studios, advertising agencies, or other professional organizations. Additionally, the program met at sites in Oakland, Berkeley, Alameda, and San Francisco to "meet students where they are" because "a lot of kids don't have experience crossing the bridge."

YOUTH MOVEMENT RECORDS (YMR)

I approached Youth Movement Records on the recommendation of Principal Montes. Montes was one of the first people I met when I moved to California from the East Coast. He founded an after-school youth leadership development and arts program called Urban Arts Academy, was principal and teacher at UPA and later a teacher at

MetWest, and eventually became a district leader in Oakland Unified. So, I considered his referral to YMR an expert recommendation. Montes put me in contact with YMR founder Chris Wiltsee and executive director Ryan Nicole Peters, who welcomed me to their program at the newly renovated Oakland School for the Arts in the Fox Theater downtown.

YMR was founded in 2003 as a media arts nonprofit providing music production and entrepreneurship training to young people ages thirteen through nineteen.[31] The first day of the summer program, Peters introduced the program, holding the rapt attention of about thirty teens at an opening "company meeting." In my notebook, I scribbled:

> Peters flips on a PowerPoint and gives some background about the history of YMR. It was founded in 2003 and was originally located at La Peña Cultural Center in Berkeley. The organization recently moved to Oakland School for the Arts in January 2009. Ryan says, "Other groups have been doing this, *but we're the dopest*." She repeats that all classes are free and do not overlap, so students can take everything. She explains they also have "friendships" with Pixar (nearby in Emeryville), Ex'pressions Center for Digital Arts, and other organizations "and we can plug you into them." She tells students that they can record demos, make music videos, and "package you as individuals." They also do compilations of YMR artists, have an artist development award, and community events like concerts, parties, and festivals including "Uptown Unveiled" and Hood Games this summer.[32] She flips to some recent pictures—they just sent students to Guatemala with Loco Bloco, another youth development and arts organization based in San Francisco.[33] She notes that they have a meet and greet with Drake next week—and a meeting with Trey Songz this week at Clear Channel.

Teens' eyes lit up around me.

Peters explained that the structure of the program included "company meetings" on Mondays, followed by "listening parties" for artist development, with a critique by peers. She said in these critiques,

"There's no hating, it's real warm. There are guest critiques on things like bios, press kits, everything it takes to be an artist." Other days, there were workshops in audio and visual media, so teens could learn skills for all parts of the music recording industry. Peters emphasized and encouraged teens' participation in the technical aspects of music production (e.g., Pro Tools workshops); she said these skills would be powerful in the recording industry. She also described the level of professionalism of the program, including employing experts in their field as instructors, and the importance of teens' overall commitment. She said:

> There's lots of people who are interested in performance, but we also offer things like Pro Tools, where you can become an engineer, run the boards—that's powerful because everyone wants you and it's the quickest way to get paid. Now, everybody can take everything—none of the classes overlap. If you have the time, it's free. Everyone who teaches does the thing they teach—it's not just a cat who read the book and thinks they can teach. . . .
>
> The process is, as a member you attend company meetings on Mondays. You plug in, figure out how you can promote yourself, do whatever is needed, attend everything. All-stars are people who plug in, who are grinding, hustling. That could take a couple months to years. But, if you're not pushing, we're not pushing. We'll help you, but we need all-stars. Our star is constantly rising. We're not about promoting nonsense. [Remember] you represent you well and us well.

Around the room, teens nodded—they understood the commitment and were ready to work.

In the middle of the meeting, a Black female named Rae with hair pulled back in long thick braids stood up next to me and announced her specific interest in the technical aspects of music, in what seemed to be an affirmation of Peters's explanation of the program. She declared to the group, "I am a vocalist and go to Oakland School for the Arts. I want to learn Pro Tools." At the time, I was impressed but not surprised by her announcement. Like Rae, many teens in other technology-related programs across the country were excited to hone their skills.

RADIO ARTE

Back in Chicago, I visited another program running during the summer called Radio Arte, an award-winning youth-run bilingual (Spanish-English) radio station. It was established in 1997 as a "Latin alternative" station owned by the National Museum of Mexican Art, which purchased it from the Boys and Girls Club and changed its call letters from WCYC to WRTE. From 1997 to 2012, the station trained teens to present bilingual programming and produce live music shows that promoted emerging Latinx artists. Facing financial issues, the museum sold the station in 2012.[34] Chicago Public Media bought it and folded it into WBEZ Chicago's sister station, Vocalo, a community-based station created in 2007 to focus on the Michigan, Illinois, and Indiana region. Although the youth training program no longer exists, some of its graduates continue to embody Radio Arte's vision at Vocalo, including Vocalo managing director Silvia Rivera and former WRTE program director Jesús Echeverría, who cohosts the bilingual show "Domingos en Vocalo" on Sundays.[35]

At the time of my observations in 2009, the youth training program was still in full swing, located in a two-story building on the corner of Eighteenth Street and Blue Island Avenue together with Yollocalli Arts Reach, the National Museum of Mexican Art's youth art training program. I picked the program in Pilsen, an historically Latinx neighborhood, to ensure that the study included linguistic diversity.[36] Inside I walked past a classroom filled with a group of teens hard at work, despite it being midsummer. Later, entering the room I saw a clamoring of excitement as they worked to produce radio segments. One teen named Alex, a Latinx student dressed all in black down to his Converse sneakers, sat hunched over his computer. He was so engaged, he barely noticed as I sat down to watch. Finally noticing my gaze, he looked up. Catching a glimpse of my notebook and later telling me he thought I was a reporter, he flashed an effervescent smile that said, "Yeah, we both know that what I'm doing is cool," and got back to work.

I DIG ZAMBIA—FIELD MUSEUM (CHICAGO) + GLOBAL KIDS (NEW YORK CITY)

Still in Chicago, I visited one side of a multicity summer program called I Dig Zambia, which was a unique collaboration between the Field Museum in Chicago and GK in New York. Unlike many other programs, instead of technology being the primary focus, teens developed their skill with a variety of technologies (Second Life software; blogs; Encyclopedia of Life, a digital platform hosted by the Smithsonian's Museum of Natural History) to learn about paleontology, scientific field research, global health, climate change, and culture. They followed an international research team doing a fossil dig in Africa in real time via Skype and simulated the dig in Second Life. Each program site (Chicago, New York) also visited the local natural history museum (the Field Museum and the American Museum of National History) and other related museums and science centers, met with scientists in person, and created blogs and other multimedia presentations to reflect on the process of scientific inquiry and what they learned.[37] Lasting two weeks, I observed one week in Chicago, then one week in New York, with all students participating online and the group of students I observed in person depending on my location.

I was introduced to I Dig Zambia through Rockman et al and the DML network. Rafi Santo, senior program associate for GK, emailed curriculum materials so I would know what to expect in both cities. I joined the Field Museum in Chicago on its second day, in the same room where WhyReef took place later in the fall. Instructor Beth Sanzenbacher led a group of eight teens sitting at tables organized into a square. Near her was a teen teaching assistant (a white male named Ethan who lived in a nearby suburb and had worked with GK in the past). The Field Museum side of the program connected with the GK side through Skype and Second Life, working in cross-program teams. For example, the Blue Team was made up of two Chicago area teens including Amber (a soft-spoken Black female with glasses, who on the first day explained she traveled from a working/middle-class area on the city's West Side) and Ashok (a friendly, tall Asian male who said he lived in an affluent western suburb). The team also included three teens in New York: Bisi (an outgoing African male who was always at the ready to help his group), Morgana (a tall, studious Black female), and Amira (a Black female with dimples and an easy laugh).

The first day of the program included an introductory overview, a paleontology workshop, a workshop on ecotourism, training in how to use Second Life—including keyboard commands to edit and move their avatars, how to communicate with Chat, how to make and edit objects ("prims," or "primitives," that the teens in BAVC's 3D gaming talked about), and how to take pictures in the virtual environment—and how to blog. When I arrived, there was a workshop on evolution, another workshop about excavation, a virtual dig where teens applied the technology skills learned the day before. This application included putting excavation tools together in Second Life, an exchange with youth in Zambia, and blogging. As I watched the teens move through these activities, I noted how technology learning was embedded and what they did to learn to each tool.

Rik Panganiban at GK, an Asian male instructor with an exuberant energy that matched the teens' excitement, introduced everyone to the technical activity in Second Life wherein students had to figure out how to put a rock hammer together (including purchasing parts). In my notes, I wrote:

Rik (*via Skype to Chicago*): Okay, [in Second Life] right or apple click the toolbox and buy [the hammer parts]. Won't cost you any linden [Second Life currency]. Your task is to form the head of the rock hammer. You saw what it looks like in the video. Get it, put in your inventory, then put the hammer together, then do linking thing. Hold the shift key while you're holding them close. You did that yesterday. Everybody go to your tents and look for toolbox.

Some teens in Chicago struggled with the activity, and the instructors told students to ask for help. Ethan, the teen teaching assistant, moved around helping people, as did other students who figured out the task. Charlie, a thirteen-year-old white male who had participated in a previous program called I Dig Tanzania, helped Kayla a thirteen-year-old Native American female. Kayla's sister Samantha participated in I Dig Tanzania the year before with Charlie and returned again this year with her sister. Charlie helped Kayla put together and pick up parts for the rock hammer, by saying "press Shift and now Control-Alt"—teaching her shortcuts that would help her figure out how to use Second Life.

On New York side of I Dig Zambia at GK, the first day of my visit (the second week of the program), I met Rafi and Rik in person—both had an easy rapport with students. They briefly introduced me to other GK instructors Shawna, Rebecca, and Krista. In total, there were eleven program participants—one African, eight Black, and two Latinx, with six girls and five boys. They sat at tables in front of laptops, chatting, laughing, and joking. In the first session I observed in New York, their goal was to work with teammates in Chicago to put simulated fossil pieces together like the scientists they were following were doing in real life in Zambia—similar to building excavation tools. They watched a short video about dinosaurs, visualizations of what the various dinosaurs looked like and how they moved, a video about dinosaur anatomy, and a video about Tyrannosaurus rex. Finally, Rik showed a video about how to put fossils together and said, "See if you recognize anyone! This is from last year and I Dig Tanzania." At the end of the fossil video, Rik said, "It's like a puzzle. A very, very fragile puzzle."

Over Skype, Shawna (a white woman with dark straight hair, large eyes, and a big smile) said to both New York and Chicago teens that they had sixteen fossils to put together to figure out what their dinosaur ate, the environment the animal lived in, and generally what it was like.

Rik said they had to work in teams, and a staff member would help each team. Everyone had to execute two steps in Second Life: "friend" all team members and give everyone "rights," such as "being able to move around the fossils, assemble fossils as a group." In New York, a Latinx teen named Israel with curly hair tucked in a ponytail, turned around to help Keisha, a Black female whose family was from Guyana. She seemed a bit confused, so Israel helped her to friend and grant rights. Caleb, a Black male with silver-framed glasses and a gentle approach to helping others, also looked over Keisha's shoulder to help and said, "See that box right there? Just check all of those people. Well, Israel (*to Israel*), you on her team?" Israel responded, "Yeah." Caleb turned back to Keisha, "Yeah, so do that. Start with that." Keisha smiled and nodded and said something to Victoria, a Black female sitting next to her whose smile revealed sparkling braces. They were all invested in the activities and made sure their peers were following along.

MOUSE/GEEK SQUAD SUMMER ACADEMY

Finally, in New York City I visited the Mouse/Geek Squad Summer Academy. When I first learned about Mouse while I taught at UPA, there were three components: Mouse Squad, a program that helped schools create student technology squads (like an in-house IT department); Mouse Corps, a program in youth leadership development and career readiness; and TechSource, a research and policy initiative to continuously improve school programs and provide information and leadership about technology use in urban school districts.[38] Although Mouse no longer runs these specific programs, it continues to provide creative STEM and computer science programs and professional development across the United States. When in 2009 I contacted Marc Lesser, who was then Mouse's education director, he told me they were offering a new summer training program in collaboration with Best Buy's Geek Squad, and I was welcomed to come observe. Marc—white, tall, and bearded—seemed to fit the stereotypical tech geek. But the work he did fought against just that stereotype. Meeting at a café before my observations, he said that students from all over New York City self-selected to spend their free summer days increasing their tech skills and I'd find a diverse group of tech-savvy teens.

On the first day, roughly 100 teens gathered onboard the USS *Intrepid*, a World War II aircraft carrier floating on the Hudson River. They were younger teens about the age of students in WhyReef. They were diverse—Dominican, Puerto Rican, Black, white, Asian, female, male. Inside the ship on an upper level was the Great Hall, a carpeted room with floor-to-ceiling windows out to the Hudson River. There, the entire group of teens gathered with some parents, teachers, and principals. They listened to an introduction of what would happen during the camp, which ran Tuesday through Friday from 9:30 a.m. to 4:00 p.m. There were approximately twenty instructors with the group, identified by their shirts with emblazoned Geek Squad logos.

Marc stood in front and welcomed everyone to the Summer Academy. He explained that students in the camp would take "positive risks" to learn new things. As a first step, he asked everyone to introduce themselves to someone they didn't know. Excitedly, the teens and their parents turned to the people around them to say hello. Marc explained that the instructors in the room were volunteers and the teens were going to learn all kinds of things, from taking computers apart to designing websites. An instructor stepped in, asking students to come up with "group agreements." Teens called out, "Respect!" "Safety." "Teamwork." Another instructor wrote down the group agreements on a large piece of chart paper fastened to a wall. After going over ground rules, another instructor announced group names and who was in them (separated by gender), such as Digital Divas, Hacksters, and F-emails. Finally, an instructor explained that they do call-and-response in the camp. "So, when I say 'Cool?' you say, 'Very cool!' Cool?" Teens (*smiling*): "Very cool!" "Okay, great, let's go out by group."

I followed thirteen girls (the F-emails) and five male instructors into a class called PC Build. Joe, a short, energetic, twentysomething white male with a buzz cut, asked the group if anyone had built a computer before. One student raised her hand. Joe told the group to attach an ESD (electrostatic discharge) strap to the table and to their wrist "for static." The girls found the straps and carefully hooked themselves to their tables with the help of other instructors. Joe then lifted up a motherboard and explained what it did. He next held up a stick of RAM (random-access memory) and asked, "What does this do?" An Asian teen named Julia suggested, "It's memory storage." Joe nodded and moved on to the hard drive and the modem—making jokes about slow dial-up internet.

Joe showed the girls a NIC (network interface card). Maya, a Black girl with a keen expression, asked, "Is that where you connect a router?" Joe responded, "Yes, very good! Anyone have any questions?" Maya asked, "What are these? They look like batteries?" as she held up a computer part in her hand. Tom, a white male instructor with shaggy brown hair, explained, "Yes, they are little batteries—capacitors—they store energy and make sure it gets to the right place." Joe talked about "add-ons" and showed a graphics card and expansion slots on the motherboard where the graphics card could be inserted to "support advanced graphics." He also showed students the power supply, CD-ROM drive, and optical drive.

Tom walked around the room handing out flash drives so students could save the work they created throughout camp. At 11:00 a.m., Joe announced they were going to do a relay race in three groups. Students lined up in two groups of four and one group of five. Joe explained that he was going to call out a part and they should try to find it and spell out the name. For example, he said, RAM means "Random Access Memory," and CPU means "Central Processing Unit." The girls enthusiastically played the game for about ten minutes and, although they got many of the terms wrong, the room filled with laughter, as though mistakes were something to be celebrated.

MOUSE SQUAD CALIFORNIA (MSCA)

Although some of the programs I observed after school or during the summer also occurred during school, the only program I observed in school was Mouse Squad California (MSCA). While teaching in Oakland, I learned about MSCA and had been in touch with director Jan

Half. I emailed her again in 2009 about visiting. She generously invited me to observe three facets of their school-based programs: an after-school program based at a school, a teacher training, and implementation of MSCA during the school day at a second school site. This way, I could get an overall sense of how MSCA worked in schools and talk to students and teachers involved.

Whereas the broader national organization began in 1997, MSCA began in 2004 in five Silicon Valley middle schools and grew to 135 sites throughout the state by 2015 (the year Half retired). During its first eleven years, MSCA served nearly twenty thousand students. In 2015 alone, MSCA partnered with twenty counties and sixty school districts to serve more than four thousand youth.[39] I first visited MSCA's school-based programs at Giannini Middle School, where MSCA collaborated with the Sunset Neighborhood Beacon Center to provide after-school tech education. When I visited in the 2009–2010 school year, 49.3 percent of students received free or reduced-price lunch, and the student body was 69.8 percent Asian, Filipino, or Pacific Islander; 9.6 percent white; 9.2 percent Latinx; and 5 percent Black.[40]

When I arrived, students were working on projects about internet safety, making PowerPoint presentations about the topic to present to other students at their school. Instructors invited me to move around and talk to students—there were ten teens present, although the program served more. Eight were Asian (six boys, two girls) and two were Latinx (boys). When I started talking to students, Eunice, a girl with neatly trimmed bangs, piped up. She had been in the program for a while and said she had "learned a lot!" What helped her learn new technologies? She took an "exploring" approach, keeping track of the steps she'd taken. She also tried to have the attitude she'd "get over it" if she encountered a problem, which would help her "get through it faster." If she couldn't figure out what to do, she'd "try different things, comparing something new to ones [she] already knew." I scribbled furiously as Eunice continued to enumerate her tricks, as I recognized many of the technology learning habits I'd seen in other programs.

Campbell Middle School, where I observed the in-school program, at the time included grades five through eight but has since been renamed Campbell School of Innovation and started transitioning to a K-8 school in 2017.[41] School demographics at the time included 45.9 percent receiving free or reduced-price meals, 29.4 percent designated as English Learners, and a racial/ethnic makeup of 57.8 percent Latinx; 21.7 percent white; 10.2 percent Asian, Filipino, or Pacific Islander; 7.3 percent Black, 2.6 percent multiracial; and less than 1 percent Native American.[42] There, I met the school's technology teacher, Carrie Tibbs, a white woman with a love for science and technology who had been at Campbell for twenty-one years, as a sixth-grade teacher for seven years specializing in science education and then working on computer integration into core curriculum. In her room, I walked into a familiar "organized chaos" as students moved between two rooms reorganizing equipment. They were clearly engaged in what they were doing, despite it being early in the school year. Carrie introduced me to several of her students, who were cheerfully ready to talk tech with a complete stranger, as if they couldn't imagine anything more fun.

Deciphering the Habits

After observations and interviews, I looked for patterns across all programs to identify the habits that helped these tech-savvy teens learn new technologies. This approach was informed by research on learning and cognitive research indicating that a range of learning strategies and strategy types (thoughts, feelings, actions) can better support learning and while early learning involves conscious decisions, these become automatic (habits) as they advance.[43] It was also informed by sociological theory that suggests *competence* is defined within a field as embodied cultural capital or *habitus* (including thoughts, feelings, actions).[44] Therefore, the learning habits taught and practiced by teens in the programs defined competence in these technology learning contexts.

My observations and interviews were in service to three goals. My first goal was to better conceptualize the construct (what helped students not give up). This conceptualization moved me from the idea of "persistence" to "digital adaptability," or the development of learning habits that support continual learning. My second goal was to enumerate and describe possible habits (how many there were and what they looked like). I had a long list of possible habits, but I had more steps to go to confirm which habits best defined digital adaptability. And my third and final goal was to move toward quantitative measurement. With these steps, both qualitative and quantitative methods were intertwined in the initial portion of the study.

DEVELOPING AND REFINING MEASUREMENT: HOW MANY AND WHICH HABITS?

Based on observation and interview data, I initially landed on eleven learning habits, some general and others technology specific. But I knew this number was too many. So, to figure out which habits composed digital adaptability, I used an integrated qualitative and quantitative approach. I first translated the list of eleven habits into twenty-two questions modeled after measures like those of the Motivated Strategies for Learning Questionnaire (MSLQ) and the "grit" scale that ask people to rate how much statements are "like them," with two items per habit (one negatively worded and one positively worded).[45] One might think such a self-rated measure could introduce bias, like self-assessments of knowledge and skill.[46] Yet methodological research shows that survey items that ask about how students perceive their typical learning approach can yield valid and reliable data.[47] I used a six-point scale with a 1 meaning "not like me at all" and a 6 meaning "exactly like me."[48]

As a next step in addressing "content validity" (i.e., whether the instrument appears to measure the concept) and methodological rigor, I presented the items to a group of six faculty experts in communication, sociology, and education to ask for their qualitative assessment.[49] Three of these people were methodological experts, including a director of the Center for Survey Research at the US Census Bureau and another who was an international leader in educational statistics on the US National Education Sciences Board and other technical advisory committees for international assessments such as the Programme for International Student Assessment. They suggested a few tweaks—for example, simplifying statements and adding items to compare the word *technology* to more specific terminology for hardware, software, and internet use.

I next pretested initial items by asking teens to read and think aloud about how they understood the items. I did these qualitative "cognitive interviews" with twenty-five teens, ages twelve through sixteen, and included twelve students I'd observed earlier in the tech-related programs, making sure to take English language development into account.[50] I asked students to interpret key terms, especially the word *technology*, which they interpreted as intended: as the consumer electronics they encountered in their everyday life. I also asked students to restate items in their own words, and I revised or removed confusing phrases. Using edited items and student language, I expanded to sixty-six items for piloting and *factor analysis*, which tests whether items load together and whether items measure the same construct (i.e., demonstrate convergent validity).

In the pilot, I again used a target population—this time, the average Chicago Public Schools (CPS) student. When I piloted the measure in 2010–2011, most CPS students were from low-income families, and the two largest racial/ethnic groups were Latinx and Black students, at 44.1 percent and 41.6 percent, respectively.[51] Therefore, I sampled two low-income regular neighborhood schools with no admissions criteria or application; one of the schools served mostly Latinx students and the other served mostly Black students. Unlike my experience in the Bay Area, most Chicago schools had a technology teacher or someone knowledgeable about technology on staff, so I worked with the technology teachers at each school. I included 243 rising or graduating eighth graders in the schools (i.e., an average of two classes of about thirty students per grade level per school). I picked eighth graders to validate the measure with younger adolescents with a range of literacy levels, so that items could potentially work for middle and high school students. Pilot test demographics are presented in table A.2.

TABLE A.2. Sample vs. CPS demographics (pilot test)

Indicator	Percent of sample (N = 243)	Percent of eighth-grade population, 2010–2011[a] (N = 28,303)
Gender		
Female	52%	51%[b]
Race/ethnicity		
Asian	1%	3%
Black	41%	44%
Latinx	57%	43%
Multiracial	<1%	<1%
Native American	<1%	<1%
White	1%	8%
Socioeconomic status		
Eligible for free or reduced-price lunch[c]	95%	86%
Other characteristics		
Has Individualized Education Program (IEP) for disability	13%	15%
Designated English Language Learner (ELL)	9%	7%

[a]Includes rising and graduating eighth graders. For space considerations, I list CPS eighth-grade demographics in 2010–2011; these are similar for seventh graders.

[b]Gender based on CPS data reported to Illinois State Board of Education for entire district.

[c]Students who live in households at or below 130% of the federal poverty level or are "categorically" eligible (i.e., participate in SNAP, TANF, FDPIR, Head Start; are foster, migrant, homeless, runaway) can receive free lunch. Students who live in households between 130% and 185% of the federal poverty level are eligible for reduced-price meals. In 2010–2011 the poverty level was $18,310 for a three-person household.

Source: Adapted from Cassidy Puckett, "Digital Adaptability: A New Measure for Digital Inequality Research," *Social Science Computer Review* (2020), https://doi.org/10.1177/0894439320926087.

Students filled out the pilot using pencil and paper; they completed the survey in about twenty-five minutes. They were asked to circle confusing items, and I manually reviewed each paper survey as they turned them in, asking students to answer blank items, so there were no missing responses. As a thank-you, I gave each student a multicolored pencil, which they seemed genuinely excited to receive. Later, I also checked for patterns indicating that a tired or otherwise uninterested student might have circled all the same response number, but very few students filled out the survey in that manner—they seemed supportive of the project (perceiving me as a student, on my way to becoming a teacher, which a few students told me while I helped out in class after they finished the surveys). Once the survey was complete, regular technology class activities resumed and I assisted the teacher, further solidifying the perception that I was a student-teacher. During this time, several students shared with me their technology interests, including the kinds of video games they liked to play.

After collecting and cleaning pilot data, I used confirmatory factor analysis to narrow to seven habits measured by four items for a total of twenty-eight items; a model which showed sufficient but not perfect fit.[52] I made changes to items that students had circled. I also analyzed the eighteen items that included terminology specific to hardware, software, and the internet (based on expert panel advice). But, the models using specific terminology were worse fitting and not significantly different from the model using the general term *technology*. So, I took those items out.

Next, I used the measure from the pilot (now seven habits measured by four items each for a total of twenty-eight items) with a stratified random sample of CPS eighth graders during the 2012–2013 school year ($N = 897$, which was 3.2 percent of the 27,873 eighth-grade population in 2012–2013).[53] Full test demographics are presented in table A.3.

To sample, I first created a list of all regular neighborhood schools serving eighth-grade students based on CPS 2011–2012 enrollment data, then separated schools by Title I status, a designation that provides supplemental funding if at least 40 percent of students are eligible for free or reduced-price lunch. From these lists, I drew a random sample of twenty-eight non–Title I schools and fifty-six Title I schools for recruitment. In total, twenty-seven schools agreed to participate, including eighteen Title I schools (in which 632 students participated) and nine non–Title I schools (265 students participated). In most schools, I recruited the help of the technology teacher, providing the school with a donation for their help and gift cards for each teacher. I also provided an incentive to students for a returned consent form (a three-dollar Subway gift card), regardless of their participation.

As shown in table A.3, the sample for the "full test" of the measure was roughly representative of CPS students, except by social class and some racial groups because I oversampled more-affluent and white students—this oversampling was so that I could compare Title I and non–Title I schools. Finally, although not a sampling goal, I also asked students for the zip code and name of the neighborhood in which they

TABLE A.3 Sample vs. CPS demographics (full test)

Indicator	Percent of sample (N = 897)	Percent of CPS eighth-grade population, 2012–2013 (N = 27,873)
Gender		
Female	53%	51%
Race and ethnicity		
Asian	3%	3%
Black	41%	42%
Latinx	38%	45%
Multiracial	<1%	1%
Native American	<1%	<1%
White	18%	9%
Socioeconomic status		
Eligible for free or reduced-price lunch[a]	78%	87%
Parents' highest education		
High school or less	14%	NA
More than high school, less than bachelor's degree	28%	NA
Bachelor's degree or above	33%	NA
Unknown	26%	NA
Other characteristics		
Has learning disability	13%	15%
Designated English Language Learner (ELL)	9%	7%
Grades in past year		
Mostly As	18%	NA
As and Bs	32%	NA
Mostly Bs	9%	NA
Bs and Cs	24%	NA
Mostly Cs	9%	NA
Cs, Ds, and Fs	8%	NA

[a]In 2012–2013, eligibility was based on a federal poverty level of $19,090 for a three-person household.

Note: NA = not available.

Source: Adapted from Cassidy Puckett, "Digital Adaptability: A New Measure for Digital Inequality Research," *Social Science Computer Review* (2020), https://doi.org/10.1177/0894439320926087.

lived and triangulated this information with school boundary data. Based on these data, I could see that students represented a range of geographic areas, with at least one student living in almost every city zip code (indicated by shading in figure A.1).

To collect survey data, I drove an old VW Golf all over Chicago in fall and winter (through snowstorms) during the 2012–2013 school year, dragging a classroom set of iPads with the help of a homeschooled high school student I met at YOUmedia. On a few occasions, his college-aged brother or other graduate students helped with data collection. The iPads were fitted with OtterBox covers to avoid damage, tucked

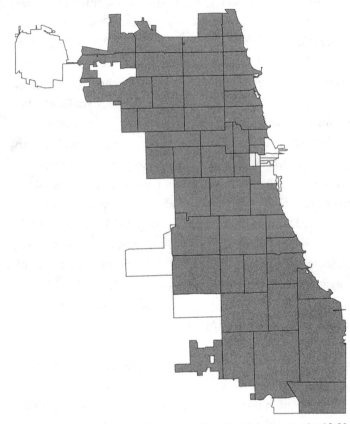

FIGURE A.1 Geographic representation in Chicago study (full test)
Source: Atul Varma.

into portable plastic file containers, and wheeled around in utility carts. In schools with no elevator, we dragged the heavy carts upstairs by hand—data collection was no easy feat.

Inside classrooms, I set up a secure local network and used my laptop as a server, together with hypertext markup language (HTML) interface viewable on web browsers on the iPads, and Python code developed with the help of Atul Varma, who at the time worked with the Mozilla

Foundation, to compile data to my laptop. I surveyed almost all eighth-grade students in each school. On average, one or two students per classroom did not participate if absent or they forgot their consent form, rather than refusing participation. Overall, students seemed very interested in the nature of the study and the use of the iPad, even though they could only take the survey on the device. The survey took one class period and included the DAS and questions about the social contexts where they might learn about technology (home, school, friends, and out-of-school—although because of a technical issue, data for the last context was unfortunately lost).

I used the same data analysis approach as in the pilot (confirmatory factor analysis) to refine the DAS, narrowing to 5 habits measured by 3 items each; a model which demonstrated best overall fit. I also replicated the fit of this model during a postdoctoral fellowship at the Tufts University Center for Engineering Education and Outreach (CEEO) with data from a school district in the Boston area, involving a survey of 1285 high school students.[54] At the end of this process, I had identified, defined, and operationalized digital adaptability.

OBSERVING AND EXPLAINING VARIATION

The measure allowed one way of observing variation in teens' technology learning habits. I also observed it in action by selecting eight survey respondents—half in one Title I school and half in one non–Title I school, including two girls and two boys in each school, one of each gender who scored higher and one who scored lower on the DAS (like high-scoring Sumalee and low-scoring Anandi). I asked each student to learn Scratch—a visual programming software developed at the Massachusetts Institute of Technology used to teach basic coding, computer science concepts and activities, and computational thinking—to accomplish a task.[55] To do the task, they watched a brief video describing Scratch and then had ten minutes to explore and ten minutes to solve the problem of moving a cat figure from the left to the right side of the screen (described in chapter 4). Students rated higher on the DAS completed the task, while those rated lower did not, although I did not systematically test for the point on the scale that might predict success or failure with the task—something future research could explore.

This performance task is similar to the demands of the entry-level computer science course requirements. In fact, the fourth unit of the Exploring Computer Science curriculum developed by the national Computer Science for All initiative focuses on programming and includes using Scratch to do a similar task of moving a "sprite" (the cat figure) on instructional days five and six.[56] Thus, a difference in the ability to do the task and related scores on the DAS suggest different levels of readiness for basic computer science. Whereas I conducted this task with a small strategic sample, and the students who failed the task might learn how to do it if given more time or instruction, it shows that the DAS is sensitive to differences in students' technology learning habits—and shows what students do when trying to learn new technologies that can help or hinder the learning process.[57]

I also shadowed these students throughout their day for one week during the school year and one week in summer for a total of approximately eighty hours per student. I met them at their home and walked with them to school, visited their classes at school, and joined them after school until just before dinner. In this process, I observed and collected data on the technology practices students encountered in each social sphere and the habits students carried across spheres, and how these interacted. Although shadowing involved following individual students, these observations also involved teachers, parents, siblings, other family members (grandparents, uncles, and aunts), other students, and friends.

Students also completed technology journals for two weeks to gather information without my presence potentially influencing practices at home and school. I conducted in-depth interviews focusing on students' experiences of technology learning over time and their perceptions of how they should approach technology learning in various social spheres. To triangulate data, I also conducted informal interviews with parents and teachers, which focused on how families and schools define and develop technological competence in students. Before collecting any information, I collected a parent consent and child assent, offering a stipend of fifty dollars for each week of observation and interviews, and no parent or child refused participation. Later, I interviewed the same students again in high school.

These observations, journals, and interviews revealed important information about dynamics within and between social spheres that could explain variation in their learning habits. What I learned through these shadow observations and interviews, as well as through the larger survey, is that schools largely do not influence students' technology learning habits. The one exception was schools that make a concerted effort, which I found in the survey was indicated by the presence of technology plans no longer required by the district or state.[58] I continue to analyze dynamics across social contexts.

CONNECTING LEARNING HABITS TO STUDENTS' FUTURES

In the larger survey in Chicago, the replication study outside of Boston, and interviews with the eight CPS students while they were in middle and high school, I asked students about their future educational plans and aspirations. Qualitative and quantitative findings in Chicago informed the replication study outside of Boston, and findings from the replication study confirmed earlier findings in Chicago. Overall, each type of data in each study seemed to verify a relationship between students' technology learning habits and their plans and aspirations, as described in chapter 5.

For the replication study I joined a larger ongoing study by Dr. Brian Gravel at Tufts. The study took place in a small, diverse urban school district near Boston. The district was chosen because of its extensive STEM offerings, including technology and engineering-related electives; extracurricular technology activities including Robotics, Computer Club, Technovation (a program for girls), a "makerspace" where students do hands-on activities; and a 1:1 school-wide laptop program.[59] For the project, we collected 998 hours of observation throughout the school day and after school over the course of the first two years of the project (2014–2016, including the second year when I was embedded in the school); interviews with 29 students, 31 teachers, 6 guidance counselors, 2 district administrators, and the principal; and a survey of 1,285 of its high school students.

We conducted the survey in 2015–2016, and I included the DAS and questions asking about students' educational plans and occupational aspirations to see whether findings from Chicago would replicate in Boston with an older cohort of students. We drew a large, representative sample of 1,285 of the district's 1,849 high school students, about 67 percent of the total population. Study demographics are presented in the Table A.4. The survey confirmed the statistical properties of the

TABLE A.4. Boston survey demographics

Indicator	Survey respondents ($n = 1,285$)	District data ($N = 1,849$)
Gender		
Female	54% (692)	50% (921)
Race/ethnicity		
Asian	30% (386)	25% (451)
Black	20% (257)	23% (422)
Latinx	18% (235)	20% (359)
Multiracial	3% (41)	4% (67)
Native American	< 1% (4)	<1% (8)
White	27% (353)	29% (526)
Socioeconomic status		
Eligible for free or reduced-price lunch[a]	61% (744)	63% (1078)
Father's education		
Less than college degree	50% (647)	NA
College degree or above	19% (239)	NA
Do not know	30% (398)	NA
Mother's education		
Less than college degree	53% (686)	NA
College or above	21% (277)	NA
Do not know	25% (322)	NA
Other characteristics		
In special education program	8% (102)	13% (241)
Limited English proficiency (LEP)	10% (132)	13% (241)

[a]In 2015–2016 eligibility was based on a federal poverty level of $20,090 for a three-person household.

Note: NA = not available.

Source: Adapted from Cassidy Puckett, "Digital Adaptability: A New Measure for Digital Inequality Research," *Social Science Computer Review* (2020), https://doi.org/10.1177/0894439320926087.

measurement model of the DAS in Chicago (i.e., the five habits, measured by three items each), as well as the relationship between students' technology learning habits and their educational plans and future aspirations.[60]

MIXED METHODS FOR THEORY BUILDING

Overall, this project adds to the growing body of mixed-methods research, showing ways scholars can conceptualize and engage in this approach. As I noted at the beginning of this appendix, this work falls between the two ends of a spectrum of mixed-methods approaches—at times distinct but always intertwined. My approach of iterating with each method also draws on the logic of the abductive analysis for theory building, where initial theories may be tested and retested through systematic observation of variation across students, settings, and—in this case—types of methods.[61] While predominantly used for qualitative research, the conceptual roots of abductive analysis can be applied to mixed-methods studies to help build new ideas about how the world works.

Notes

INTRODUCTION

1   My own students, who are now adults, gave permission to use their real names in the book (e.g., the aforementioned Amairani). All names of other students mentioned are pseudonyms. In many cases, I also made adjustments to make students less specifically identifiable, such as combining information about multiple students into one composite student or describing them in a slightly different way than they actually appeared (e.g., short when tall, long hair when short).

2   Yu Xie, Michael Fang, and Kimberlee Shauman, 2015. "STEM Education," *Annual Review of Sociology* 41 (2015): 331–57; David N. Beede et al., *Women in STEM: A Gender Gap to Innovation*, Economics and Statistics Administration Issue Brief No. 04–11 (August 1, 2011), https://doi.org/10.2139/ssrn.1964782. Throughout the book I draw on research in STEM as a whole, but my research specifically focuses on technology.

3   Sapna Cheryan et al., "Ambient Belonging: How Stereotypical Cues Impact Gender Participation in Computer Science," *Journal of Personality and Social Psychology* 97, no. 6 (2009): 1045–60.

4   Nicole R. Zarrett and Oksana Malanchuk, "Who's Computing? Gender and Race Differences in Young Adults' Decisions to Pursue an Information Technology Career," *New Directions for Child and Adolescent Development*, no. 110 (Winter 2005): 65–84.

5   Bruno Latour, *Science in Action: How to Follow Scientists and Engineers through Society* (Cambridge, MA: Harvard University Press, 1987).

265

6   I borrow from Roli Varma's use of Roland Barthes's definition of myth, applied
    to geek culture: "[Barthes] conceptualized myth not as a fictitious or unverified
    thing, but as a socially constructed reality, which is passed off as 'natural' despite
    having little actual connection to history." Roli Varma, "Women in Computing:
    The Role of Geek Culture," *Science as Culture* 16, no. 4 (2007): 359–76, at 361.
7   Billy Wong, "'I'm Good, But Not That Good': Digitally-Skilled Young People's
    Identity in Computing," *Computer Science Education* 26, no. 4 (2016): 299–317.

Asian immigrants and Asian Americans' inclusion in tech stereotypes is a
more recent phenomenon that tracks with immigration policy tied to the rise
of the tech industry in Silicon Valley. Yet the stereotype conceals important
challenges that these groups have faced in tech fields. The increase in Asian
groups' participation in tech began with passage of the amended Immigration
and Naturalization Act of 1965, also known as the Hart-Celler Act, a policy
intended to help family reunification and attract skilled labor. The act lifted
quota restrictions for immigrants from non-European countries, giving all countries an allocation of twenty thousand visas per year and setting up a preference
system whereby 74 percent of visas were granted for family reunification, 20
percent for skilled labor and professionals, and 6 percent for political refugees.
Further, by including skilled labor as a criterion, it boosted the occupational
profile of educated immigrants from China and India in particular, who came
to the United States seeking educational opportunities, better jobs, and greater
political stability and freedom. This immigration context was in contrast to that
of Filipino and Vietnamese immigrants, who were largely political refugees flee-
ing economic and political conditions in their home countries and who worked
in lower-wage jobs upon arrival in the United States.

In 1990, another immigration act designed to attract more educated labor-
ers further increased the number of Asian immigrants to the United States. That
act increased professional employment-based visas to 140,000. It also established the H-1B, a work visa that permitted migrants with "special skills" to work
in the United States for six years to pursue a green card. The H-1B visas were
initially capped at 65,000, with the bulk going to computer-related occupations.
Then, in 1998 at the request of tech companies, Congress passed another bill
to increase the H-1B visa numbers to 115,000 for 1999 and 2000. Finally, the
American Competitiveness in the Twenty-First Century Act of 2000 increased
the limit of H-1B visas to 195,000 for each of the next three years. All together,
these policies created a powerful pull for non-US-born Asian male computer
scientists and engineers to immigrate to the United States. These policies also
coincided with China's opening up to more immigration and trade, improved US
relations with China and India, and growing economies in these countries that
helped produce more educated professionals.

As a result of these policies, non-US-born Asian groups' representation in
tech grew to the point that in the first decade of the twenty-first century, approximately one-third of the engineers and scientists in Santa Clara County were
born outside the United States—primarily from China and India. This increase
in (some) Asian groups' representation in Silicon Valley gave rise to the stereo-

type that *all* Asians are tech savvy. Yet, only certain Asian groups are in fact represented in these fields. For example, in an analysis of demographic data on US occupations from 1960 to 2009, Alegria and Branch found that in computing, non-US-born Asian men dramatically outnumbered and outpaced placement in tech fields as compared to their US-born counterparts. In 1960, they composed only 0.48 percent of the computing workforce, but by 2009 that representation had increased to 14.14 percent. In contrast, in 1960, US-born Asian men made up 1.25 percent of the computing workforce, and in 2009, they remained at a similar 1.82 percent of that labor force. See Sharla N. Alegria and Enobong Hannah Branch, "Causes and Consequences of Inequality in the STEM: Diversity and its Discontents," *International Journal of Gender, Science and Technology* 7, no. 3 (2015): 322–42. Further, those within tech fields have faced substantial challenges; many have encountered a "bamboo ceiling" or "silicon ceiling" in being passed over for managerial positions, and many are subject to precarious employment through contract labor.

See also Roli Varma, "High Tech Coolies: Asian Immigrants in the US Science and Engineering Workforce," *Science as Culture* 11, no. 3 (2002): 337–61; James M. Freeman, *Hearts of Sorrow: Vietnamese American Lives* (Redwood City, CA: Stanford University Press, 1989); Benito Manalo Vergara, *Pinoy Capital: The Filipino Nation in Daly City* (Philadelphia: Temple University Press, 2008); AnnaLee Saxenian, "Silicon Valley's New Immigrant High-Growth Entrepreneurs," *Economic Development Quarterly* 16, no. 1 (2002):20–31; Bernard P. Wong, *The Chinese in Silicon Valley: Globalization, Social Networks, and Ethnic Identity* (Lanham, MD: Rowman & Littlefield, 2006); Payal Banerjee, "Indian Information Technology Workers in the United States: The H-1B Visa, Flexible Production, and the Racialization of Labor," *Critical Sociology* 32, no. 2–3 (2006): 425–45.

8   Research shows, for example, that there are few differences in skill (or even perception of skill) between men and women in engineering and that inequities may be better explained by signals that communicate the notion that women do not "fit" heavily sex-typed fields (what scholars call "professional role confidence"). Other research shows there are many disadvantaged students motivated to learn STEM (and supportive families of these children), but they face substantial barriers to opportunity. See: Erin Cech et al., "Professional Role Confidence and Gendered Persistence in Engineering," *American Sociological Review* 76, no. 5 (2011): 641–66; S. Craig Watkins et al., *The Digital Edge: How Black and Latino Youth Navigate Digital Inequality* (New York: New York University Press, 2018).

9   Barry Fishman and BaoHui Zhang, "Planning for Technology: The Link Between Intentions and Use," *Educational Technology* 43, no. 4 (2003): 14–18.

10 David Figlio and Susanna Loeb, "School Accountability," in *Handbook of the Economics of Education*, vol. 3, ed. Eric A. Hanushek, Stephen Machin, and Ludger Woessmann (Amsterdam: North-Holland, 2011), 383–421.

11 Before I began my study, these definitions included but were not limited to (in chronological order): NETS (ISTE 1998); information and communication

technologies (ICT) literacy (ETS ICT Literacy Panel 2002); twenty-first century skills framework (Partnership for 21st Century Skills 2002); digital age literacy, inventive thinking, effective communication, and high productivity (Metiri/ NCREL 2003); technical competence defined as operating electronic devices and information literacy (Mossberger, Tolbert, and Stansbury 2003); computer literacy, information literacy, multimedia literacy, and computer mediated communication literacy (Warschauer 2004); machine interactivity (Page and Uncles 2004); internet skill and digital literacy (Hargittai 2005, 2002); operational skill, information skill, and strategic skill (van Dijk 2005); neomillennial learning styles (Dede 2005); new skills needed for "participatory cultures" including play, performance, simulation, appropriation, multitasking, distributed cognition, collective intelligence, judgment, transmedia navigation, networking, and negotiation (Jenkins et al. 2006); ICT skills and digital literacy (International Society for Technology in Education 2007); and Web 2.0 skills (Dede 2009).

See International Society for Technology in Education (ISTE), *National Education Technology Standards for Students* (Washington, DC: ISTE, 1998); ETS ICT Literacy Panel, *Digital Transformation: A Framework for ICT Literacy*, (Princeton, NJ: Educational Testing Service, 2002); Partnership for 21st Century Skills, *Framework for 21st Century Learning* (Washington, DC: 2002); Laboratory, Metiri Group/North Central Regional Educational Laboratory (NCREL), *Engauge 21st Century Skills* (Naperville, IL: NCREL, 2003); Karen Mossberger, Caroline J. Tolbert, and Mary Stansbury, *Virtual Inequality: Beyond the Digital Divide* (Washington DC: Georgetown University Press, 2003); Mark Warschauer, *Technology and Social Inclusion: Rethinking the Digital Divide* (Cambridge, MA: MIT Press, 2004); Kelly Page and Mark Uncles, "Consumer Knowledge of the World Wide Web: Conceptualization and Measurement," *Psychology and Marketing* 21, no. 8 (2004): 573–91; Eszter Hargittai, "Survey Measures of Web-Oriented Digital Literacy," *Social Science Computer Review* 23, no. 3 (2005): 371–79; Eszter Hargittai, "Second-Level Digital Divide: Differences in People's Online Skills," *First Monday* 7, no. 4 (2002): 1–20; Jan A. G. M. van Dijk, *The Deepening Divide: Inequality in the Information Society* (Thousand Oaks, CA: Sage, 2005); Chris Dede, "Planning for Neomillennial Learning Styles," *EDUCAUSE Quarterly* 28, no. 1 (2005): 7–12; Henry Jenkins et al., *Confronting the Challenges of Participatory Culture: Media Education for the 21st Century* (Chicago: MacArthur Foundation, 2006); ISTE, *National Education Technology Standards for Students*, 2nd ed. (Washington, DC: ISTE, 2007); Chris Dede, "Comments on Greenhow, Robelia, and Hughes: Technologies That Facilitate Generating Knowledge and Possibly Wisdom," *Educational Researcher* 38, no. 4 (2009): 260–63.

12 ISTE, *National Education Technology Standards* (1998); ISTE, *National Education Technology Standards*, 2nd ed. (2007); ISTE, *National Education Technology Standards for Students* (Washington, DC: ISTE, 2016), https://www.iste.org /standards/for-students.

13 ISTE, *National Education Technology Standards* (1998).

14 Mary M. Somerville, Gordon W. Smith, and Alexius Smith Macklin, "The ETS iSkills Assessment: A Digital Age Tool, *Electronic Library* 26, no. 2 (2008): 158–71.

15 Warschauer, *Technology and Social Inclusion*; van Dijk, *Deepening Divide*.

16 John Palfrey and Urs Gasser, *Born Digital: Understanding the First Generation of Digital Natives* (New York: Basic Books, 2008); Marc Prensky, "Digital Natives, Digital Immigrants," *On the Horizon* 9, no. 5 (2001): 1–6; Susan Bennett, Karl Maton, and Lisa Kervin, "The 'Digital Natives' Debate: A Critical Review of the Evidence," *British Journal of Educational Technology* 39, no. 5 (2009): 775–86.

17 ISTE, *National Education Technology Standards* (2016).

18 US Department of Education, *Toward a New Golden Age in American Education: How the Internet, the Law and Today's Students Are Revolutionizing Expectations; National Education Technology Plan 2004* (Washington, DC: US Department of Education, 2004), 11.

19 Bennett, Maton, and Kervin, "'Digital Natives' Debate."

20 Sapna Cheryan et al., "Why Are Some STEM Fields More Gender Balanced Than Others?" *Psychological Bulletin* 143, no. 1 (2017): 1–35.

21 James Damore, "Google's Ideological Echo Chamber: How Bias Clouds Our Thinking About Diversity and Inclusion," Internet Archive Wayback Machine, July 2017, https://diversitymemo-static.s3-us-west-2.amazonaws.com/Googles-Ideological-Echo-Chamber.pdf; Omar Etman, "Google Employee's Leaked Anti-Diversity Memo Sparks Evaluation of Tech Culture," in *PBS Newshour*, August 6, 2017, https://www.pbs.org/newshour/nation/google-anti-diversity-memo-leaked-women-tech.

22 I believe this was the result of the enrollment of a core group of friends—Cindy, Maria, Meihong—which likely encouraged other eighth-grade girls to join.

23 Catherine Riegle-Crumb and Chelsea Moore, "The Gender Gap in High School Physics: Considering the Context of Local Communities," *Social Science Quarterly* 95, no. 1 (2013): 253–68; Sapna Cheryan et al., "The Stereotypical Computer Scientist: Gendered Media Representations as a Barrier to Inclusion for Women," *Sex Roles* 69 (2013): 58–71.

24 I used a protocol similar to the "Draw A Computer User" test described in Mark Jeremy Brosnan, "A New Methodology, an Old Story? Gender Differences in the 'Draw-a-Computer-User' Test," *European Journal of Psychology of Education* 14, no. 3 (1999): 375–85.

25 Sean F. Reardon et al., "Gender Achievement Gaps in U.S. School Districts" (working paper, Stanford CEPA [Center for Education Policy Analysis], Stanford, CA, 2018).

26 Celia L. Ridgeway, *Framed by Gender: How Gender Inequality Persists in the Modern World* (New York: Oxford University Press, 2011).

27 Mary K. Eamon, "Digital Divide in Computer Access and Use between Poor and Non-Poor Youth," *Journal of Sociology and Social Welfare* 31, no. 2 (2004): 91–113.

28 My initial study while I was teaching middle school tech classes included surveys, observations, interviews, and the collection of artifacts from the class, with the permission of my students and their parents. For the survey and interviews, I used a modified version of Dr. Brigid Barron's instruments, which included the "Draw-A-Computer-Type-Person" drawing task I described in note 23. At the time, Dr. Barron was working on the Bermuda Computing Curriculum Project, a collaborative project between Stanford and Bermuda Public

Schools to develop and evaluate computing curriculum focused on programming. I helped analyze data from that project as preliminary training for my early research in this area.

29   Alexander J. A. M. van Deursen and Jan A. G. M. van Dijk, "The Digital Divide Shifts to Differences in Usage," *New Media and Society* 16, no. 3 (2013): 507–26. On access to broadband in rural communities, see Brian E. Whitacre, "The Diffusion of Internet Technologies to Rural Communities: A Portrait of Broadband Supply and Demand," *American Behavioral Scientist* 53, no. 9 (2011): 1283–1303.

30   See Paul Attewell, "Comment: The First and Second Digital Divides," *Sociology of Education* 74, no. 3 (2001): 252–59; Hargittai, "Second-Level Digital Divide"; Paul DiMaggio et al., "From Unequal Access to Differentiated Use: A Literature Review and Agenda for Research on Digital Inequality," in *Social Inequality*, ed. Kathryn Neckerman (New York: Russell Sage Foundation, 2004), 355–400.

31   DiMaggio et al., "From Unequal Access to Differentiated Use." See also, Hargittai, "Survey Measures of Web-Oriented Digital Literacy"; Eszter Hargittai, "An Update on Survey Measures of Web-Oriented Digital Literacy," *Social Science Computer Review* 27, no. 1 (2009): 130–37; Eszter Hargittai and Yuli Patrick Hsieh, "Succinct Survey Measures of Web-Use Skills," *Social Science Computer Review* 30, no. 1 (2012): 95–107.

32   Angela L. Duckworth et al., "Grit: Perseverance and Passion for Long-Term Goal," *Journal of Personality and Social Psychology* 92, no. 6 (2007): 1087–101.

33   Benjamin Herold, "Is 'Grit' Racist?" *Digital Education* (blog), *Education Week*, January 24, 2015, http://blogs.edweek.org/edweek/DigitalEducation/2015/01/is_grit_racist.html.

34   Claudia Buchmann, Thomas A. DiPrete, and Anne McDaniel, "Gender Inequalities in Education," *Annual Review of Sociology* 34 (2008): 319–37.

35   Xie, Fang, and Shauman, "STEM Education."

36   Charity Anderson et al., "On the Meaning of Grit . . . and Hope . . . and Fate Control . . . and Alienation . . . and Locus of Control . . . and . . . Self-Efficacy . . . and . . . Effort Optimism . . . and. . . ." *Urban Review* 48, no. 2 (2016): 198–219.

37   There are debates over whether HTML and CSS are, in fact, coding or programming languages. Some make the distinction between "front end" languages that define the form of interfaces and "back end" languages that define function, with the latter characterized as the "real" programming languages. Often, this distinction is coupled with an assumption that front-end development (i.e., what people see and interact with) is less difficult or less skilled work than back-end development (i.e., what people don't see, how things function), something that has been intertwined with the devaluation of women's work in tech. See Nalini P. Kotamraju, "Art Versus Code: The Gendered Evolution of Web Design Skills," in *Society Online: The Internet in Context*, ed. Philip N. Howard and Steve Jones (Thousand Oaks, CA: Sage, 2004), 189–200.

38   At the time, my thinking was largely influenced by sociocultural theories of how social context shapes learning based on Lev Vygotsky (later, I combined this with sociological theory and research). Lev Vygotsky, *Mind in Society: The Development of Higher Psychological Processes* (Cambridge, MA: Harvard University

Press, 1978); Lev Vygotsky, *Thought and Language* (Cambridge, MA: MIT Press, 1986).

39   Carol Dweck, *Mindset: The New Psychology of Success* (New York: Ballantine Books, 2006).

40   For a summary, see Carol Dweck, Gregory M. Walton, and Geoffrey L. Cohen, *Academic Tenacity: Mindset and Skills That Promote Long Term Learning.* (Seattle, WA: Bill and Melinda Gates Foundation, 2014).

41   Lisa S. Blackwell, Kali H. Trzesniewski, and Carol S. Dweck, "Implicit Theories of Intelligence Predict Achievement across an Adolescent Transition: A Longitudinal Study and an Intervention," *Child Development* 78, no. 1 (January–February 2007): 246–63.

42   This approach follows the philosophy of Barrie Thorne, described in depth in her 1993 book *Gender Play: Girls and Boys in School* (New Brunswick, NJ: Rutgers University Press). Thorne argued that "kids" should be taken seriously and on their own terms—I wholeheartedly agree.

43   I further validated the measure in a replication study of almost 1,300 high school students in a diverse school district just outside of Boston.

44   Adam V. Maltese and Robert H. Tai, "Pipeline Persistence: Examining the Association of Educational Experiences with Earned Degrees in STEM among U.S. Students," *Science Education* 95, no. 5 (2011): 877–907.

45   This quote is an excerpt from Cassidy Puckett and Jennifer L. Nelson, "The Geek Instinct: Theorizing Cultural Alignment in Disadvantaged Contexts," *Qualitative Sociology* 42, no. 1 (2019): 25–48.

46   This study is the first, to my knowledge, to show this potential with quantitative evidence. However, there are others who demonstrate similar findings through qualitative means. See, for example: Matthew H. Rafalow, "Disciplining Play: Digital Youth Culture as Capital at School," *American Journal of Sociology* 123, no. 5 (2018): 1416–52; Watkins et al., *Digital Edge*; Jane Margolis et al., *Stuck in the Shallow End* (Cambridge, MA: MIT Press, 2008).

47   Alicia Headlam Hines, Alondra Nelson, and Thuy Linh N. Tu, *Technicolor: Race, Technology, and Everyday Life* (New York: New York University Press, 2001), 3–10.

CHAPTER ONE

1   On research suggesting that more accessible and in-depth technology education is critical to a more equitable and democratic society, see Larry Irving et al., *Falling Through the Net: Defining the Digital Divide; A Report on the Telecommunications and Information Technology Gap in America* (Washington, DC: National Telecommunications and Information Administration, US Department of Commerce, 1999); Megan Smith, "Computer Science for All," *White House* (blog), January 30, 2016, https://obamawhitehouse.archives.gov/blog/2016/01/30/computer-science-all.

2   Laura Robinson et al., "Digital Inequalities and Why They Matter," *Information, Communication and Society* 18, no. 5 (2015): 569–82.

3   Virginia Eubanks, *Automating Inequality: How High-Tech Tools Profile, Police, and Punish the Poor* (New York: Picador, 2018); Catherine L. Besteman and Hugh Gusterson, eds., *Life by Algorithms: How Roboprocesses Are Remaking Our World* (Chicago: University of Chicago Press, 2019)

4   On maintaining social hierarchies in education, see Samuel R. Lucas, "Effectively Maintained Inequality: Education Transitions, Track Mobility, and Social Background Effects," *American Journal of Sociology* 106, no. 6 (2001): 1642–90; David F. Labaree, *A Perfect Mess: The Unlikely Ascendancy of American Higher Education.* (Chicago: University of Chicago Press, 2017). On opportunity hoarding and exclusion see Jessica McCrory Calarco, *Negotiating Opportunities: How the Middle Class Secures Advantages in School* (Oxford: Oxford University Press, 2018); Amanda E. Lewis and John B. Diamond, *Despite the Best Intentions: How Racial Inequality Thrives in Good Schools.* (New York: Oxford University Press, 2015).

5   Here I apply David Labaree's argument that, historically, there have been three ways of understanding the purpose of education and learning in general in the United States—for democratic equality (benefit to society), social efficiency (benefit to employers), and social mobility (benefit to individuals). He argues that these goals are competing and ultimately accept different overall societal forms—the latter two are predicated upon an unequal society. Only the first moves toward equality. See David F. Labaree, "Public Goods, Private Goods: The American Struggle over Educational Goals," *American Educational Research Journal* 34, no. 1 (1997): 39–81; David F. Labaree, *How to Succeed in School without Really Learning* (New Haven, CT: Yale University Press, 1997).

6   Labaree, "Public Goods, Private Goods"; Labaree, *How to Succeed in School without Really Learning.*

7   Labaree, "Public Goods, Private Goods"; Labaree, *How to Succeed in School without Really Learning*, 20.

8   Len Masterman, *Teaching the Media* (London: Comedia Books, 1985), 13.

9   I put "low-skill" and "high-skill" in quotation marks to note that these categories are social constructions, with biases embedded into conceptions of "skill." I would argue that it takes just as much skill to fix a car, for example, as it does to fix a software bug—but we pay disparate wages for these jobs. See: Paul Attewell, "What Is Skill," *Work and Occupations* 17, no. 4 (1990): 422–48. On skill-biased technological change, see Edward L. Glaeser, "Inequality" (NBER Working Paper 11511, National Bureau of Economic Research, Cambridge, MA, 2005); David Autor, Lawrence Katz, and Melissa S. Kearney, "Trends in U.S. Wage Inequality: Revising the Revisionists," *Review of Economics and Statistics* 90, no. 2 (2008): 300–323; Eric Brynjolfsson and Brian Kahin, *Understanding the Digital Economy: Data, Tools, and Research* (Cambridge, MA: MIT Press, 2000); Maarten Goos, Alan Manning, and Anna Salomons, "Explaining Job Polarization: Routine-Biased Technological Change and Offshoring," *American Economic Review* 104, no. 8 (2014): 2509–26.

10   Simon Kuznets, "Economic Growth and Income Inequality," *American Economic Review* 45, no. 1 (1955): 1–28.

11   David Autor, Lawrence Katz, and Alan Krueger, "Computing Inequality: Have

Computers Changed the Labor Market?" *Quarterly Journal of Economics* 113, no. 4 (November 1998): 1169–1213.

12 Claudia Goldin and Lawrence F. Katz, *The Race Between Technology and Education* (Cambridge, MA: Harvard University Press, 2008).

13 Goldin and Katz, *Race Between Technology and Education*; Jeffrey J. Kuenzi, Christine M. Matthew, and Bonnie F. Mangan, "Science, Technology, Engineering, and Mathematics (STEM) Education Issues and Legislative Options," in *Progress in Education*, vol. 14 (New York: Nova Science Publishers, 2007), 161–89; National Research Council, *Rising above the Gathering Storm: Energizing and Employing America for a Brighter Economic Future* (Washington, DC: National Academies Press, 2007). One critique of this work I've discussed elsewhere is that this research and other related work conceptualizes technological competence as the skill demanded by jobs and uses biased proxy measures such as educational credentials, ratings created through expert review of jobs, or worker ratings. See Cassidy Puckett, "Digital Adaptability: A New Measure for Digital Inequality Research." *Social Science Computer Review*, July 16, 2020, https://doi.org/10.1177/0894439320926087. See also Daron Acemoglu and David Autor, "Skills, Tasks and Technologies: Implications for Employment and Earnings," in *Handbook of Labor Economics*, vol. 4, edited by Orley Ashenfelter and David Card (Amsterdam: North Holland, 2010); Yujia Liu and David B. Grusky, "The Payoff to Skill in the Third Industrial Revolution," *American Journal of Sociology* 118, no. 5 (2013): 1330–74; Guy Michaels, Ashwini Natraj, and John Van Reenen, "Has ICT Polarized Skill Demand? Evidence from Eleven Countries over 25 Years," *Review of Economics and Statistics* 96, no. 1 (2014): 60–77, https://doi.org/10.1162/REST_a_00366. Job skill ratings, for example, are prone to rater biases about social hierarchies, overrating the skills required in higher-paying jobs (cf. Attewell, "What Is Skill"). They may also introduce gender- or race-based biases; see Cheryan et al, "Why Are Some STEM Fields More Gender Balanced?"; David I. Miller, Alice H. Eagly, and Marcia C. Linn, "Women's Representation in Science Predicts National Gender-Science Stereotypes: Evidence from 66 Nations," *Journal of Educational Psychology* 107, no. 3 (2015): 631–44, https://doi.org/10.1037/edu0000005; Ridgeway, *Framed by Gender*. Historically, computer programming was considered lower-skill administrative work in its early years when female-dominated but reframed as higher-skill work when it later became male-dominated; see Nathan Ensmenger, *The Computer Boys Take Over: Computers, Programmers, and the Politics of Technical Expertise* (Cambridge, MA: MIT Press, 2010); Misa, Thomas J., ed, *Gender Codes: Why Women Are Leaving Computing.* (Hoboken, NJ: IEEE Computer Society and John Wiley & Sons, 2010). While this research suggests technological change demands new skill and therefore adaptability, it only measures skill (indirectly and likely with bias), leaving an empirical gap that I fill with my redefinition of technological competence as skill, literacies, and the habits I describe in this book.

14 Attewell, "Comment."

15 Labaree, "Public Goods, Private Goods"; Labaree, *How to Succeed in School without Really Learning.*

16   Larry Cuban, *Oversold and Underused: Computers in the Classroom* (Cambridge, MA: Harvard University Press, 2003), 12.

17   Cuban, *Oversold and Underused*, 15.

18   National Telecommunications and Information Administration, *Falling through the Net: A Survey of the "Have Nots" in Rural and Urban America* (Washington, DC: US Department of Commerce, 1995); National Telecommunications and Information Administration, *Falling through the Net II: New Data on the Digital Divide* (Washington, DC: US Department of Commerce, 1998).

19   Jennifer Light, "Rethinking the Digital Divide," *Harvard Educational Review* 71, no. 4 (2001): 710–34, at 711.

20   Light, "Rethinking the Digital Divide," 716.

21   Joy Lisi Rankin, *A People's History of Computing in the United States.* (Cambridge, MA: Harvard University Press, 2018), 4.

22   Rankin, *People's History of Computing*, 4.

23   Laura DeNardis, *The Global War for Internet Governance* (New Haven, CT: Yale University Press, 2014).

24   National Telecommunications and Information Administration, *The National Information Infrastructure: Agenda for Action* (Washington, DC: US Department of Commerce, 1993).

25   On whites being more likely to have internet access, see National Telecommunications and Information Administration, *Falling through the Net*. On controlling for socioeconomic background, see Debabrata Talukdar and Dinesh K. Gauri, "Home Internet Access and Usage in the USA: Trends in the Socio-Economic Digital Divide," *Communications of the Association for Information Systems* 28, no. 7 (2011): 85–98.

26   Hiroshi Ono and Madeline Zavodny, "Immigrants, English Ability and the Digital Divide," *Social Forces* 86, no. 4 (June 2008): 1455–80; Lu Wei and Douglas Blanks Hindman, "Does the Digital Divide Matter More? Comparing the Effects of New Media and Old Media Use on the Education-Based Knowledge Gap," *Mass Communication and Society* 14, no. 2 (2011): 216–35.

27   Celeste Campos-Castillo, "Revisiting the First-Level Digital Divide in the United States: Gender and Race/Ethnicity Patterns, 2007-2012," *Social Science Computer Review* 33, no. 4 (2015): 423–39.

28   Amy Gonzales, "The Contemporary US Digital Divide: From Initial Access to Technology Maintenance," *Information, Communication and Society* 19, no. 2 (2015): 234–48.

29   This disparity was first called the "differentiated use" perspective, rather than the second level of the digital divide. See DiMaggio et al., "From Unequal Access to Differentiated Use"; van Deursen and van Dijk, "Digital Divide Shifts"; Attewell, "Comment"; Hargittai, "Second-Level Digital Divide."

30   On new media literacies, see New London Group, "A Pedagogy of Multiliteracies: Designing Social Futures." *Harvard Educational Review* 66, no. 1 (April 1996): 60–92. On information, media, and technology skills, see Partnership for 21st Century Skills, *Framework for 21st Century Learning*. On computer, information, multimedia, and computer mediated communication literacies, see Warschauer, *Technology and Social Inclusion*. On "participatory culture" skill,

see Jenkins et al., "Confronting the Challenges of Participatory Culture." On Web 2.0 skill, see Chris Dede, "A Seismic Shift in Epistemology," *EDUCAUSE Review* 43, no. 3 (2008): 80–81. On operational, information, and strategic skill, see van Deursen and van Dijk, "Internet Skills and the Digital Divide." On computer skill, see Maria Paino and Linda A. Renzulli, "Digital Dimension of Cultural Capital: The (In)Visible Advantages for Students Who Exhibit Computer Skills," *Sociology of Education* 86, no. 2 (2013): 124–38. On web use skill, see Hargittai, "Survey Measures of Web-Oriented Digital Literacy." On internet skill, see Alexander J. A. M. van Deursen, Ellen J. Helsper, and Rebecca Eynon, "Development and Validation of the Internet Skills Scale (ISS)," *Information, Communication and Society* 19, no. 6 (2016): 804–23.

31 Paul DiMaggio and Bart Bonikowski, "Make Money Surfing the Web? The Impact of Internet Use on the Earnings of U.S. Workers." *American Sociological Review* 73, no. 2 (April 2008): 227–50; Kerry Dobransky and Eszter Hargittai, "Inquiring Minds Acquiring Wellness: Uses of Online and Offline Sources for Health Information," *Health Communication* 27, no. 4 (2012): 331–43; Paino and Renzulli, "Digital Dimension of Cultural Capital."

32 Margolis et al., *Stuck in the Shallow End.*

33 Margolis et al., *Stuck in the Shallow End*, chap. 2, esp. pp. 36–37.

34 Margolis et al., *Stuck in the Shallow End*, chap. 4.

35 Jane Margolis and Allan Fisher, *Unlocking the Clubhouse: Women in Computing* (Cambridge, MA: MIT Press, 2002).

36 Catherine Hill, Christianne Corbett, and Andresse St. Rose, *Why So Few? Women in Science, Technology, Engineering, and Mathematics* (Washington, DC: American Association of University Women, 2010); Linda J. Sax et al., "Anatomy of an Enduring Gender Gap: The Evolution of Women's Participation in Computer Science," *Journal of Higher Education* 88, no. 2 (2017): 258–93; Wendy DuBow and J. J. Gonzalez, *NCWIT Scorecard: The Status of Women in Technology* (Boulder, CO: National Center for Women and Information Technology, 2020).

37 DiMaggio et al., "From Unequal Access to Differentiated Use."

38 Richard Arum and Josipa Roksa, *Academically Adrift: Limited Learning on College Campuses* (Chicago: University of Chicago Press, 2011); Randall Collins, *The Credential Society: An Historical Sociology of Education and Stratification* (New York: Academic Press, 1979).

39 Hargittai and Hsieh, "Succinct Survey Measures of Web-Use Skills"; van Deursen and van Dijk, "Internet Skills and the Digital Divide."

40 Cassidy Puckett, "CS4Some? Differences in Technology Learning Readiness." *Harvard Educational Review* 89, no. 4 (2019): 554–87; M. Smith, "Computer Science for All."

41 Yasmiyn Irizarry, "Selling Students Short: Racial Differences in Teachers' Evaluations of High, Average, and Low Performing Students," *Social Science Research* 52 (July 2015): 522–38; Douglas C. Ready and David L. Wright, "Accuracy and Inaccuracy in Teachers' Perceptions of Young Children's Cognitive Abilities: The Role of Child Background and Classroom Context," *American Educational Research Journal* 48, no. 2 (2011): 335–60.

42   For a full discussion of skills, literacies, and the ability to adapt to technological change, see Puckett, "Digital Adaptability."

43   See Alexander J. A. M. van Deursen and Ellen J. Helsper, "The Third-Level Digital Divide: Who Benefits Most from Being Online?" in *Communication and Information Technologies Annual Studies in Media and Communications*, ed. Laura Robinson et al. (Bingley, UK: Emerald Group, 2015), 29–52. I view this work as similar to a "capabilities" approach in economics, where the central concern is if individuals are able to convert resources into reward and live a full life, rather than just focusing on whether they can access resources. See Martha C. Nussbaum and Amartya K. Sen, *The Quality of Life* (Oxford: Clarendon Press, 1993).

44   Van Deursen and Helsper, "Third-Level Digital Divide."

45   Janet Abbate, *Recoding Gender: Women's Changing Participation in Computing* (Cambridge, MA: MIT Press, 2012).

46   Rafalow, "Disciplining Play."

47   Safiya Umoja Noble, *Algorithms of Oppression: How Search Engines Reinforce Racism* (New York: NYU Press, 2018).

48   Joy Buolamwini and Timnit Gebru, "Gender Shades: Intersectional Accuracy Disparities in Commercial Gender Classification," in *Proceedings of Machine Learning Research* 81 (2018): 1–15, https://proceedings.mlr.press/v81/buolamwini18a/buolamwini18a.pdf. See also Ruha Benjamin, *Race After Technology: Abolitionist Tools for the New Jim Code* (Medford, MA: Polity, 2019).

49   On how democratic equality suggests schools develop in students a common set of broad competencies, see Labaree, *How to Succeed in School without Really Learning*, 19–22; Labaree, "Public Goods, Private Goods," 43–46.

50   Janet Abbate, "Code Switch: Alternative Visions of Computer Expertise as Empowerment from the 1960s to the 2010s," *Technology and Culture* 59, no. 4 (2018): S134–S59.

51   Labaree, *How to Succeed in School without Really Learning*, 18.

52   Labaree, *How to Succeed in School without Really Learning*, 18.

53   Andrew Hussey and Michael Jetter, "Long Term Trends in Fair and Unfair Inequality in the United States," *Applied Economics* 29, no. 1 (2016): 1–17.

54   US Department of Education National Commission of Excellence in Education, *A Nation at Risk: The Imperative for Educational Reform* (Washington, D.C.: US Government Printing Office, 1983), 5.

55   National Research Council, *Rising above the Gathering Storm*, 3–4.

56   Rafael Alarcon, "Recruitment Processes among Foreign-Born Engineers and Scientists in Silicon Valley," *American Behavioral Scientist* 42, no. 9 (1999): 1381–97; Alejandro Portes and Rubén G. Rumbaut, *Immigrant America: A Portrait*, 3rd ed. (Berkeley, CA: University of California Press, 2006).

57   For example, see Sylvia Hurtado et al., "Diversifying Science: Underrepresented Students' Experiences in Structured Research Programs," *Research in Higher Education* 50, no. 2 (March 2009): 189–214. They state in their introduction on page 189, "Increasing the number of students completing advanced scientific degrees that lead to scientific research careers is critical to national interests. A declining cadre of skilled workers for scientific fields portends a decline in U.S. global competitiveness and the exportation of high-skill jobs to

other countries. . . . National efforts are now focused on purposefully reversing these trends. Indeed, *Rising above the Gathering Storm* . . . was a strong call to action that resulted in passage of the 2007 America Competes Act to strengthen science-related education, programs, and research," which implies that increased competitiveness will improve society—yet, the growth of the tech industry and increasing inequality suggests otherwise. At the same time, it should be noted that the authors demonstrate the role that racism plays in barring well-qualified undergraduate students from STEM fields.

58   Labaree, *How to Succeed in School without Really Learning*, 25.

59   Abbate, "Code Switch."

60   In fact, "high-skill" jobs have seen a slowdown—see David Autor, "Why Are There Still So Many Jobs? The History and Future of Workplace Automation," *Journal of Economic Perspectives* 29, no. 3 (2015): 3–30.

61   Stephen J. McNamee and Robert K. Miller Jr., *The Meritocracy Myth* (Lanham, MD: Rowman and Littlefield, 2004).

62   Ensmenger, *Computer Boys Take Over*.

63   Ensmenger, *Computer Boys Take Over*, 62.

64   Abbate, *Recoding Gender*; Clive Thompson, *Coders: The Making of a New Tribe and the Remaking of the World* (New York: Penguin, 2019); Ensmenger, *Computer Boys Take Over*.

65   Ensmenger, *Computer Boys Take Over*, 77–78.

66   Abbate, *Recoding Gender*; Thompson, *Coders*.

67   Ensmenger, *Computer Boys Take Over*, 78–79.

68   Ensmenger, *Computer Boys Take Over*, 80.

69   For studies of Asian groups (both US-born and non-US-born) in Silicon Valley in the 1990s, see Wong, *Chinese in Silicon Valley*; Shalini Shankar, *Desi Land: Teen Culture, Class, and Success in Silicon Valley* (Durham, NC: Duke University Press, 2008).

70   Labaree, *How to Succeed in School without Really Learning*.

71   Labaree, *How to Succeed in School without Really Learning*, 18.

72   *If offered* is a key phrase here. Many low-income urban school districts, like Oakland, offer few technology courses—particularly at the time that I was teaching (in the first decade of the twenty-first century). In some cities this inequity is changing with "Computer Science For All" or "CS4All" initiatives. See Office of Innovation and Improvement, *Computer Science For All Fact Sheet*. (Washington, DC: U.S. Department of Education, 2016). On STEM education as preparation for college technology courses leading to higher-skill, higher-wage technology jobs, see Xie, Fang, and Shauman, "STEM Education"; Arne L. Kalleberg, *Good Jobs, Bad Jobs: The Rise of Polarized and Precarious Employment Systems in the United States, 1970s–2000s*, American Sociological Association Rose Series in Sociology (New York: Russell Sage Foundation, 2011); D. Langdon et al., *STEM: Good Jobs Now and for the Future*. (Washington, DC: US Department of Commerce Economics and Statistics Administration, 2011), https://files.eric.ed.gov /fulltext/ED522129.pdf.

73   Margolis et al., *Stuck in the Shallow End*; Margolis and Fisher, *Unlocking the Clubhouse*; Abbate, *Recoding Gender*; Thompson, *Coders*; Alison T. Wynn and Shelley

Correll, "Puncturing the Pipeline: Do Technology Companies Alienate Women in Recruiting Sessions?" *Social Studies of Science* 48, no. 1 (2018): 149–64.

74 Amy J. Binder, Daniel B. Davis, and Nick Bloom. 2016. "Career Funneling: How Elite Students Learn to Define and Desire 'Prestigious' Jobs," *Sociology of Education* 89, no. 1 (2016): 20–39.

75 As Ensmenger notes, computer programmers and other technology-related workers have "assumed an increasingly active and visible role in the shaping of our modern information society. . . . In recent years, 'computer people' have become some of our wealthiest citizens, most important business leaders and philanthropists, and most recognized celebrities." Ensmenger, *Computer Boys Take Over*, 1.

76 Stephen B. Adams, "Growing Where You Are Planted: Exogenous Firms and the Seeding of Silicon Valley," *Research Policy* 40, no. 3 (2011): 368–79.

77 Citing sociologist Ulrich Bech, education historian David Labaree suggests that this "elevator effect" occurs in education when "educational access steadily grows, average levels of schooling keep rising, and the relative advantage among social groups remains the same. . . . Every time you raise the floor, you also raise the ceiling." Labaree, *Perfect Mess*, 97. This dynamic suggests that if the *individual advantage* perspective continues to dominate technology education and occupations, as initiatives like Hour of Code and CSforAll increase access to computing education, new qualifications may be added at advanced tiers to justify the continued exclusion of women and historically marginalized groups from more powerful and well-compensated roles.

78 Anne Witz, *Professions and Patriarchy* (New York: Routledge, 1992); Ron D. Dempsey, *The Role of Engineering Technology as a Pathway for African Americans into the Field of Engineering* (Atlanta: Georgia Institute of Technology, 2018).

79 Labaree, *How to Succeed in School without Really Learning*, 19.

80 Robert Post, "Democracy and Equality," *Annals of the American Academy of Political and Social Science* 603 (January 2006): 24–36, at 28.

81 Peggy A. Ertmer and Timothy J. Newby, "The Expert Learner: Strategic, Self-Regulated, and Reflective," *Instructional Science* 24, no. 1 (January 1996): 1–24, at 1.

82 John Bransford, Anne L. Brown, and Rodney R. Cocking, *How People Learn: Brain, Mind, Experience, and School*, expanded ed. (Washington, DC: National Academies Press, 2000); Fernand Gobet, *Understanding Expertise: A Multi-Disciplinary Approach* (London: Palgrave, 2016).

83 Habit was a central concept in early sociological theory, then became less so with the advent of behaviorism, then made a resurgence in more recent scholarship. See: Charles Camic, "The Matter of Habit," *American Journal of Sociology* 91, no. 5 (1986): 1039–87; Neil Gross, "A Pragmatist Theory of Social Mechanisms," *American Sociological Review* 74, no. 3 (June 2009): 358–79. In this book, I primarily draw on Bourdieu's concept of "habitus" and theory of fields, applied to technological fields. See Pierre Bourdieu, *Distinction: A Social Critique of the Judgement of Taste* (Cambridge, MA: Harvard University Press, 1984).

84 Cheryan et al., "Ambient Belonging"; Cheryan et al., "Stereotypical Computer Scientist"; Aparna Joshi, "By Whom and When Is Women's Expertise Recog-

nized? The Interactive Effects of Gender and Education in Science and Engineering Teams," *Administrative Science Quarterly* 59, no. 2 (2014): 202–39.

85 Research shows that extracurriculars are crucial for all students' development, but particularly for historically marginalized students. The skills, habits, knowledge, and connections students develop in such experiences can help increase self-esteem and resilience, academic performance, entry into college, job earnings, and even the likelihood of voting and engaging in politics. In STEM, extracurricular participation supports students' aspirations and later achievement in these fields, in higher education and beyond. This participation is important for historically marginalized students because they can gain more from these experiences than already advantaged students. For technology learning more specifically, research shows less tech learning occurs *during* the school day than *outside* school. Extracurricular programs are a key site for technology learning that can serve a wide range of students, if observing in the right places. Yet, more affluent white and Asian males do dominate STEM extracurricular activities. See Amy F. Feldman and Jennifer L. Matjask, "The Role of School-Based Extracurricular Activities in Adolescent Development: A Comprehensive Review and Future Directions," *Review of Educational Research* 75, no. 2 (2005): 159–210; Benjamin G. Gibbs et al., "Extracurricular Associations and College Enrollment," *Social Science Research* 50 (March 2015): 367–81; Jennifer Glanville, "Political Socialization or Selection? Adolescent Extracurricular Participation and Political Activity in Early Adulthood," *Social Science Quarterly* 80, no. 2 (1999): 279–90; Katherine P. Dabney et al., "Out-of-School Time Science Activities and Their Association with Career Interest in STEM," *International Journal of Science Education* 2, no. 1 (2012): 63–79; Joseph A. Kitchen, Gerhard Sonnert, and Philip M. Sadler, "The Impact of College- and University-Run High School Summer Programs on Students' End of High School STEM Career Aspirations," *Science Education* 102, no. 3 (May 2018): 529–47; Elizabeth Covay and William Carbonaro, "After the Bell: Participation in Extracurricular Activities, Classroom Behavior, and Academic Achievement," *Sociology of Education* 83, no. 1 (2010): 20–45; Ann Meier, Benjamin Swartz Hartmann, and Ryan Larson, "A Quarter Century of Participation in School-Based Extracurricular Activities: Inequalities by Race, Class, Gender and Age?" *Journal of Youth and Adolescence* 47, no. 6 (2018): 1299–1316; Ingrid A. Nelson, *Why Afterschool Matters* (New Brunswick, NJ: Rutgers University Press, 2016).

86 The term *historically marginalized* places the onus for their exclusion on gatekeepers, as compared to the term *underrepresented*, which does not specify the mechanism of exclusion, so I use the former throughout the book, as part of my argument that gatekeeping is what needs to be fixed, not the kids. I include in this group African American/Black (in the book, I use the terms interchangeably), African (immigrated from an African country, or I specify country if the student shared this information), Native American, and Latinx (I observed primarily students who were born in or have families from Puerto Rico, the Dominican Republic, Mexico, or Central American countries). It should be noted that there is much contention over the term *Latinx* and the category of "Hispanic," see Mark Hugo Lopez, Jens Manuel Krogstad, and Jeffrey S.

Passel, "Who Is Hispanic?" Fact Tank, Pew Research Center, September 15, 2020, https://www.pewresearch.org/fact-tank/2019/11/11/who-is-hispanic/). Although I did not ask students to self-identify by race, ethnicity, gender, or socioeconomic status, I requested general demographic information from programs and noted when students self-identified along these dimensions during observations or interviews. I also identify program director and instructor race throughout the book, as I believe it is key to note the fact that many (although not all) programs are representative of the students they serve.

Research suggests that the context of learning defines what is and is not "legitimate" practice, which shapes whether or not student STEM skills are recognized as such. See, for example: Christo Sims, "From Differentiated Use to Differentiating Practices: Negotiating Legitimate Participation and the Production of Privileged Identities," *Information, Communication and Society* 17, no. 6 2014): 670–82; Na'ilah Suad Nasir, Victoria Hand, and Edd V. Taylor, "Culture and Mathematics in School: Boundaries between "Cultural" and "Domain" Knowledge in the Mathematics Classroom and Beyond," *Review of Research in Education* 32 (2008): 187–240. In tech specifically, research also shows there are ongoing barriers to full participation in tech fields, despite nascent talent among historically marginalized groups. See Watkins et al., *Digital Edge*.

87   Many researchers and educators only use the acronym STEAM, which adds an *A* for arts embedded in STEM-related activities. I see creative activity as fundamentally intertwined in STEM, and arts activities were included in all the programs I observed, including ones focused specifically on science or technology. I also speak to a literature that solely uses the STEM acronym, so I chose not to use STEAM in the majority of this book. However, I understand and agree with those who argue for the addition of the *A* as a political move for the inclusion of arts/creative production. See Kylie Peppler and Karen Wohlwend, "Theorizing the Nexus of STEAM Practice." *Arts Education Policy Review* 119, no. 2 (2018): 88–99; Kylie Peppler, "STEAM-Powered Computing Education: Using E-Textiles to Integrate the Arts and STEM," *Computer* 46 (September 2013): 38–43, https://www.computer.org/csdl/magazine/co/2013/09/mco2013090038/13rRUxoxPP9.

88   Brigid Barron et al., *The Digital Youth Network: Cultivating Digital Media Citizenship in Urban Communities* (Cambridge, MA: MIT Press, 2014). In Chicago, a 2018 report on computer science learning opportunities produced by the Chicago City of Learning at Northwestern's School of Education and Social Policy Office of Community Education Partnerships showed there were at least forty-two organizations—like the ones described in this chapter—providing technology learning opportunities. Out of Chicago's seventy-seven neighborhoods, they found that sixty-seven had at least one program teaching some form of computer science, although it is crucial to note that few offered training beyond the introductory level and of course not all teens participate in these introductory programs. Chicago's recent Computer Science For All (CS4All) Initiative introduced more computer science courses into many high schools and some elementary and middle schools, but this initiative is also far from providing

universal access to technology training. So, while there are a substantial number of programs serving tech-savvy historically marginalized students, there is still a need for more technology training, particularly in terms of training for advanced technological skills. See Elena Smith, Chicago's Informal Computer Science Learning Landscape: Identifying and Connecting Chicago's Computer Science Learning Opportunities for Youth. (Chicago: Chicago City of Learning at the Northwestern School of Education and Social Policy Office of Community Education Partnerships, 2018); Puckett, "CS4Some?"

89 See, e.g., Michael Cole and the Distributed Literacy Consortium, *The Fifth Dimension: An After-School Program Built on Diversity* (New York: Russell Sage Foundation, 2006); Yasmin B. Kafai, Kylie Peppler, and Robbin Chapman, *The Computer Clubhouse: Constructionism and Creativity in Youth Communities* (New York: Teachers College Press, 2009); James-Burdumy et al., *When Schools Stay Open Late: The National Evaluation of the 21st Century Community Learning Centers Program; Final Report* (Washington, DC: US Department of Education, Institute of Education Sciences, National Center for Education Evaluation and Regional Assistance, 2005).

90 Skyline is a Title I school (i.e., 40 percent or more students are from low-income families) in Oakland, CA and is predominantly Black and Latinx (31% and 40%, respectively, according to 2017–2018 data from the National Center for Education Statistics). "Christine" is a pseudonym; as explained in note 1 to the introduction, all names of students in this book, other than my own students (who are now adults and gave permission to use their real names in the book), are pseudonyms. In many cases, I also made adjustments to such descriptors as height or hair color or used composites to make students less specifically identifiable.

91 At the time, Campbell Middle School included grades 5–8. The student body composition was 57.8 percent Latinx; 21.7 percent white; 10.2 percent Asian, Filipino, or Pacific Islander; 7.3 percent Black; 2.6 percent Multiracial; and less than 1 percent Native American. Among these students, 45.9 percent were eligible for free or reduced-price meals, and 29.4 percent were designated English Learners. The school has since been renamed Campbell School of Innovation, and it started transitioning to a K-8 school (kindergarten through eighth grade) in 2017. See Jasmin Levya, "Campbell Middle School Will Get a New Name Next Summer," *Mercury News* (San Francisco Bay Area), September 30, 2017, https://www.mercurynews.com/2017/09/30/campbell-middle-school-will-get-a-new-name-next-summer/.

CHAPTER TWO

1 See Christopher Emdin, "The Rap Cypher, the Battle, and Reality Pedagogy: Developing Communication and Argumentation in Urban Science Education," in *Schooling Hip-Hop: Expanding Hip-Hop Based Education across the Curriculum*, ed. M. L. Hill and E. Petchauer (New York: Teachers College Press, 2013), 11–27.

2   This approach borrows from research in cognitive psychology on how people learn, where expertise is studied to understand and develop it in learners. See Gobet, *Understanding Expertise.*

3   Patricia A. Alexander and Judith E. Judy, "The Interaction of Domain-Specific and Strategic Knowledge in Academic Performance," *Review of Educational Research* 58, no. 4 (1988): 375–404; John H. Flavell, "Metacognition and Cognitive Monitoring: A New Area of Cognitive–Developmental Inquiry," *American Psychologist* 34, no. 10 (1979): 906–11; Ruth Schoenbach et al., "Apprenticing Adolescents to Reading in Subject-Area Classrooms," *Phi Delta Kappan* 85, no. 2 (October 2003): 133–38.

4   Karin Knorr Cetina, *Epistemic Cultures: How the Sciences Make Knowledge* (Cambridge, MA: Harvard University Press, 1999).

5   USB, which stands for *universal serial bus*, is a standardized serial computer interface that allows simplified attachment of peripherals, such as a mouse or a flash drive. CPU stands for *central processing unit*, the component of a computer system that performs the basic operations (such as processing data) of the system, that exchanges data with the system's memory or peripherals, and that manages the system's other components.

6   Albert Bandura, "Self-Efficacy: Toward a Unifying Theory of Behavioral Change," *Psychological Review* 84, no. 2 (1977): 191–215, at 193.

7   There is some ongoing controversy on this point—whether there is a distinction between being "willing" or being "able." See Shawn P. Cahill et al., "Willing or Able? The Meanings of Self-Efficacy," *Journal of Social and Clinical Psychology* 25, no. 2 (2006): 196–209; Albert Bandura, "Much Ado over a Faulty Conception of Self-Perceived Efficacy Grounded in Faulty Experimentation," *Journal of Social and Clinical Psychology* 26, no. 6 (2007): 641–58.

8   Hubbard High School in Chicago was 94.37 percent low income in 2009–2010, according to Chicago Public Schools data. Chicago Public Schools, "District Data Demographics," https://www.cps.edu/about/district-data/demographics/.

9   Ramsey F. Hamade, Hassan A. Artail, and Mohamad Y. Jaber, "A Study of the Impact of the Willingness-to-Learn of CAD Novice Users on their Competence Development," *Computers and Industrial Engineering* 61, no. 3 (2011): 709–20.

10   Amber Simpson and Adam V. Maltese, "'Failure Is a Major Component of Learning Anything': The Role of Failure in the Development of STEM Professionals," *Journal of Science Education and Technology* 26, no. 2 (2017): 223–37; Christian Sandvig, "How Technical Is Technology Research?" in *Research Confidential: Solutions to Problems Most Social Scientists Pretend They Never Have*, ed. Eszter Hargittai (Ann Arbor: University of Michigan Press, 2009).

11   Dweck, *Mindset*; Jeni L. Burnette et al., "Mindsets Matter: A Meta-Analytic Review of Implicit Theories and Self-Regulation," *Psychological Bulletin* 139, no. 3 (2013): 655–701.

12   Na'ilah Suad Nasir, *Racialized Identities: Race and Achievement among African American Youth* (Stanford, CA: Stanford University Press, 2011); Geneva Gay, *Culturally Responsive Teaching: Theory, Research, and Practice*, 3rd ed. (New York:

Teachers College Press, 2018); Gloria Ladson-Billings, "Culturally Relevant Pedagogy 2.0: a.k.a. the Remix," *Harvard Educational Review* 84, no. 1 (2014): 74–84.

13 Dale H. Schunk, "Inherent Details of Self-Regulated Learning Include Student Perceptions," *Educational Psychologist* 30, no. 4 (1995): 213–16; Monique Boekaerts, "Self-Regulated Learning: Where We Are Today," *International Journal of Educational Research* 31, no. 6 (1999): 445–57.

14 Bandura, "Much Ado over a Faulty Conception," 647.

15 In 2008–2009, 57.8 percent of students at Galileo High were eligible for free and reduced-price meals (FRPM), according to a California Department of Education (CDE) DataQuest query (selecting "school level," "free and reduced price meals," "2008-2009," and "Galileo High"), accessed June 1, 2021, https://dq.cde.ca.gov/dataquest/dataquest.asp. More recent school-level downloadable data files are available on the CDE Student Poverty FRPM Data webpage, https://www.cde.ca.gov/ds/ad/filessp.asp.

16 Carole Ames and Jennifer Archer, "Achievement Goals in the Classroom: Students' Learning Strategies and Motivation Processes," *Journal of Educational Psychology* 80, no. 3 (1988): 260–67; Carole Ames, "Classrooms: Goals, Structures, and Student Motivation," *Journal of Educational Psychology* 84, no. 3 (1992): 261–71; Carol Dweck and Lisa A. Sorich, "Mastery-Oriented Thinking," in *Coping: The Psychology of What Works*, ed. C. R. Snyder (New York: Oxford University Press, 1999), 232–51.

17 Mihaly Csikszentmihalyi, *Flow: The Psychology of Optimal Experience* (New York: HarperCollins, 1990)s; Mihaly Csikszentmihalyi, *The Systems Model of Creativity: The Collected Works of Mihaly Csikszentmihalyi* (Dordrecht, Neth.: Springer, 2014).

18 Mihaly Csikszentmihalyi, Monica N. Montijo, and Angela R. Mouton, "Flow Theory: Optimizing Elite Performance in the Creative Realm," in *APA Handbook of Giftedness and Talent*, ed. Steven I. Pfeiffer, Elizabeth Shaunessy-Dedrick, and Megan Foley-Nicpon (Washington, DC: American Psychological Association, 2018), 215–29.

19 Michael Cole and Yrjö Engeström, "A Cultural-Historical Approach to Distributed Cognition," in *Distributed Cognitions: Psychological and Educational Considerations*, ed. Gavriel Salomon (New York: Cambridge University Press, 1993), 88–110; Yrjö Engeström, *Learning by Expanding: An Activity-Theoretical Approach to Developmental Research* (1987; repr., New York: Cambridge University Press, 2015); Kris D. Gutiérrez and Barbara Rogoff, "Cultural Ways of Learning: Individual Traits or Repertoires of Practice," *Educational Researcher* 32, no. 5 (2003): 19–25.

20 Sandvig, "How Technical Is Technology Research?" 153–54.

21 Sandvig, "How Technical Is Technology Research?" 151.

22 Gina Neff and David Stark, "Permanently Beta: Responsive Organization in the Internet Era," in *Society Online: The Internet in Context*, ed. Philip Howard and Steve Jones (Thousand Oaks, CA: Sage, 2004), 173–88, at 175.

23 M. Kay Alderman, *Motivation for Achievement: Possibilities for Teaching and*

Learning (New York: Routledge, 2008); Dale H. Schunk and Barry J. Zimmerman, *Motivation and Self-Regulated Learning: Theory, Research, and Applications* (New York: Erlbaum, 2008).

24 Dale H. Schunk, "Self-Efficacy for Reading and Writing: Influence of Modeling, Goal Setting, and Self-Evaluation," *Reading and Writing Quarterly* 19, no. 2 (2003): 159–72.

25 Dale H. Schunk, "Social Cognitive Theory and Self-Regulated Learning., in *Self-Regulated Learning and Academic Achievement: Theoretical Perspectives*, ed. Barry J. Zimmerman and Dale H. Schunk (New York: Erlbaum), 125–51.

26 Research on mentors, for example, shows that having multiple mentors as a networked resource can be helpful to learning and development, in education and in the workplace. See L. L. Phillips-Jones, *Mentors and Protégés* (New York: Arbor House, 1982); S. Gayle Baugh and Terri A. Scandura, "The Effect of Multiple Mentors on Protégés' Attitudes toward the Work Setting," *Journal of Social Behavior and Personality* 14, no. 4 (1999): 503–21.

27 Campos-Castillo, "Revisiting the First-Level Digital Divide"; Edward Carlson and Justin Gross, "The State of the Urban/Rural Digital Divide," National Telecommunications and Information Administration (blog), August 10, 2016, https://www.ntia.doc.gov/blog/2016/state-urbanrural-digital-divide; Margolis et al., *Stuck in the Shallow End*.

28 On talent being devalued or policed, see Rafalow, "Disciplining Play"; Sims, "From Differentiated Use to Differentiating Practices."

CHAPTER THREE

1 On differences in computer science participation by gender, see Cheryan et al., "Why Are Some STEM Fields More Gender Balanced?"

2 Watkins et al., *Digital Edge*.

3 Jessica McCrory Calarco, "'I Need Help!' Social Class and Children's Help-Seeking in Elementary School," *American Sociological Review* 76, no. 6 (2011): 862–82; Annette Lareau, *Unequal Childhoods: Class, Race, and Family Life*, 2nd ed. (Los Angeles: University of California Press, 2011).

4 James H. Stronge, Thomas J. Ward, and Leslie W. Grant, "What Makes Good Teachers Good? A Cross-Case Analysis of the Connection between Teacher Effectiveness and Student Achievement," *Journal of Teacher Education* 62, no. 4 (2011): 339–55; James H. Stronge, *Qualities of Effective Teachers*, 3rd ed. (Alexandria, VA: Association for Supervision and Curriculum Development, 2018).

5 In related qualitative and quantitative work, I find that students' technology learning habits are linked with the practices they experience at home, but not family resources, most school practices, or school resources. See Puckett and Nelson, "Geek Instinct"; Puckett "CS4Some?"; Cassidy Puckett, "Technological Change, Digital Adaptability, and Social Inequality" (PhD diss., Evanston, IL: Northwestern University, 2015).

6 Human-centered design suggests that "successful" design feels "natural," congruent with expectations, and therefore the logic should take little to no effort

to understand. See Donald Norman, *The Design of Everyday Things* (New York: Basic Books, 1988). However, technologies are designed with particular users and logics in mind and therefore less "seamless" to those who do not fit the particular user profile. For example, Safiya Umoja Noble argues that even "neutral" algorithms baked into the design of technological systems are shaped by social processes and have biases embedded within them. See Umoja Noble, *Algorithms of Oppression.*

7   Renee Hobbs, "Multiple Visions of Multimedia Literacy: Emerging Areas of Synthesis," in *International Handbook of Literacy and Technology*, vol. 2, ed. Michael C. McKenna et al. (Mahwah, NJ: Erlbaum, 2006); Patricia Aufderheide, *Media Literacy: A Report of the National Leadership Conference on Media Literacy* (Queenstown, MD: Aspen Institute, 1993); New London Group, "Pedagogy of Multiliteracies."

8   This emphasis on English (and math) has been particularly true since No Child Left Behind (NCLB), an initiative which focuses heavily on testing in English and mathematics. Research shows that when things are quantified, people change their behavior in reaction to what is measured (called "reactivity"). In this case, as a result of NCLB's focus on English and math achievement, schools spend less time on other subject areas. See Wendy Nelson Espeland and Michael Sauder, "Rankings and Reactivity: How Public Measures Recreate Social Worlds," *American Journal of Sociology* 113, no. 1 (July 2007): 1–40; Jennifer McMurrer, *Choices, Changes, Challenges: Curriculum and Instruction in the NCLB Era* (Washington, DC: Center on Education Policy, 2007); Jennifer McMurrer, *Instructional Time in Elementary Schools: A Closer Look at Changes for Specific Subjects* (Washington, DC: Center on Education Policy, 2008); Kathleen K. Manzo, "Social Studies Losing Out to Reading, Math," *Education Week* 24, no. 27 (2005): 1–17.

9   Renee Hobbs, "The Seven Great Debates in the Media Literacy Movement," *Journal of Communication* 48, no. 1 (2006): 16–32.

10 James Paul Gee, *What Video Games Have to Teach Us about Learning and Literacy*, 2nd ed. (New York: St. Martin's Press, 2007).

11 Gee, *What Video Games Have to Teach Us*, 32.

12 Human-centered design calls this "affordances" (the range of possible things one can do with an object) and "constraints" (limitations to use). Donald Norman also discusses this; see Norman, *Design of Everyday Things.*

13 Constance Steinkuehler, foreword to *Connected Gaming: What Making Video Games Can Teach Us about Learning and Literacy*, ed. Yasmin B. Kafai and Quinn Burke (Cambridge, MA: MIT Press, 2016), xxii.

14 Philip Golden, Hervé Dedieu, and Krista S. Jacobsen, *Fundamentals of DSL Technology* (Boca Raton, FL: Auerbach Publications, 2006).

15 The "CoolSwitch" was once a technical term used to describe the keyboard command to switch between running programs (i.e., holding down the Alt or Command key and pressing the Tab key at the same time). See "Using Sneaky Key Commands" in Woody Leonhard, *Windows 7 All-in-One for Dummies* (Hoboken, NJ: Wiley, 2009).

16 Joel Krantz, *Pro Tools 10: Advanced Post Production Techniques* (Boston: Cengage Learning, 2013), 148–49.

17   Ulf Mellström, "Machines and Masculine Subjectivity: Technology as an Integral Part of Men's Life Experiences," *Men and Masculinities* 6, no. 4 (2004): 368–82, at 373 (emphasis mine).
18   Puckett, "CS4Some?"
19   Puckett, "Technological Change, Digital Adaptability, and Social Inequality."
20   Mellström, "Machines and Masculine Subjectivity," 375.
21   Ulf Mellström, "The Intersection of Gender, Race and Cultural Boundaries, or Why Is Computer Science in Malaysia Dominated by Women?" *Social Studies of Science* 39, no. 6 (2009): 885–907, at 886.
22   In chapter 4, I describe in brief the history and politics of measurement in education and how this context shaped my approach to measuring the five learning habits. For a related and extensive history of the Scholastic Aptitude Test (SAT), see Nicholas Lemann, *The Big Test: The Secret History of the American Meritocracy* (New York: Farrar, Straus and Giroux, 2000).
23   Lincoln Quillian et al., "Meta-Analysis of Field Experiments Shows No Change in Racial Discrimination in Hiring Over Time," *Proceedings of the National Academy of Sciences of the United States of America* 114, no. 41 (2017): 10870–75.
24   Joanna N. Lahey and Douglas R. Oxley, "Discrimination at the Intersection of Age, Race, and Gender: Evidence from a Lab-in-the-field Experiment (NBER Working Paper No. 25357, National Bureau of Economic Research, Cambridge, MA, 2018), 5.

CHAPTER FOUR

1   Prensky, "Digital Natives, Digital Immigrants."
2   Mitchel Resnick, "Sowing the Seeds for a More Creative Society," *Learning and Leading with Technology* 35, no. 4 (2007): 18–22.
3   George A. Bekey, *Autonomous Robots: From Biological Inspiration to Implementation and Control* (Cambridge, MA: MIT Press, 2005).
4   For debates about the notion of the "digital native," see Prensky, "Digital Natives, Digital Immigrants"; Palfrey and Gasser, *Born Digital*; Bennett, Maton, and Kervin, "'Digital Natives' Debate"; Eszter Hargittai, "Digital Na(t)ives? Variation in Internet Skills and Uses among Members of the 'Net Generation,'" *Sociological Inquiry* 80, no. 1 (February 2010): 92–113.
5   For example, Sumalee, whom I describe later in this chapter, solved the Scratch task without using mathematical knowledge; Scratch was created in such a way that students may apply existing mathematical knowledge, learn more about mathematics in service to learning the software, and/or apply the "design logic" of other programs to learn Scratch (like how to use design software).
6   Understanding brokerage has a long history in sociological research, although that is not the focus of this book. Brokering has been understood in different ways. It was first described in 1950 by Georg Simmel, based on the interaction of groups of three people, who theorized that a third-party influence (broker) could act as arbiter to unify or split the group, as the beneficiary of a separation between two others, or as social divider. See Georg Simmel, *The Sociology*

of Georg Simmel, ed. Kurt Wolff (New York: Free Press, 1950). In 1982, Peter V. Marsden defined *brokers* as intermediaries who facilitated connection to others, and in 2012, Katherine Stovel and Lynnette Shaw suggested brokers can connect individuals to resources. See Peter V. Marsden, "Brokerage Behavior in Restricted Exchange Networks," in *Social Structure and Network Analysis*, ed. Peter V. Marsden and Nan Lin (Beverly Hills, CA: Sage, 1982), 201–18; Katherine Stovel and Lynnette Shaw, "Brokerage," *Annual Review of Sociology* 38 (2012): 138–58. https://doi.org/10.1146/annurev-soc-081309-150054. For a comprehensive review, see Nir Halevy, Eliran Halali, and Julian J. Zlatev, "Brokerage and Brokering: An Integrative Review and Organizing Framework for Third Party Influence," *Academy of Management Annals* 13, no. 1 (2019): 215–39. Here, I use the term *learning broker* to emphasize the importance of these individuals for access to technology learning resources, following the work of Brigid Barron, Caitlin Kennedy Martin, Lori Takeuchi, and Rachel Fithian; See Brigid Barron et al., "Parents as Learning Partners in the Development of Technological Fluency," *International Journal of Learning and Media* 1, no. 2 (2009): 55–77. Also, although not focused on brokerage, in my survey of Chicago Public School students, I found that family practice was the most important factor in explaining differences in students' learning habits, net of the contribution of school (see Puckett, "CS4Some?").

7   Puckett and Nelson, "Geek Instinct."

8   "Think alouds" are also known as "protocol analysis," a common technique in cognitive science, psychology, and learning sciences, and in industry for usability or user experience (UX) research. See K. Anders Ericsson and Herbert A. Simon, *Protocol Analysis: Verbal Reports as Data*, rev. ed. (Boston, MA: MIT Press, 1993).

9   For perspectives on the definition and development of interest, see Jacquelynne S. Eccles, Allen Wigfield, and U. Schiefele, "Motivation to Succeed," in *Handbook of Child Psychology*, vol. 3, *Social, Emotional, and Personality Development*, 5th ed., edited by N. Eisenberg and W. Damon (New York: Wiley, 1998).

10   John Dewey, *Interest and Effort in Education* (Boston: Riverside, 1913).

11   Ann K. Renninger and Suzanne Hidi, *The Power of Interest for Motivation and Engagement* (New York: Routledge, 2016).

12   Suzanne Hidi and K. Ann Renninger, "The Four Phase Model of Interest Development," *Educational Psychologist* 41, no. 2 (2006): 111–27.

13   Dewey, *Interest and Effort in Education*, 197.

14   Dewey, *Interest and Effort in Education*, 197.

15   For a wonderful history about how social science, through the development of measures, influenced how people in the United States understand what it means to be American, see Sarah Igo, *The Averaged American: Surveys, Citizens, and the Making of a Mass Public* (Cambridge, MA: Harvard University Press, 2008).

16   See Robert J. Wright, *Educational Assessment: Tests and Measurements in the Age of Accountability* (Los Angeles: Sage, 2007), on the pros and cons of various forms of assessment, including portfolio assessments, which while time-consuming do have additional learning benefits.

17   Puckett, "CS4Some?"

18   Wendy Nelson Espeland and Mitchell Stevens, "Commensuration as a Social Process," *Annual Review of Sociology* 24 (1998): 313–43.

19   Ensmenger, *Computer Boys Take Over*, 69.

20   Roy Freedle, "Correcting the SAT's Ethnic and Social-Class Bias: A Method for Reestimating SAT Scores," *Harvard Educational Review* 73, no. 1 (2003): 1–43.

21   Maria Veronica Santelices and Mark Wilson, "Unfair Treatment? The Case of Freedle, the SAT, and the Standardization Approach to Differential Item Functioning," *Harvard Educational Review* 80, no. 1 (2010): 106–34.

22   Valerie Strauss, "Record Number of Colleges Drop SAT or ACT Admissions Requirement amid Growing Disenchantment with Standardized Tests," *Washington Post*, October 18, 2019, https://www.washingtonpost.com/education /2019/10/18/record-number-colleges-drop-satact-admissions-requirement -amid-growing-disenchantment-with-standardized-tests/.

23   Bruce L. Brown and Dawson Hedges, "Use and Misuse of Quantitative Methods: Data Collection, Calculation, and Presentation," in *The Handbook of Social Research Ethics*, ed. Donna M. Mertens and Pauline E. Ginsberg (Thousand Oaks, CA: Sage, 2009), 373–86, at 375.

24   On the "grit scale," see Duckworth et al., "Grit"; Teresa Garcia Duncan and Wilbert J. McKeachie, "The Making of the Motivated Strategies for Learning Questionnaire," *Educational Psychologist* 40, no. 2 (2005): 117–28.

25   Oliver P. John and Richard W. Robins, "Accuracy and Bias in Self-Perception: Individual Differences in Self-Enhancement and the Role of Narcissism," *Journal of Personality and Social Psychology* 66, no. 1 (1994): 206–19.

26   Paul R. Pintrich et al., "Reliability and Predictive Validity of the Motivated Strategies for Learning Questionnaire (MSLQ)," *Educational and Psychological Measurement* 53, no. 3 (1993): 801–13.

27   On content review, which is a common approach to scale development, see Robert F. DeVellis, *Scale Development: Theory and Applications* (Thousand Oaks, CA: Sage, 2012); Jum C. Nunnally and Ira H. Bernstein, *Psychometric Theory*, 3rd ed. (New York: McGraw-Hill, 1994). On cognitive interviews, see Laura M. Desimone and Kerstin Carlson Le Floch, "Are We Asking the Right Questions? Using Cognitive Interviews to Improve Surveys in Education Research," *Educational Evaluation and Policy Analysis* 26, no. 1 (2004): 1–22. On "average" CPS students, see Chicago Public Schools (CPS), *School Data: Demographics* (Chicago: CPS, 2019).

28   Linda K. Muthén and Bengt O. Muthén, *Mplus User's Guide, 7th ed.* (Los Angeles, CA: Muthén and Muthén, 2012); Rebecca Weston and Paul A. Gore Jr., "A Brief Guide to Structural Equation Modeling," *Counseling Psychologist* 34, no. 5 (2006): 719–51.

29   Donald T. Campbell and Donald W. Fiske, "Convergent and Discriminant Validation by the Multitrait-Multimethod Matrix," *Psychological Bulletin* 56, no. 2 (1959): 81–105.

30   For detailed methodological information about the development of the DAS, see Puckett, "Digital Adaptability: A New Measure for Digital Inequality Research."

31   Gail Chapman, "ECS Unit 4: Introduction to Programming; Introduction

and Daily Overview," CS for All Teachers, published March 28, 2013, https://csforallteachers.org/resource/ecs-unit-4-introduction-programming.

32   Puckett, "Digital Adaptability"; Puckett and Nelson, "Geek Instinct"; Puckett, "CS4Some?"

33   Lemann, *Big Test*.

34   Alan Schoenfeld, "Learning to Think Mathematically: Problem Solving, Metacognition, and Sense Making in Mathematics," in *Handbook for Research on Mathematics Teaching and Learning*, ed. Douglas Grouws (New York: MacMillan, 1992), 334–70.

35   Elaine Allensworth et al., "College Preparatory Curriculum for All: Academic Consequences of Requiring Algebra and English I for Ninth Graders in Chicago," *Educational Evaluation and Policy Analysis* 31, no. 4 (2009): 367–91; Thurston Domina et al., "Aiming High and Falling Short: California's Eighth-Grade Algebra-for-All Effort," *Educational Evaluation and Policy Analysis* 37, no. 3 (September 2015): 275–95; Frances R. Spielhagen, "Closing the Achievement Gap in Math: The Long-Term Effects of Eighth-Grade Algebra," *Journal of Advanced Academics* 18, no. 1 (2006): 34–59; Xueli Wang, "Why Students Choose STEM Majors: Motivation, High School Learning, and Postsecondary Context of Support," *American Educational Research Journal* 50, no. 5 (2013): 1081–1121.

36   There are extensive debates about the optimal number of points on a scale. See Jihyun Lee and Insu Paek, "In Search of the Optimal Number of Response Categories in a Rating Scale," *Journal of Psychoeducational Assessment* 32, no. 7 (2014): 663–73. I chose 6, with no midpoint, because, conceptually, I wanted respondents to make a decision (no/yes) and indicate the strength of that choice (1–3 or 4–6).

37   Puckett, "Digital Adaptability."

38   Laura Robinson et al., "Digital Inequalities and Why They Matter," *Information, Communication and Society* 18, no. 5 (2015): 569–82.

39   Chicago Public Schools (CPS), *New CPS Computer Science Graduation Requirement to Prepare Students for Jobs of the Future* (Chicago: CPS Office of Communications, 2016); Puckett, "CS4Some?"

40   On students' orienting beliefs, see, for example, Alan Schoenfeld's work on mathematics beliefs and learning—e.g., Alan H. Schoenfeld, "Students' Beliefs about Mathematics and Their Effects on Mathematical Performance: A Questionnaire Analysis" (paper presented at the annual meeting of the American Educational Research Association, New Orleans, 1985), ERIC Reproduction Service Document 259950; Alan H. Schoenfeld, "Explorations of Students' Mathematical Beliefs and Behavior," *Journal for Research in Mathematics Education* 20, no. 4 (1985): 338–55.

41   In the survey, I asked about twenty-one activities, based on a measure developed by Brigid Barron, and used the sum of these activities in my analysis. Activities included the following: created a multimedia presentation with pictures or movies using a program like PowerPoint; wrote code using a programming language like C, Java, Logo, Perl; made a publication such as a brochure using a program like Word; started your own newsgroup or discussion group on the internet; created a website using an application like Dreamweaver; made a

website using HTML [hypertext markup language]; published a site on the web so other people could see it; created a piece of art using an authoring tool like Photoshop or Aviary; designed a 2D or 3D model using a tool like AutoCAD or Modelshop; built a robot or created an invention of any kind using technology; used a simulation to model a real-life situation or set of data; made a database or created a spreadsheet in a program; created a digital movie; created an animation or cartoon; created a computer game using software like GameMaker, Scratch, etc.; created a piece of digital music using software like Pro Tools, GarageBand, etc.; played games using a computer or handheld device; analyzed data or calculated something using software like Excel; wrote a paper using a computer program like Microsoft Word; went online to get help from experts or mentors about a topic that interests me; participated in online projects (WebQuests, etc.). See Brigid Barron, "Learning Ecologies for Technological Fluency: Gender and Experience Differences," *Journal of Educational Computing Research* 31, no. 1 (2004): 1–36; Puckett, "CS4Some?"

42   Paino and Renzulli, "Digital Dimension of Cultural Capital."

43   Irizarry, "Selling Students Short"; Ready and Wright, "Accuracy and Inaccuracy in Teachers' Perceptions."

44   Margolis et al., *Stuck in the Shallow End*; Margolis and Fisher, *Unlocking the Clubhouse*; Sims, "From Differentiated Use to Differentiating Practices"; Rafalow, "Disciplining Play."

45   Cheryan et al., "Ambient Belonging."

CHAPTER FIVE

1   Maltese and Tai, "Pipeline Persistence."

2   For example, with a cultural shift in the "college-for-all" era, most students now aspire to go to college and will "hold steady" with these aspirations, even when they encounter barriers or are underprepared for college. See James Rosenbaum, *Beyond College for All* (New York: Russell Sage Foundation, 2001); Kelly Nielsen, "'Fake It 'til You Make It': Why Community College Students' Aspirations 'Hold Steady,'" *Sociology of Education* 88, no. 4 (2015): 265–83.

3   Puckett, "CS4Some?"

4   Jay W. Rojewski, "Occupational Aspirations: Constructs, Meanings, and Application," in *Career Development and Counseling: Putting Theory and Research to Work*, ed. Steven D. Brown and Robert W. Lent (Hoboken, NJ: John Wiley & Sons, 2005), 131–54, at 132.

5   See, e.g., Ashton D. Trice, "Stability of Children's Career Aspirations," *Journal of Genetic Psychology* 152, no. 1 (1991): 137–39; Ashton D. Trice and Nancy McClellan, "Do Children's Career Aspirations Predict Adult Occupations? An Answer from a Secondary Analysis of a Longitudinal Study," *Psychological Reports* 72, no. 2 (1993): 368–70; William H. Sewell, Archibald O. Haller, and Alejandro Portes, "The Educational and Early Occupational Attainment Process," *American Sociological Review* 34, no. 1 (1969): 82–92; Wei-Cheng Mau and

Lynette Heim Bikos, "Educational and Vocational Aspirations of Minority and Female Students: A Longitudinal Study," *Journal of Counseling and Development* 78, no. 2 (2000): 186–94; Kevin Marjoribanks, "Family Background, Individual and Environmental Influences, Aspirations and Young Adults' Educational Attainment: A Follow-Up Study," *Educational Studies* 29, no. 2–3 (2003): 233–42.

6   Ingrid Schoon, "Teenage Job Aspirations and Career Attainment in Adulthood: A 17-Year Follow-up Study of Teenagers Who Aspired to Become Scientists, Health Professionals, or Engineers," *International Journal of Behavioral Development* 25, no. 2 (2001): 124–32.

7   Sue A. Maple and Frances K. Stage, "Influences on the Choice of Math/Science Major by Gender and Ethnicity," *American Educational Research Journal* 28, no. 1 (1991): 37–60; Wang, "Why Students Choose STEM Majors"; Wei-Cheng Mau, "Factors that Influence Persistence in Science and Engineering Career Aspirations," *Career Development Quarterly* 51, no. 3 (2003): 234–43. Here, it should be noted that the majority of this research focuses on science and mathematics-related fields, not technology or engineering, although some research does include these fields. See also Adam V. Maltese and Robert H. Tai, "Eyeballs in the Fridge: Sources of Early Interest in Science," *International Journal of Science Education* 32, no. 5 (2010): 669–85; Maltese and Tai, "Pipeline Persistence"; Yu Xie and Kimberlee Shauman, *Women in Science: Career Processes and Outcomes* (Cambridge, MA: Harvard University Press, 2003); Joscha Legewie and Thomas A. DiPrete, "Pathways to Science and Engineering Bachelor's Degrees for Men and Women," *Sociological Science* 1 (February 18, 2014): 41–48.

8   Robert H. Tai et al., "Planning Early for Careers in Science," *Science* 312, no. 5777 (2006): 1143–44.

9   Steven L. Morgan, Dafna Gelbgiser, and Kim Weeden, "Feeding the Pipeline: Gender, Occupational Plans, and College Major Selection," *Social Science Research* 42, no. 4 (2013): 989–1005. For a comprehensive overview of the research on aspirations that takes an international perspective, see Maria Charles, "Venus, Mars, and Math: Gender, Societal Affluence, and Eighth Graders' Aspirations for STEM," *Socius* 3:1–16, published March 6, 2017, https://doi.org/10.1177/2378023117697179.

10   Tai et al., "Planning Early for Careers in Science."

11   Linda Seligman, Leslie Weinstock, and E. Neil Heflin, "The Career Development of 10 Year Olds," *Elementary School Guidance and Counseling* 25, no. 3 (1991): 172–81.

12   Richard W. Auger, Anne E. Blackhurst, and Kay Herting Wahl, "The Development of Elementary-Aged Children's Career Aspirations and Expectations," *Professional School Counseling* 8, no. 4 (2005): 322–29; Linda S. Gottfredson and Richard T. Lapan, "Assessing Gender-Based Circumscription of Occupational Aspirations," *Journal of Career Assessment* 5, no. 4 (1997): 419–41.

13   Albert Bandura et al., "Self Efficacy Beliefs as Shapers of Children's Aspirations and Career Trajectories," *Child Development* 72, no. 1 (2001): 187–206; Jacquelynne S. Eccles, "Understanding Women's Educational and Occupational Choices," *Psychology of Women Quarterly* 18, no. 4 (1994): 585–609.

14   Arthur L. Costa and Bena Kallick, *Learning and Leading with Habits of Mind: 16 Essential Characteristics for Success* (Alexandria, VA: Association for Supervision and Curriculum Development, 2008).

15   Erving Goffman, "On Cooling the Mark Out," *Psychiatry* 15, no. 4 (1952): 451–63; Jay MacLeod, *Ain't No Making It: Aspirations and Attainment in a Low-Income Neighborhood* (Boulder, CO: Westview Press, 1995); Burton R. Clark, "The 'Cooling Out' Function in Higher Education," *American Journal of Sociology* 65, no. 6 (1960): 569–76; Rosenbaum, *Beyond College for All*; Nielsen, "'Fake It 'til You Make It'"; Sarah M. Ovink, "In Today's Society, It's a Necessity: Latino/a Postsecondary Plans in the College-for-all Era," *Social Currents* 4, no. 2 (2016): 128–45.

16   Alexandria Walton Radford, *Top Student, Top School? How Social Class Shapes Where Valedictorians Go to College* (Chicago: University of Chicago Press, 2013).

17   Louise Archer, Jennifer DeWitt, and Billy Wong, "Spheres of Influence: What Shapes Young People's Aspirations at Age 12/13 and What Are the Implications for Education Policy?" *Journal of Education Policy* 29, no. 1 (2014): 58–85; Nancy E. Hill et al., "Parent Academic Involvement as Related to School Behavior, Achievement, and Aspirations: Demographic Variations across Adolescence," *Child Development* 75, no. 5 (2004): 1491–1509.

18   Jill M. Bystydzienski, Margaret Eisenhart, and Monica Bruning, "High School Is Not Too Late: Developing Girls' Interest and Engagement in Engineering Careers," *Career Development Quarterly* 63, no. 1 (2015): 88–95.

19   Shelley J. Correll, "Constraints into Preferences: Gender, Status and Emerging Career Aspirations," *American Sociological Review* 69, no. 1 (February 2004): 93–133; Grace Kao and Marta Tienda, "Educational Aspirations of Minority Youth," *American Journal of Education* 106, no. 3 (May 1998): 349–84; Trice and McClellan, "Do Children's Career Aspirations Predict Adult Occupations?"

20   Morgan, Gelbgiser, and Weeden, "Feeding the Pipeline"; Jonathan Osborne, Shirley Simon, and Sue Collins, "Attitudes Toward Science: A Review of the Literature and its Implications," *International Journal of Science Education* 25, no. 9 (2003): 1049–79; Xie, Fang, and Shauman, "STEM Education."

21   Puckett, "CS4Some?"; Charles, "Venus, Mars, and Math." While beyond the scope of this book, it's important to note that the large majority of research on gender disparities in STEM has treated gender as strictly binary, particularly at the K–12 level. For example, in an analysis of how articles published in the *Journal of Engineering Education* (*JEE*) 1998–2012 analyzed gender, Alice L. Pawley, Corey Schimpf, and Lindsey Nelson noted that the terms *cisgender*, *transgender*, and *agender* did not appear in any article. However, students may self-identify as "nonbinary," "non-gender-conforming," "gender fluid," "gender queer," and other ways to identify gender and sexuality—and these groups are likely to experience marginalization in STEM. For example, in a recent study of lesbian, gay, bisexual, transgender, and queer (LGBTQ) college students enrolled in eight US engineering programs, Erin A. Cech and William R. Rothwell found that these groups face greater marginalization, devaluation, and health difficulties than their non-LGBTQ peers. Similarly, using a nationally representative data set of college students, Bryce E. Hughes found that lesbian, gay, bisexual,

and queer students are less likely to persist in STEM compared to their heterosexual peers. More research treating gender in a nonbinary way is needed at the K–12 level. See Alice L. Pawley, Corey Schimpf, and Lindsey Nelson, "Gender in Engineering Education Research: A Content Analysis of Research in *JEE*," *Journal of Engineering Education* 105, no. 3 (July 2016): 508–28; Erin A. Cech and William R. Rothwell, "LGBTQ Inequality in Engineering Education," *Journal of Engineering Education* 107, no. 4 (2018): 583–610; and Bryce E. Hughes, "Coming Out in STEM: Factors Affecting Retention of Sexual Minority STEM Students," *Science Advances* 4, no. 3 (March 2018): eaao6373.

22 Mau and Heim Bikos, "Educational and Vocational Aspirations of Minority and Female Students"; Hill, Corbett, and St. Rose, "Why So Few?"

23 Joscha Legewie and Thomas A. DiPrete, "The High School Environment and the Gender Gap in Science and Engineering," *Sociology of Education* 87, no. 4 (October 2014): 259–80; Lynn S. Liben, Rebecca S. Bigler, and Holleen R. Krogh, "Pink and Blue Collar Jobs: Children's Judgments of Job Status and Job Aspirations in Relation to Sex of Worker," *Journal of Experimental Child Psychology* 79, no. 4 (August 2001): 346–63; Carol Lynn Martin, Carolyn H. Wood, and Jane K. Little, "The Development of Gender Stereotype Components," *Child Development* 61, no. 6 (December 1990): 1891–1904; J. McGee and J. Stockard, "From a Child's View: Children's Occupational Knowledge and Perceptions of Occupational Characteristics," *Sociological Studies of Child Development* 4 (1991): 113–36.

24 Xie and Shauman, *Women in Science*.

25 Sara M. Lindberg et al., "New Trends in Gender and Mathematics Performance: A Meta-Analysis," *Psychological Bulletin* 136, no. 6 (2010): 1123–35; Christianne Corbett, Catherine Hill, and Andresse St. Rose, *Where the Girls Are: The Facts about Gender Equity in Education*, American Association of University Women, published May 2008, https://ww3.aauw.org/files/2013/02/Where-the-Girls -Are-The-Facts-About-Gender-Equity-in-Education.pdf.

26 On gender gaps in test scores having largely disappeared, see Janet S. Hyde et al., "Gender Similarities Characterize Math Performance," *Science* 321, no. 5888 (2008): 494–95. On the remaining differences being too small to explain gender disparities in major and degree attainment and employment, see Richard M. Simon and George Farkas, "Sex, Class, and Physical Science Educational Attainment: Portions Due to Achievement Versus Recruitment," *Journal of Women and Minorities in Science and Engineering* 14, no. 3 (2008): 30–46; Xie and Shauman, *Women in Science*.

27 Sabrina Sobieraj and Nicole C. Krämer, "The Impacts of Gender and Subject on Experience of Competence and Autonomy in STEM," *Frontiers in Psychology* 10, no. 1432 (2019): 1–16.

28 Shelley J. Correll, "Gender and the Career Choice Process: The Role of Biased Self-Assessments," *American Journal of Sociology* 106, no. 6 (2001): 1691–1730.

29 Charles, "Venus, Mars, and Math"; Sean Reardon et al., "Gender Achievement Gaps in U.S. School Districts," *American Educational Research Journal* 56, no. 6 (2019): 2474–2508.

30 In a series of initial regression analyses looking at the factors that shape gen

der gaps in various technology-related careers, I found that gender gaps in technology-related aspirations vary by school affluence, where there are smaller gaps in Title I schools than in non–Title I schools. Also, comparing particular careers (e.g., tech teacher vs. computer programmer), girls in Title I schools also seem to selectively aspire to more male-stereotypical roles (e.g., computer programmer) rather than roles that might be closer to more female-stereotypical roles (e.g., tech teacher). In all regressions, the DAS was significantly associated with students' future aspirations, even when taking other well-established factors into account (achievement, parental education, etc.). But, given the complexities of these dynamics, delving into further depth is beyond the scope of this book—indeed, entire books have been devoted to this topic. Instead, here I focus on findings that establish a relationship between students' technology learning habits and their educational plans and occupational aspirations and will continue to pursue this topic in greater depth in future work. See Louise Archer and Jennifer DeWitt, *Understanding Young People's Science Aspirations* (London: Routledge, 2016).

31   Michela Musto, "Brilliant or Bad: The Gendered Social Construction of Exceptionalism in Early Adolescence," *American Sociological Review* 84, no. 3 (2019): 369–93; Cheryan et al., "Ambient Belonging"; Cheryan et al., "Why Are Some STEM Fields More Gender Balanced?"

32   Sarah Thébaud and Maria Charles, "Segregation, Stereotypes, and STEM," *Social Sciences* 7, no. 7 (2018): 1–18.

33   Margolis et al., *Stuck in the Shallow End*; Stacy B. Erlich, Sue E. Sporte, and Penny Bender Sebring, *The Use of Technology in Chicago Public Schools* (Chicago: Consortium on Chicago School Research, 2013); E. Smith, *Chicago's Informal Computer Science Learning Landscape*.

34   Puckett, "CS4Some?" The exception of schools with technology plans is an interesting one—these were previously required by most school districts for access to technology-related funding but are typically no longer required. Given this, at present, a plan might indicate a higher level of coordinated effort to provide robust technology learning experiences for students.

35   Heather G. Peske and Kati Haycock, *Teaching Inequality: How Poor and Minority Students Are Shortchanged on Teacher Quality* (Washington, DC: Education Trust, 2006).

36   Marjoribanks, "Family Background, Individual and Environmental Influences, Aspirations and Young Adults' Educational Attainment."

37   Diane Reay, Miriam David, and Stephen Ball, "Making a Difference? Institutional Habituses and Higher Education Choice," *Sociological Research Online* 5, no. 4 (2001): 126–42; Maureen E. Kenny et al., "The Role of Perceived Barriers and Relational Support in the Educational and Vocational Lives of Urban High School Students," *Journal of Counseling Psychology* 50, no. 2 (2003): 142–55.

38   Louise Archer et al., "Science Aspirations, Capital, and Family Habitus: How Families Shape Children's Engagement and Identification With Science," *American Educational Research Journal* 49, no. 1 (2012): 1–28; Xie, Fang, and Shauman, "STEM Education."

39   Puckett, "CS4Some?"; Puckett and Nelson, "Geek Instinct."

40 There is a huge body of literature on this topic. For example, see Grace Kao and Jennifer S. Thompson, "Racial and Ethnic Stratification in Educational Achievement and Attainment," *Annual Review of Sociology* 29 (2003): 417–42; Dennis J. Condron et al., "Racial Segregation and the Black/White Achievement Gap, 1992 to 2009," *Sociological Quarterly* 54, no. 1 (2013): 130–57; Dennis J. Condron, and Vincent J. Roscigno, "Disparities Within: Unequal Spending and Achievement in an Urban School District," *Sociology of Education* 76, no. 1 (2003): 18–36; Charles T. Clotfelter, Helen F. Ladd, and Jacob L. Vigdor, "Teacher Credentials and Student Achievement in High School: A Cross-Subject Analysis with Student Fixed Effects," *Journal of Human Resources* 45, no. 3 (2010): 655–81; Charles Clotfelter et al., "High Poverty Schools and the Distribution of Principals and Teachers," *North Carolina Law Review* 85, no. 5 (2007): 1345–79; Terris Ross et al., *Higher Education: Gaps in Access and Persistence Study*, Statistical Analysis Report NCES 2012–046 (Washington, DC: National Center for Education Statistics, 2012); Xie, Fang, and Shauman, "STEM Education"; Sean F. Reardon, "The Widening Academic Achievement Gap between the Rich and the Poor: New Evidence and Possible Explanations," *Whither Opportunity? Rising Inequality, Schools, and Children's Life Chances*, ed. Greg J. Duncan and Richard J. Murnane (New York: Russell Sage Foundation, 2011), 91–116.

41 Margolis et al., *Stuck in the Shallow End*; Calarco, *Negotiating Opportunities*; Lewis and Diamond, *Despite the Best Intentions*.

42 Harriet R. Tenenbaum and Martin D. Ruck, "Are Teachers' Expectations Different for Racial Minority than for European American Students? A Meta-Analysis," *Journal of Educational Psychology* 99, no. 2 (2007): 253–73; Jeannie Oakes, *Keeping Track: How Schools Structure Inequality*, 2nd ed. (New Haven, CT: Yale University Press, 2005).

43 Xianglei Chen and Matthew Soldner, *STEM Attrition: College Students' Paths Into and Out of STEM Fields* (Washington, DC: National Center for Education Statistics, 2014).

44 Xie, Fang, and Shauman, "STEM Education."

45 Catherine Riegle-Crumb, Chelsea Moore, and Aida Ramos-Wada, "Who Wants to Have a Career in Science or Math? Exploring Adolescents' Future Aspirations by Gender and Race/Ethnicity," *Science Education* 95, no. 3 (2011): 458–76, at 472–73.

46 Barbara Rogoff et al., "The Organization of Informal Learning," *Review of Research in Education* 40 (2016): 356–401.

47 Legewie and DiPrete, "High School Environment and Gender Gap in Science and Engineering."

48 For research showing that time outside school plays a pivotal role in learning, see Herbert J. Walberg, "Families as Partners in Educational Productivity," *Phi Delta Kappan* 65, no. 6 (1984): 397–400; Douglas B. Downey, David M. Quinn, and Melissa Alcaraz, "The Distribution of School Quality: Do Schools Serving Mostly White and High-SES Children Produce the Most Learning?" *Sociology of Education* 92, no. 4 (2019): 386–403; Douglas B. Downey, *How Schools Really Matter: Why Our Assumption about Schools and Inequality Is Mostly Wrong* (Chicago: University of Chicago Press, 2019). For research on the broader

"social supports" that can help aspirations, see Julie Wall, Katherine Covell, and Peter D. MacIntyre, "Implications of Social Supports for Adolescents' Education and Career Aspirations," *Canadian Journal of Behavioral Science* 31, no. 2 (1999): 63–71; George V. Gushue and Melissa L. Whitson, "The Relationship among Support, Ethnic Identity, Career Decision Self-Efficacy, and Outcome Expectations in African American High School Students: Applying Social Cognitive Career Theory," *Journal of Career Development* 33, no. 2 (2006): 112–24.

49 Philip M. Sadler et al., "The Influence of Teachers' Knowledge on Student Learning in Middle School Physical Science Classrooms," *American Educational Research Journal* 50, no. 5 (2013): 1020–49; Claudia Buchmann and Ben Dalton, "Interpersonal Influences and Educational Aspirations in 12 Countries: The Importance of Institutional Context," *Sociology of Education* 75, no. 2 (2002): 99–122.

50 Kao and Tienda, "Educational Aspirations of Minority Youth"; Stephanie C. Berzin, "Educational Aspirations among Low-Income Youths: Examining Multiple Conceptual Models," *Children and Schools* 32, no. 2 (2010): 112–24; John U. Ogbu, "Minority Coping Responses and School Experience," *Journal of Psychohistory* 18, no. 4 (Spring 1991): 433–56; Wei-Cheng Mau, "Educational Planning and Academic Achievement of Middle School Students: A Racial and Cultural Comparison," *Journal of Counseling and Development* 73, no. 5 (1995): 518–26; Gloria Crisp, Nora Amaury, and Amanda Taggart, "Student Characteristics, Pre-College, College, and Environmental Factors as Predictors of Majoring in and Earning a STEM Degree: An Analysis of Students Attending a Hispanic Serving Institution," *American Educational Research Journal* 46, no. 4 (2009): 924–42.

51 Barron et al., *Digital Youth Network*, 231–32.

52 Lewis and Diamond, *Despite the Best Intentions*; Margolis et al., *Stuck in the Shallow End*.

CHAPTER SIX

1 The idea of a "learning ecology" is extensively used in the field of learning sciences but surprisingly less so in sociology. See Urie Bronfenbrenner, *The Ecology of Human Development: Experiments by Nature and Design* (Cambridge, MA: Harvard University Press, 1979); Brigid Barron, "Interest and Self-Sustained Learning as Catalysts of Development: A Learning Ecology Perspective," *Human Development* 49, no. 4 (2006): 193–224; Douglas S. Massey and Stefanie Brodmann, *Spheres of Influence: The Social Ecology of Racial and Class Inequality* (New York: Russell Sage Foundation, 2014).

2 Puckett, "CS4Some?"

3 Brosnan, "A New Methodology, an Old Story?"; Margaret Mead and Rhoda Métraux, "Image of Scientists Among High School Students," *Science* 126, no. 3270 (1957): 384–90.

4 Emma Mercier, Brigid Barron, and K. M. O'Connor, "Images of Self and Others

as Computer Users: The Role of Gender and Experience," *Journal of Computer Assisted Learning* 22, no. 5 (October 2006): 335–48; Cheryan et al., "Stereotypical Computer Scientist"; Allison Master, Sapna Cheryan, and Andrew N. Meltzoff, "Computing Whether She Belongs: Stereotypes Undermine Girls' Interest and Sense of Belonging in Computer Science," *Journal of Educational Psychology* 108, no. 3 (2016): 424–37.

5   Xie and Shauman, *Women in Science*; Asia A. Eaton et al., "How Gender and Race Stereotypes Impact the Advancement of Scholars in STEM: Professors' Biased Evaluations of Physics and Biology Post-Doctoral Candidates," *Sex Roles* 82, no. 3–4 (February 2020): 127–41.

6   Musto, "Brilliant or Bad"; Jacquelynne S. Eccles, Janis E. Jacobs, and Rena D. Harold, "Gender Role Stereotypes, Expectancy Effects, and Parents' Socialization of Gender Differences," *Journal of Social Issues* 46, no. 2 (Summer 1990): 183–201.

7   On both men and women believing scientists are typically male, see L. L. Carli, L. Alawa, Y. Lee, B. Zhao, and E. Kim, "Stereotypes about Gender and Science: Women ≠ Scientists," *Psychology of Women Quarterly* 40, no. 2 (2016): 244–60; Cheryan et al., "Stereotypical Computer Scientist." On men in male-dominated fields believing that men are better in math and science than women, see Sarah Banchefsky, and Bernadette Park, "Negative Gender Ideologies and Gender-Science Stereotypes Are More Pervasive in Male-Dominated Academic Disciplines," *Social Sciences* 7, no. 2 (2018): 27.

8   For example, in a classic study of stereotypes of scientists, Margaret Mead and Rhoda Métraux asked 35,000 students to describe their ideas about scientists, from which they drew a random sample. The dominant image was a negative one: an isolated middle-aged (presumably white) male with glasses and a lab coat running scientific experiments. See Mead and Métraux, "Image of Scientists among High School Students." Studies of middle and high school students from the late twentieth and early twenty-first centuries suggest that this image persists. See Deborah C. Fort and Heather L. Varney, "How Students See Scientists: Mostly Male, Mostly White, and Mostly Benevolent," *Science and Children* 26, no. 8 (May 1989): 8–13; Kevin D. Finson, "Drawing a Scientist: What We Do and Do Not Know after Fifty Years of Drawings," *School Science and Mathematics* 102, no. 7 (2002): 335–45; Mercier, Barron, and O'Connor, "Images of Self and Others as Computer Users." On these persistent views being consistent across gender and racial groups in the United States, see Kevin D. Finson, "Applicability of the DAST-C to the Images of Scientists Drawn by Students of Different Racial Groups," *Journal of Elementary Science Education* 15, no. 1 (Spring 1989): 15–26; Fort and Varney, "How Students See Scientists"; Renato A. Schibeci and Irene Sorensen, "Elementary School Children's Perceptions of Scientists," *School Science and Mathematics* 83, no. 1 (January 1983): 14–20.

9   Brian A. Nosek et al., "Pervasiveness and Correlates of Implicit Attitudes and Stereotypes," *European Review of Social Psychology* 18 (2007): 36–88.

10   Wynn and Correll, "Puncturing the Pipeline"; Alison T. Wynn and Shelley Correll, "Gendered Perceptions of Cultural and Skill Alignment in Technology

Companies," *Social Sciences* 6, no. 2 (2017): 45; M. A. Beasley and M. J. Fischer, "Why They Leave: The Impact of Stereotype Threat on the Attrition of Women and Minorities from Science, Math and Engineering Majors," *Social Psychology of Education* 15, no. 4 (2012): 427–48; Madeleine E. Heilman, "Gender Stereotypes and Workplace Bias," *Research in Organizational Behavior* 32 (2012) 113–35; A. Smeding, "Women in Science, Technology, Engineering, and Mathematics (STEM): An Investigation of Their Implicit Gender Stereotypes and Stereotypes' Connectedness to Math Performance," *Sex Roles* 67, no. 11–12 (2012): 617–29.

11   Ron Eglash, "Race, Sex, and Nerds: From Black Geeks to Asian American Hipsters," *Social Text* 20, no. 2 (2002): 49–64.

12   Ridgeway, *Framed by Gender*.

13   Thorne, *Gender Play*, 159.

14   Puckett, "CS4Some?"

15   I describe this notion of "readiness" and other research on the importance of readiness in further detail in Puckett, "CS4Some?"

16   Puckett and Nelson, "Geek Instinct."

17   Khe Foon Hew and Thomas Brush, "Integrating Technology into K-12 Teaching and Learning: Current Knowledge Gaps and Recommendations for Future Research," *Educational Technology Research and Development* 55, no. 3 (June 2007): 223–52.

18   Puckett and Nelson, "Geek Instinct."

19   I examined how students interpreted of the term technology using cognitive interviews with a range of students. See Puckett, "Digital Adaptability."

20   Puckett and Nelson, "Geek Instinct"; Puckett, "CS4Some?"

21   Barron et al., "Parents as Learning Partners"; Brigid Barron et al., "Predictors of Creative Computing Participation and Profiles of Experience in Two Silicon Valley Middle Schools," *Computers and Education* 54, no. 1 (2010): 178–89; Sandra D. Simpkins, Pamela E. Davis-Kean, and Jacquelynne S. Eccles, "Parents' Socializing Behavior and Children's Participation in Math, Science, and Computer Out-of-School Activities," *Applied Developmental Science* 9, no. 1 (2005): 14–30.

22   Margolis and Fisher, *Unlocking the Clubhouse*.

23   Rachael Robnett and Campbell Leaper, "Friendship Groups, Personal Motivations, and Gender in Relation to High School Students' STEM Career Interest," *Journal of Research on Adolescence* 23, no. 4 (2012): 652–64.

24   Toby Parcel, Mikaela J. Dufur, and Rena Cornell Zito, "Capital at Home and at School: A Review and Synthesis," *Journal of Marriage and Family* 72, no. 4 (August 2010): 828–46; Puckett, "Technological Change, Digital Adaptability, and Social Inequality."

25   In the survey in Chicago, I did in fact ask these questions. But unfortunately due to a technical issue, that segment of the survey data was lost, so I was unable to include it in my analysis. I encourage research in the future to do so, as my observations and a number of other qualitative studies demonstrate the importance of out-of-school experiences in tech, and quantitative studies have long noted the importance of these experiences for STEM pathways in general.

26 Ricarose Roque, "Family Creative Learning," in *Makeology: The Maker Movement and the Future of Learning*, ed. Kylie Peppler, Yasmin B. Kafai, and Erica Rosenfeld Halverson (New York: Routledge, 2016), 47–63.

27 Chicago Learning Exchange, "Our Community," accessed May 14, 2021, https://chicagolx.org/community; Hive New York, "Brokering Youth Pathways," accessed May 14, 2021, http://hivenyc.org/.

28 Puckett and Nelson, "Geek Instinct," 38.

29 Jacquelynne Eccles and Jennifer Appleton Gootman, *Community Programs to Promote Youth Development* (Washington, D.C.: National Academies Press, 2002).

30 Barron et al., *Digital Youth Network*.

31 Barron et al., *Digital Youth Network*, 112.

32 Etienne Wenger, *Communities of Practice: Learning, Meaning, and Identity* (Cambridge: Cambridge University Press, 1998).

33 Tom Page, "Skeuomorphism or Flat Design: Future Directions in Mobile Device User Interface (UI) Design Education," *International Journal of Mobile Learning and Organization* 8, no. 2 (2014): 130–42.

34 Andrew Eisele, *Sound Design and Mixing in Reason* (New York: Hal Leonard, 2012), chap. 5.

35 Victor Ray, "A Theory of Racialized Organizations," *American Sociological Review* 84, no. 1 (2019): 26–53; Joan Acker, "Inequality Regimes: Gender, Class, and Race in Organizations," *Gender and Society* 20, no. 4 (2006): 441–64.

36 Ray, "Theory of Racialized Organizations"; Acker, "Inequality Regimes"; Thurston Domina, Andrew Penner, and Emily Penner, "Categorical Inequality: Schools as Sorting Machines," *Annual Review of Sociology* 43 (2017): 311–30; Christo Sims, *Disruptive Fixation: School Reform and the Pitfalls of Techno-Idealism* (Princeton, NJ: Princeton University Press, 2017); Matthew H. Rafalow, *Digital Divisions: How Schools Create Inequality in the Tech Era* (Chicago: University of Chicago Press, 2020).

37 Adapted from Nasir, *Racialized Identities*, 163.

38 Thorne, *Gender Play*, 163–67.

39 Barron et al., *Digital Youth Network*.

40 Puckett, "CS4Some?"

41 Margolis and Fisher, *Unlocking the Clubhouse: Women in Computing*; Carnegie Mellon University, "CMU's Proportion of Undergraduate Women in Computer Science and Engineering Soars above National Averages," September 12, 2016, https://www.cmu.edu/news/stories/archives/2016/september/undergrad-women-engineering-computer-science.html.

42 Joshi, "By Whom and When Is Women's Expertise Recognized?" 203.

43 Alice H. Eagly and Steven J. Karau, "Gender and the Emergence of Leaders: A Meta-Analysis," *Journal of Personality and Social Psychology* 60, no. 5 (1991): 685–710; Alice H. Eagly, Mona G. Makhijani, and Bruce G. Klonsky, "Gender and the Evaluation of Leaders: A Meta-Analysis," *Psychological Bulletin* 111, no. 1 (1992): 3–22; Barbara F. Reskin, Debra B. McBrier, and Julie A. Kmec, "The Determinants and Consequences of Workplace Sex and Race Composition,"

Annual Review of Sociology 25 (1999): 335–61; Cecilia L. Ridgeway and Lynn Smith-Lovin, "The Gender System and Interaction," *Annual Review of Sociology* 25 (1999): 191–216.

44 Donald Tomaskovic-Devey, "The Relational Generation of Workplace Inequalities," *Social Currents* 1, no. 1 (2014): 51–73, at 59.

45 Donald Tomaskovic-Devey and Sheryl Skaggs, "Sex Segregation, Labor Process Organization, and Gender Earnings Inequality," *American Journal of Sociology* 108, no. 1 (2002): 102–28; Sherry N. Mong and Vincent J. Roscigno, "African American Men and the Experience of Employment Discrimination," *Qualitative Sociology* 33, no. 1 (2010): 1–21.

46 Attewell, "What Is Skill."

47 Abbate, "Code Switch."

48 Thompson, *Coders*, 345.

49 Some research calls into question the idea that people learn very much in school, particularly in higher education, arguing that credentials are not reflective of actual skill. See Collins, *Credential Society*; Arum and Roksa, *Academically Adrift*.

50 Abbate, *Recoding Gender*; Thompson, *Coders*.

51 Abbate, *Recoding Gender*, 4.

52 Abbate, *Recoding Gender*, 4.

53 Margolis and Fisher, *Unlocking the Clubhouse*.

54 Quillian et al., "Meta-Analysis of Field Experiments."

55 There is a long-standing debate about mechanisms for workplace inequality—whether by devaluation of the work done by women and historically marginalized groups or by "queuing" and discrimination in the hiring process, whereby these groups are placed into lower-paying positions. There is evidence for both mechanisms, although they may vary by group, with greater evidence for devaluation in terms of gender inequality and discrimination in hiring for racial inequality—and overlapping inequities at the intersection of race and gender, particularly among Black women. See, e.g., Julie Kmec, "Minority Concentration and Wages," *Social Problems* 50, no. 1 (February 2003): 38–50; Matt L. Huffman and Philip M. Cohen, "Racial Wage Inequality: Job Segregation and Devaluation Across U.S. Labor Markets," *American Journal of Sociology* 109, no. 4 (January 2004): 902–36; Irene Browne and Joya Misra, "The Intersection of Gender and Race in the Labor Market," *Annual Review of Sociology* 29 (August 2003): 487–513.

56 Asaf Levanon, Paula England, and Paul Allison, "Occupational Feminization and Pay: Assessing Causal Dynamics Using 1950–2000 U.S. Census Data," *Social Forces* 88, no. 2 (2009): 865–91.

57 Eagly and Karau, "Gender and the Emergence of Leaders"; Eagly, Makhijani, and Klonsky, "Gender and the Evaluation of Leaders."

58 Ridgeway and Smith-Lovin, "Gender System and Interaction"; Linda L. Carli, "Gender and Group Behavior," in *Handbook of Gender Research in Psychology*, vol. 2, *Gender Research in Social and Applied Psychology*, ed. J. C. Chrisler and D. R. McCreary (New York: Springer Science + Business Media, 2010), 337–58.

59 This suggestion is based on the recommendations of Ridgeway, *Framed by Gen-*

der, for gender-based inequities, but I argue it can also be applied to class- and race-based inequities.

60 Ridgeway, *Framed by Gender*, 194.

61 Kotamraju, "Art Versus Code."

62 Tomaskovic-Devey, "Relational Generation of Workplace Inequalities"; Donald Tomaskovic-Devey and Sheryl Skaggs, "An Establishment-Level Test of the Statistical Discrimination Hypothesis," *Work and Occupations* 26, no. 4 (1999): 422–45.

63 Cedric Herring, "Does Diversity Pay? Race, Gender, and the Business Case for Diversity," *American Sociological Review* 74, no. 2 (2009): 208–24.

64 Acker, "Inequality Regimes," 455.

65 Acker, "Inequality Regimes," 455.

66 Schoenfeld, "Explorations of Students' Mathematical Beliefs and Behavior."

67 Schoenfeld, "Learning to Think Mathematically."

68 Puckett, "CS4Some?"

69 Margot Lee Shetterly, *Hidden Figures: The American Dream and the Untold Story of the Black Women Who Helped Win the Space Race* (New York: Harper Collins, 2016); *Hidden Figures*, directed by Theodore Melfi (20th Century Fox, 2016).

70 For a collection that includes Black and white women, see Margaret A. M. Murray, *Women Becoming Mathematicians: Creating a Professional Identity in Post–World War II America* (Cambridge, MA: MIT Press, 2000).

71 Buolamwini and Gebru, "Gender Shades."

72 Some historians and archivists are trying to remedy this oversight by unearthing documentation such as *Ebony* magazine's coverage of African Americans working in computing fields from 1959 to 1969, otherwise unavailable in "official" labor documentation. Of this, R. Arvid Nelsen writes, "Between 1959 and 1996, fifty-seven profiles in the 'Speaking of People' column featured individuals employed in positions in or related to computing. . . . The fact that so many people active in computing professions can be found within the pages of a magazine aimed at a general audience of African American readers whereas so little information has been found in traditional sources of archival materials from the computing field(s) suggests that, rather than focusing on what the computing industry has had to say about persons of color, it may be more profitable to examine what communities of color have had to say about computing." R. Arvid Nelsen, "Race and Computing: The Problem of Sources, the Potential of Prosopography, and the Lesson of Ebony Magazine," *IEEE Annals of the History of Computing* 39, no. 1 (2017): 29–51, at 38. According to a 2017 article from the Point Mugu, California, Naval Air Warfare Center Weapons Division (NAWCWD), one of the women depicted in the "Speaking of People" column, Gwendolyn Elliott Hunt, was a mathematician with a bachelor's degree from Tennessee State University, who first worked for IBM in the 1950s before joining Pacific Missile Test Center in 1961. When photographed for *Ebony* in November 1969, Hunt was a systems analysis programming supervisor. The article went on to add, "She was featured again in July 1971 in an article titled 'New Careers for the New Woman.' Hunt noted that while African-American women in civil service might have an easier time getting promoted than in corporate America,

there were certainly boundaries to being the 'first' woman in any position or indeed in getting a foot in the door to begin with. So she worked to help others break that boundary down." See Kimberly Brown, "Black History Month: Point Mugu's Own 'Hidden Figures,'" Story #NNS170221-15, Naval Air Warfare Center, Weapons Division Public Affairs, February 20, 2017, https://www.dvidshub .net/news/236774/black-history-month-point-mugus-own-hidden-figures.

73 Recent research also suggests that creating a "balanced prototype," or idea of who is best suited for certain positions, can be accomplished by carefully "inverting" the prototype. For example, feminized traits may be emphasized as essential to largely masculinized jobs to create this balance. See Felix Danbold and Corinne Bendersky, "Balancing Professional Prototypes Increases the Valuation of Women in Male-Dominated Professions," *Organization Science* 31, no. 1 (2020): 119–40.

CONCLUSION

1 In one of the first academic conferences I ever attended, the 2003 National Council of Teachers of English Assembly for Research (NCTEAR) conference at UC Berkeley, I talked about my all-female technology class in a small interactive session with Dr. Pedro Noguera, an education scholar now at UCLA. He looked at me quizzically when I described the demographics of my class—I remember being surprised by that reaction, not expecting an all-female class to be taken as so unusual. It made me wonder: Do we know how many low-income, minoritized girls participate in technology classes and programs, or are they just *uncounted*? Do we just assume they do not exist because they are fewer in number at the higher levels of STEM? I have not answered these questions in my research—I encourage other scholars to pursue the broader question of how many "hidden techies" there are across the country.

2 Camic, "Matter of Habit"; Gross, "Pragmatist Theory of Social Mechanisms"; Bourdieu, *Distinction*; Shannon Sullivan, *Revealing Whiteness: The Unconscious Habits of Racial Privilege* (Bloomington: Indiana University Press, 2006).

3 Antar A. Tichavakunda, "An Overdue Theoretical Discourse: Pierre Bourdieu's Theory of Practice and Critical Race Theory in Education," *Educational Studies* 55, no. 6 (2019): 651–66, at 663.

4 Shawn Michell Smith, *Photography on the Color Line* (Durham, NC: Duke University Press, 2004); José Itzigsohn and Karida Brown, "Sociology and the Theory of Double Consciousness: W. E. B. Du Bois's Phenomenology of Racialized Subjectivity," *Du Bois Review: Social Science Research on Race* 12, no. 2 (2015): 231–48.

5 Ensmenger, *Computer Boys Take Over*.

6 This study is the first, to my knowledge, to show this assertion about "hidden techies" among historically marginalized groups with quantitative evidence. However, there are others who demonstrate similar findings through qualitative means. See Watkins et al., *Digital Edge*.

7 Damien Joseph et al., "Practical Intelligence in IT: Assessing Soft Skills of IT

Professionals," *Communications of the ACM* 53, no. 2 (February 2010): 149–54, https://cacm.acm.org/magazines/2010/2/69374-practical-intelligence-in-it-assessing-soft-skills-of-it-professionals/fulltext; Chris Warhurst, Irena Grugulis, and Ewart Keep, *The Skills That Matter* (London: Palgrave, 2004).

8   Krista Scott-Dixon, *Doing IT: Women Working in Information Technology* (Toronto: Sumach Press, 2004).

9   National Telecommunications and Information Administration, *Falling Through the Net*; M. Smith, "Computer Science for All."

10 Cuban, *Oversold and Underused*.

11 Rosemary E. Sutton, "Equity and Computers in the Schools: A Decade of Research," *Review of Educational Research* 61, no. 4 (1991): 475–503, at 476.

12 US Equal Employment Opportunity Commission, "Diversity in High Tech," accessed May 15, 2021, https://www.eeoc.gov/eeoc/statistics/reports/hightech/index.cfm.

13 US Equal Employment Opportunity Commission, "Advancing Opportunity for All in the Tech Industry," press release, May 18, 2016, https://www.eeoc.gov/eeoc/newsroom/release/5-18-16.cfm.

14 National Coalition for Girls and Women in Education, *Women and STEM: Preparing for a Technology-Driven Economy* (2017), 10. https://www.ncwge.org/TitleIX45/Women and STEM.pdf

15 Margolis and Fisher, *Unlocking the Clubhouse*, 6.

16 Nelson, *Why Afterschool Matters*; Xie, Fang, and Shauman, "STEM Education."

17 Calarco, *Negotiating Opportunities*; R. L'Heureux Lewis-McCoy, *Inequality in the Promised Land: Race, Resources, and Suburban Schooling* (Stanford, CA: Stanford University Press, 2014).

18 Daniel Rigney, *The Matthew Effect: How Advantage Begets Further Advantage* (New York: Columbia University Press, 2010); Robert Merton, "The Matthew Effect in Science," *Science* 159, no. 3810 (1968): 56–63.

19 Lareau, *Unequal Childhoods*; Lewis and Diamond, *Despite the Best Intentions*.

20 This notion of competition, where some win and others lose, is also true of education as a whole. See David F. Labaree, *Someone Has to Fail: The Zero-Sum Game of Public Schooling* (Cambridge, MA: Harvard University Press, 2010).

21 Abbate, "Code Switch," S155.

22 Kristen Grant et al., "Health Consequences of Exposure to E-Waste: A Systematic Review," *Lancet Global Health* 1, no. 6 (2013): e350–e61.

23 Valerio De Stefano, *The Rise of the "Just-in-Time Workforce": On-Demand Work, Crowdwork and Labour Protection in the "Gig-Economy*, Conditions of Work and Employment Series 71 (Geneva: International Labour Organisation, 2016); Gianpiero Petriglieri, Susan J. Ashford, and Amy Wrzesniewski, "Agony and Ecstasy in the Gig Economy: Cultivating Holding Environments for Precarious and Personalized Work Identities," *Administrative Science Quarterly* 64, no. 1 (2019): 124–70.

24 Rafi Santo, Sara Vogel, and Dixie Ching, *CS for What? Diverse Visions of Computer Science Education in Practice* (New York: CSforALL, 2019).

25 Hill, Corbett, and St. Rose, "Why So Few?," 13.

26 US Department of Education Office of Civil Rights, "Know Your Rights," mod-

ified June 10, 2020, https://www2.ed.gov/about/offices/list/ocr/know.html?src=ft.

27 Lemann, *Big Test*.

28 In education, biases among teachers that are shaped by school culture can influence technological gatekeeping. See Puckett and Nelson, "Geek Instinct"; Rafalow, "Disciplining Play"; Sims, "From Differentiated Use to Differentiating Practices." In employment, group biases can shape gatekeeping in tech-related fields—see Thompson, *Coders*; Abbate, "Code Switch."

29 McNamee and Miller, *Meritocracy Myth*.

30 Jonathan J. B. Mijs, "The Paradox of Inequality: Income Inequality and Belief in Meritocracy Go Hand in Hand," *Socio-Economic Review*, published ahead of print, January 23, 2019, https://doi.org/10.1093/ser/mwy051.

31 Paula England, Andrew Levine, and Emma Mishel, "Progress Toward Gender Equality in the United States Has Slowed or Stalled," *Proceedings of the National Academy of Sciences of the United States of America* 117, no. 13 (2020): 6990–97.

32 On the "social imaginary," see Charles Taylor, *Modern Social Imaginaries* (Durham, NC: Duke University Press, 2004).

33 Robin D. G. Kelley, *Freedom Dreams: The Black Radical Imagination* (Boston: Beacon Press, 2003), xii, quoted in Ruha Benjamin, *Captivating Technology: Race, Carceral Technoscience, and Liberatory Imagination in Everyday Life* (Durham, NC: Duke University Press, 2019), 13–14.

34 Benjamin, *Captivating Technology*, 12.

35 Benjamin, *Captivating Technology*, 12.

36 Jonathan Wilkins, ed., *Black Panther: The Official Movie Special* (London: Titan Comics, 2018).

APPENDIX

1 There are many ways of defining *mixed methods*. Here I use Mario Small's definition of a *mixed-methods study* as involving either "mixed data collection" that is "based on at least two kinds of data (such as field notes and administrative records) or two means of collecting them (such as interviewing and controlled experimentation)" or "mixed data–analysis studies" wherein "regardless of the number of data sources, [the studies] either employ more than one analytical technique or cross techniques and types of data (such as using regression to analyze interview transcripts)." See Mario L. Small, "How to Conduct a Mixed Method Study: Recent Trends in a Rapidly Growing Literature," *Annual Review of Sociology* 37 (2011): 55–84, at 60.

2 Randall Collins, "Statistics Versus Words." *Sociological Theory* 2 (1984): 329–62.

3 John David Brewer and Albert Hunter, *Foundations of Multimethod Research: Synthesizing Styles* (Thousand Oaks, CA: Sage, 2006); Abbas Tashakkori and Charles Teddlie, eds., *Handbook of Mixed Methods in Social and Behavioral Research* (Thousand Oaks, CA: Sage, 2003).

4 Small, "How to Conduct a Mixed Method Study."

5   Paula England and Kathryn Edin, *Unmarried Couples with Children* (New York: Russell Sage Foundation, 2007).

6   Mario L. Small, *Unanticipated Gains: Origins of Network Inequality in Everyday Life* (New York: Oxford University Press, 2009). The methods appendix of this text is robust and highly recommended but does reflect a conceptual distinction between the study's qualitative and quantitative approaches.

7   On narrative analysis that moves into formal modeling methods, see Roberto Franzosi, "From Words to Numbers: A Set Theory Framework for the Collection, Organization, and Analysis of Narrative Data," *Sociological Methods* 24 (1994): 105–36. On "fuzzy sets," see Charles C. Ragin, *Fuzzy-Set Social Science* (Chicago: University of Chicago Press, 2000), 8.

8   John W. Creswell and Vicki L. Plano Clark, *Designing and Conducting Mixed Methods Research*, 3rd ed. (Thousand Oaks, CA: Sage, 2017).

9   Campbell, and Fiske, "Convergent and Discriminant Validation by the Multitrait-Multimethod Matrix."

10   Sam D. Sieber, "The Integration of Fieldwork and Survey Methods," *American Journal of Sociology* 78, no. 6 (1973): 1335–59; K. A. Bollen and P. Paxton, "Detection and Determinants of Bias in Subjective Measures," *American Sociological Review* 63, no. 3 (1998): 465–78.

11   Contributing to the challenge of forming a professional community as a mixed-methods researcher are the historical "quant-qual" divide and the role of mathematics as a high-status gatekeeper at all levels of education—from kindergarten through graduate school—and in occupations. See Daniel Douglas and Paul Attewell, "School Mathematics as Gatekeeper," *Sociological Quarterly* 58, no. 4 (2017): 648–69; Adrienne Redmond-Sanogo, Julie Angle and Evan Davis, "Kinks in the STEM Pipeline: Tracking STEM Graduation Rates Using Science and Mathematics Performance, "*School Science and Mathematics* 116, no. 7 (2016): 378–88; Barbara Hanson, "Whither Qualitative/Quantitative? Grounds for Methodological Convergence," *Quality & Quantity* 42, no. 1 (February 2008): 97–111.

12   At present, there are four main mixed-methods publications venues, two journals that include articles about the application of mixed-methods approaches (both established in 2007; the *Journal of Mixed Method Research* and the *International Journal of Multiple Research Approaches*) and two that are methodological in nature and advance new mixed-methods techniques (*Quality & Quantity* and *Field Methods*). For writing on improving mixed-methods training, see Patricia Bazeley, *Integrating Analyses in Mixed Methods Research* (Thousand Oaks, CA: Sage, 2018); Sharlene Hesse-Biber, "The Problems and Prospects in the Teaching of Mixed Methods Research," *International Journal of Social Research Methodology* 18, no. 5 (2015): 463–77.

13   The same approach could be taken in redefining and reoperationalizing an existing construct.

14   Dawne S. Vogt, Daniel W. King, and Lynda A. King, "Focus Groups in Psychological Assessment: Enhancing Content Validity by Consulting Members of the Target Population," *Psychological Assessment* 16, no. 3 (2004): 231–43.

15   See Cole and Distributed Literacy Consortium, *Fifth Dimension*; Yasmin B. Kafai, Kylie Peppler, and Robbin Chapman, *The Computer Clubhouse: Constructionism and Creativity in Youth Communities* (New York: Teachers College Press, 2009); Peppler and Wohlwend, "Theorizing the Nexus of STEAM Practice"; Peppler, "STEAM-Powered Computing Education."

16   MacArthur Foundation, "Digital Media and Learning," accessed May 17, 2021, https://www.macfound.org/programs/learning/.

17   Barron et al., *Digital Youth Network*.

18   Kimberly Austin, Stacy B. Ehrlich, Cassidy Puckett, and Judi Singleton, *YOUmedia Chicago: Reimagining Learning, Literacies, and Libraries—A Snapshot of Year 1* (Chicago, IL: Consortium on Chicago School Research at the University of Chicago Urban Education Institute, 2011).

19   Chicago Public Library, "YOUmedia," accessed May 17, 2021, https://www.chipublib.org/programs-and-partnerships/youmedia/.

20   My undergraduates probably do not believe me when I explain that I was among a team of researchers at YOUmedia when Chance was there making mixtapes with Instrumentality and recording *10 Day*. It's been wonderful to watch some—but not all—YOUmedia teens be recognized for their incredible talents.

21   In the book I do not use pseudonyms for instructors and program directors who have already been named in previous publications or whose permission I received to use their real names, including Brother Mike, Simeon, and Raphael.

22   Penny Bender Sebring et al., "Teens, Digital Media, and the Chicago Public Library," UChicago Consortium on Chicago School Research, May 2013, 2. https://consortium.uchicago.edu/publications/teens-digital-media-and-chicago-public-library. Quotation is on page 2 of the report, downloadable via the consortium website.

23   Cody S. Jolin, "WhyReef: A Virtual Educational Program Analysis," *University of Wisconsin-Stout Journal of Student Research* 13 (2014): 335–46; Whyville, "Welcome to WhyReef," accessed May 17, 2021, http://www.whyville.net/smmk/top/gates?source=reef.

24   Kristin Bass, Ingrid Hu Dahl, and Shirin Panahandeh, "Designing the Game: How a Project-Based Media Production Program Approaches STEAM Career Readiness for Underrepresented Young Adults," *Journal of Science Education and Technology* 25, no. 6 (2016): 1009–24.

25   Bay Area Video Coalition (BAVC), *From the Beginning: Bay Area Video Coalition's Founding through to 2016* (San Francisco: BAVC, 2016).

26   California Emerging Technology Fund, *Organization Profile: Bay Area Video Coalition (BAVC)* (Oakland, CA: California Emerging Technology Fund, 2007).

27   Bay Area Video Coalition, Digital Pathways Video Curriculum, n.d., https://bavc.org/sites/default/files/resource/DigitalPathwaysVideoCurriculum.pdf.

28   J. Weststar, V. O'Meara, and M.-J. Legault, *Developer Satisfaction Survey Summary Report* (Toronto: International Game Developers Association, 2017).

29   Bass, Hu Dahl, and Panahandeh, "Designing the Game."

30   Bay Area Video Coalition, "BUMP Records," accessed April 2009, https://www.bavc.org/bump.

31   Rex Foundation, "Youth Movement Records," accessed May 18, 2021, https://www.rexfoundation.org/grantees/youth-movement-records/.

32   Rachel Swan, "Hood Games and Pipe Dreams," *East Bay Express* (Oakland, CA), July 16, 2008, https://eastbayexpress.com/hood-games-and-pipe-dreams-1/.

33   Loco Bloco, "About Us: Mission and Vision," accessed May 2020, http://loco bloco.electricembers.net/?page_id=160.

34   Deanna Isaacs, "Adios, Radio Arte?" *Chicago Reader*, May 26, 2011, https://www.chicagoreader.com/chicago/radio-arte-national-museum-of-mexican-art/Content?oid=3905398

35   Rivera began her career at Radio Arte and rose through the ranks to become general manager at Radio Arte before joining Vocalo in 2010. Of the purchase of Radio Arte by Chicago Public Media, Rivera said, "This is a natural partnership. . . . Radio Arte has been a trailblazer in representing marginalized communities and showcasing the diversity of Latino culture." Echeverría was one of the first teens involved in the design of Radio Arte. He has cohosted "Domingos en Vocalo" since 2013, in addition to his work since 2004 as an entertainment and news show producer for the Spanish-language TV network Univision. See Lynn Marek, "Chicago Public Media Buys Latino Radio Station WRTE-FM." *Crain's Chicago Business*, June 22, 2012, https://www.chicagobusiness.com/article/20120622/NEWS06/120629928/chicago-public-media-buys-latino-radio-station-wrte-fm; Seamus Doheny and Silvia Rivera. 2019. "City Scenes: Five Chicago Latinx Artists to Watch in 2019," *Slingshot* (National Public Radio), April 24, 2019, https://www.npr.org/2019/04/24/716145140/slingshot-scenes-5-chicago-latinx-artists-to-watch-in-2019; Vocalo, "Jesús Echeverría / Host," accessed May 18, 2021, https://vocalo.org/members/jesus-echeverria/.

36   Puckett, "Technological Change, Digital Adaptability, and Social Inequality."

37   The program is described in Dánielle Nicole DeVoss, Elyse Eidman-Aadahl, and Troy Hicks, *Because Digital Writing Matters: Improving Student Writing in Online and Multimedia Environments* (San Francisco: Jossey-Bass, 2010), 149; Global Kids, *Developing Youth Leaders for the Global Stage: Global Kids Annual Report, 2009–2010*, http://storage.cloversites.com/globalkids/documents/GK_Annual _Report_2009-2010.pdf.

38   Rhea Borja, "The MOUSE Squad," *Education Week*, November 2, 2004, https://www.edweek.org/leadership/the-mouse-squad/2004/11; Jennifer Demski, "They're Taking Requests: Student Techs Command the Help Desk," *T.H.E. Journal* 37, no. 8 (2010): 36–40.

39   Mouse, "Farewell to Jan Half Program Director, Mouse Squad California," *Mouse_News*, June 16, 2015, https://mouse.org/news/farewell-to-jan-half -program-director-mouse-squad-of-california.

40   Based on California Department of Education data for 2009–2010, obtained via Data Quest (https://dq.cde.ca.gov/dataquest/).

41   Levya, "Campbell Middle School Will Get a New Name."

42   Based on California Department of Education data for 2009–2010.

43   Barbara Rogoff, *The Cultural Nature of Human Development* (New York: Oxford University Press, 2003); Vygotsky, *Mind in Society*.

44 Pierre Bourdieu, *The Logic of Practice* (Stanford, CA: Stanford University Press, 1980).

45 Duckworth et al., "Grit"; Duncan and McKeachie, "Making of the Motivated Strategies for Learning Questionnaire."

46 John and Robins, "Accuracy and Bias in Self-Perception."

47 Pintrich et al., "Reliability and Predictive Validity of the Motivated Strategies for Learning Questionnaire (MSLQ)."

48 There are extensive debates about the optimal number of points on a scale. See Lee and Paek, "In Search of the Optimal Number."

49 This approach is common in scale development. See DeVellis, *Scale Development*; Nunnally and Bernstein, *Psychometric Theory*.

50 On "cognitive interviews," see Desimone and Carlson Le Floch, "Are We Asking the Right Questions?"

51 Chicago Public Schools, *School Data: Demographics*.

52 Muthén and Muthén, *Mplus User's Guide*; Weston and Gore, "Brief Guide to Structural Equation Modeling."

53 Chicago Public Schools, *School Data: Demographics*.

54 Statistical details provided in Puckett, "Digital Adaptability."

55 On Scratch, see Resnick, "Sowing the Seeds."

56 Chapman, "ECS Unit 4."

57 Puckett and Nelson, "Geek Instinct"; Puckett, "CS4Some?"

58 Puckett and Nelson, "Geek Instinct"; Puckett, "CS4Some?"

59 Cassidy Puckett and Brian Gravel, "Institutional Ambiguity and De Facto Tracking in STEM," *Teachers College Record* 122, no. 11 (2020): 9.

60 Puckett, "Digital Adaptability."

61 Iddo Tavory and Stefan Timmermans, *Abductive Analysis: Theorizing Qualitative Research* (Chicago: University of Chicago Press, 2014); Stefan Timmermans and Iddo Tavory, "Theory Construction in Qualitative Research: From Grounded Theory to Abductive Analysis," *Sociological Theory* 30, no. 3 (September 2012): 167–86.

Index

Page numbers followed by "f" or "t" refer to figures or tables, respectively.

Campbell, Donald T., 232

Campbell Middle School, 65, 72, 190. *See also* Mouse Squad California (MSCA)

Captivating Technology: Race, Carceral Technoscience, and Liberatory Imagination in Everyday Life (Benjamin), 221–22

certified knowledge, indicators of, 75

Chance the Rapper, 237

Chicago Public Library (CPL), 18, 236, 237. *See also* Digital Youth Network; Harold Washington Library Center; YOUmedia Chicago

Chicago Public Schools (CPS), 18, 92, 115, 152, 167, 255

Cisneros, Sandra, 81, 238

class-related inequalities, in STEM education, 167–69

Coders (Thompson), 200–201

cognition, distributed, 74–75

Collins, Robert, 188, 189, 242

competence. *See* technological competence

Computer Boys Take Over, The (Ensmenger), 40

computer type, collective reimagining of, 205

computing history: questioning origins of, 217; retelling of, 217–18; women in, 201–2

confirmatory factor analysis, 128, 257–60

continual learning, 10, 16, 45, 59, 83, 105, 165, 254

Coogler, Ryan, 222

cooling out process, 158

CoolSwitch, 98, 99

cooperative relations, methods for promoting, 198

Corbett, Christianne, 218

culture, organizational, changing, 198–99

Damore, James, 8

Darden, Christine, 205

DAS. *See* Digital Adaptability Scale

democratic equality, 26, 211–12; applied to technology education, 26–36, 212; learning habits as necessity for, 214; technological competence and, 16–17, 20

design grammars, internal and external, 90–91

design logic habit, 4, 18, 87–96, 98, 99, 104, 105, 106t, 110, 117, 121, 123, 146, 151, 161, 172; addressing digital inequality and, 172, 182; DAS scoring for, 132; defined, 89; designing games and, 92; distribution of DAS scores and, 134–37, 136f; distribution of scores by gender and, 140, 142f; reading

technologically and, 89–92; teaching of, 93–96, 166, 191–94, 195. *See also* efficiencies habit; management of frustration and boredom habit; use of models habit; willingness to try and fail habit

devaluation process, 202, 300n55

Dewey, John, 23, 24, 119, 207

digital adaptability, 112–13; digital native vs., 7, 112–14, 138; equitably measuring, 124–29; interest vs., 114–24; qualitative observation of, 114–24. *See also* Digital Adaptability Scale

Digital Adaptability Scale (DAS), 18, 19, 125; ability to see, 144–50; aspirations and, 159–60, 160f, 262–64; development of, 127–29, 232, 254–60; distribution of habits scores in, 134–37f; distribution of scores by gender, 139–44, 140f; enforcement of antidiscrimination laws with, 219; explaining difference with, 138–44, 260–62; formatted, 131t; for measuring gatekeeping, 173–76, 180–81; redefining technological competence and, 206; scoring, 130–34; seeing difference with, 130–38

digital divide, 9–10, 28–29; defined, 29; first-level, 29–31; inequality and, 35–36; second-level, 10, 31–33; third-level, 34–35

digital inequality: addressing, 43, 152, 170, 172–73, 204–6, 213–19, 221; bottom-up perspective of, 28–35; engines of, 26, 211–13; organizations, addressing gatekeeping and, 196–204; research and scholarship on, 17, 24, 26–28; 35–36, 43, 222; role of gatekeepers and, 20, 25, 152, 170; top-down perspective of, 27–28, understanding technology learning and, 16. *See also* inequalities

digital native: digital adaptability and, 112–14; myth of, 7, 138

Digital Youth Network (DYN), 17–18, 19, 47, 82–83, 101, 171, 185–86, 188, 195–96, 198, 210, 223, 234, 236–38

DiMaggio, Paul, 10

distractions, blocking out, 70–71

distributed cognition, 74–75

Diversity in High Tech (US Equal Employment Opportunity Commission), 212

Du Bois, W. E. B., 44, 210, 211

Dunbar-Hester, Christina, 172

Dweck, Carol, 13–14

DYN. *See* Digital Youth Network

Edin, Kathryn, 231
educational persistence. *See* persistence, educational
educational program structures, changing for equity, 198–99
Educational Testing Service (ETS), 6, 126
efficiencies habit, 18, 55, 76, 96–102, 106t, 111, 117, 122, 123, 151, 163, 166, 172, 182; becoming an insider and, 100–102; components of, 96–97; CoolSwitch example of, 97–100; DAS scoring for, 132; distribution of efficiencies scores, 134–37, 137f; distribution of scores by gender, 140, 143f; gender and, 102–5; summarized, 102; teaching of, for addressing gatekeeping, 195–96; tricks of the trade and, 98–100; use of models and, 99. *See also* design logic habit; management of frustration and boredom habit; use of models habit; willingness to try and fail habit
Eisenhart, Margaret, 160–61
elevator effect, 42
Ellingrud, Kweilin, 213
England, Paula, 231
Ensmenger, Nathan, 40, 126
ethics, quantitative research and, 126–27
experts, finding, 73–83. *See also* use of models habit
explanatory sequential design, 232
exploratory sequential design, 232
external design grammars, 90–91

Family Creative Learning program, 181
Field Museum (Chicago), 17, 18, 47, 48, 75, 223, 234, 235t, 238–39, 246–49
Fisher, Allan, 32–33, 199, 213
Fiske, Donald W., 232
flow, qualities of, 70–71
framing to learn, 64–66
Freedle, Roy, 126
Freese, Jeremy, 232
friends, as gatekeepers, 178–80
friends technology teaching scales, 178–79, 180t
frustration, management of. *See* management of frustration and boredom habit

games, designing, design logic habit and, 91–92
gatekeepers, 25, 34, 40–41, 44, 51, 114, 148, 149, 152, 161, 164, 221; addressing inequality in STEM education and, 165, 168, 171, 174, 196, 197, 206, 211; defining technological competence and, 171, 174; peers as, 178–80; role of, in digital inequality, 152; STEM occupations and, 174
gatekeeping, 17, 20, 25, 26, 169, 209, 218; addressing, for organizations, 196–204; addressing, for parents and educators, 181–96; addressing, for people in general, 204–6; addressing inequalities and, 169–70, 213–19; engines of, 211–13; home practices and, 178; in learning ecology, 176–77; measuring, 175–81; opportunity hoarding and, 201; organizational steps for addressing, 196–204; persistence of digital inequality and, 25–26, 29, 35, 36, 42; problem of, 152, 169, 170, 173–75; regulating practices of, 218; teaching design logic for, 191–94; teaching efficiencies for, 195–96; teaching management of frustration and boredom for, 184–87; teaching use of models for, 187–90; teaching willingness to try and fail for, 182–84; technological futures of students and, 173–74; workplace inequality and, 200
Gebru, Timnit, 205
Gee, James Paul, 89–91
Gelbgiser, Dafna, 157
gender: in computing history, 201–3; devaluation and, 202–3; distribution of DAS scores by, 139–44, 140f; technology-specific habits and, 102–5
gender frame, salience of, 9
gender inequality, addressing, 198–99; in STEM education, 165–67
general technology learning habits, 52–85. *See also* willingness to try and fail habit; management of frustration and boredom habit; use of models habit
Giannini Middle School, 93, 252. *See also* Mouse Squad California
gig economy, 217
Global Kids (GK), 18, 48, 210, 215, 223, 234
Goapele, 78
grammars, internal and external design, 90–91
Granville, Evelyn Boyd, 205
Gravel, Brian, 262
greater good, 26, 37, 43, 200; focusing on, 35–36. *See also* democratic equality

grit, 10–11, 13, 14; digital adaptability and, 139; scale, 127, 254. *See also* persistence, educational

growth mindset, 13–14, 60

habits, 17–18; addressing inequality and, 164–69; aspirations and, 161–64; general, 4; learning, as necessity for democratic equality, 214; learning opportunities and, 161–64; management of frustration and boredom, 62–73; purpose of identifying and describing, 44–45; reasons for focusing on, 43–45; role of, 157–61; selecting which ones to study, 45–51; summary of five, 105–7, 106t; technology-specific, 4; teens' futures and, 152–56; use of models, 73–83; willingness to try and fail, 55–62. *See also* design logic habit; efficiencies habit; general technology learning habits; management of frustration and boredom habit; use of models habit; willingness to try and fail habit

Half, Jan, 251–52

Harold Washington Library Center (Chicago), 237

Hawkins, Brother Mike, 195, 237

Hedges, Dawson, 127

Herring, Cedric, 203

Hidden Figures (Shetterly), 205

hidden techies, 21, 107, 114, 148, 150, 210; seeing, 219–23, 302n6

Hill, Catherine, 218

Hines, Alicia Headlam, 21

historical marginalization, 45, 279–80n86

hoarding, opportunity, gatekeeping and, 201, 212

Hobbs, Renee, 89–90

home practices, gatekeeping and, 178

home technology teaching scales, 178, 179t

Hopper, Grace Murray, 205

House on Mango Street, The (Cisneros), 81, 82, 186, 238

identity building, principles for, 197–98

I Dig Zambia (Chicago and New York City), 18, 48, 98, 215–16, 235, 246–49. *See also* Global Kids; Field Museum

imperfection, practicing, 66–68, 73, 184

individual access, dilemma of, 30–31

individual advantage, logic of, 17, 26, 31, 37, 38,

40–43, 211, 212, 213, 214, 215, 216; resisting framing technology learning for serving needs of, 216–17; technology learning for, 36, 40–43

inequalities: addressing digital, 43, 152, 170, 172–73, 204–6, 213–19, 221; addressing, in workplaces, 199–204; aspirations and, 164–69; class- and race-related, in STEM education, 167–69; engines of, 26, 211–13; habits and, 164–69; levels of digital divide and, 28–35; organizations, addressing gatekeeping and, 196–204; reasons organizations want to change, 203; research on technology and, 17, 24, 26–28; 35–36, 43, 222; role of gatekeepers and, 20, 25, 152, 170; in STEM education, addressing, 164–69; technological competence and, research on, 24, 27–28; top-down perspective of, 27–28; understanding technology learning and, 16; workplace, gatekeeping and, 200. *See also* digital inequality

inequality regimes, 197; reasons for difficulty of changing, 203–4. *See also* organizations

insider, becoming an, efficiencies and, 100–102

instinct: assumption of, 8; defined, 4, 44; geek, 20, 21, 221; gender-, race-, and class-based assumptions about, 8–9; technological, 4–5, 44, 86, 105

instructors, as models, 75–76. *See also* use of models habit

interest, adaptability vs., 114–24

interest-driven learning, 119–20

internal design grammars, 90–91

International Society for Technology Education (ISTE), 6–7. *See also* National Educational Technology Standards

intuitive design, 114

Johnson, Katherine, 150

Kawamura, Naomi, 240

"keeping an open mind," habit and, 55–62. *See also* willingness to try and fail habit

Kelley, Robin D. G., 221

Kuznets Curve, 28

Labaree, David, 26, 42

language development, technology learning and, 89–92

learning, interest-driven, 119–20

learning brokers, 114, 286n6

learning ecology, 173, 296n1; gatekeeping in, 176–77

learning habits. *See* general technology learning habits; habits

learning measures, biases in, 105, 125–28, 148, 170, 219, 254

Lesser, Marc, 249

Light, Jennifer, 30

literacies, technological and digital, 4, 6, 10, 24, 29, 32, 33, 34, 43, 44, 89–91, 96, 103, 113, 221, 237, 273n13, 274n30

logic, design, habit. *See* design logic habit

logics, educational: contradictory, 17, 29, 39; democratic equality, 17, 26–36; for framing technology education, 17; of individual advantage, 17, 26, 31, 37, 38, 40–43, 211–16; of serving needs of markets, 17, 25, 26, 36–40, 41, 211–17; social efficiency, 17, 25, 26, 36–40, 41, 211–17; social mobility, 17, 26, 31, 37, 38, 40–43, 211–16

MacArthur Foundation Digital Medial and Learning (DML) Initiative, 234, 237, 238, 246

management of frustration and boredom habit, 4, 18, 55, 62–73, 78, 84, 94, 96, 103, 105, 106t, 110, 117, 118, 120, 122, 123, 124, 132, 137, 140, 151, 172, 182; blocking out distractions and, 70–71; breaking down tasks and, 69–70; DAS scoring for, 132; distribution of scores, 134–37, 135f; distribution of scores by gender, 141f; enlisting others to help with, 71–73; framing to learn and, 64–66; pivoting and, 69; practicing imperfection and, 66–68; repertoire building and, 68–73; self-regulation and, 63–64; teaching, for addressing gatekeeping, 184–87. *See also* design logic habit; efficiencies habit; use of models habit; willingness to try and fail habit

Margolis, Jane, 32, 199, 213

markets, logic of, 17, 25, 26, 36–40, 41, 211–17; resisting framing technology learning for serving needs of, 211–17; technology learning for, 36–40

Masterman, Len, 26–27

mastery-oriented thinking, 68

Matthew Effect, 215

media education, 27

Mellström, Ulf, 103–4

men. *See* gender

mental models, developing, 81–83

mindsets: fixed, 13, 14; growth, 13, 14, 60; research on, 13–16

models, use of, habit. *See* use of models habit

Montes, David, 8, 174, 220, 242, 243

Moore, Chelsea, 169

Morgan, Stephen L., 157

Motivated Strategies for Learning Questionnaire (MSLQ), 254

Mouse/Geek Squad Summer Academy (New York City), 18, 48, 49, 50, 55–58, 61, 63, 64–65, 75, 95, 175, 187, 188, 210, 223, 234, 235, 236, 249–51

Mouse Squad California (MSCA; Bay Area), 18, 46–47, 50–51, 65–66, 68, 69, 72, 76, 93, 190, 210, 223, 234, 235, 251–53

multiple models, using, 74–75, 78–81, 83, 189–90. *See also* use of models habit

multitrait-multimethod matrix (MTMM), 232

Nasir, Na'ilah Suad, 197–98

Nation at Risk, A (US National Commission on Excellence in Education), 37–38

National Education Technology Standards (NETS), 6, 7. *See also* International Society for Technology Education

Neff, Gina, 75

Nelson, Alondra, 21

Noble, Safiya Umoja, 35

No Child Left Behind, 169, 285n8

Noname, 237

observation of technology learning habits: qualitative, 114–24; quantitative, 115, 124–38

online resources, as models, 74, 77

opportunities, learning, habits, aspirations, and, 161–64, 170

opportunity hoarding, gatekeeping and, 25, 201, 212, 272n4

organizational culture, changing, 198–99

organizations: addressing gatekeeping and, 196–204; reasons for addressing inequalities and, 203. *See also* inequality regimes

orienting beliefs, 138, 139, 204–5

out-of-school technology teaching scales, 180–81, 181t

Panganiban, Rik, 247-48, 249
peers: as gatekeepers, 178-80; as source of information, 76-77
People's History of Computing in the United States, A (Rankin), 30, 217-18
persistence, educational: explanations of, 10-16; research on, 233. *See also* grit
Peters, Ryan Nicole, 188, 243
Pinkard, Nichole, 237
pivoting, 63, 69, 84, 184, 186

qualitative observation of technology learning habits, 114-24; ethics and, 126-27
quantitative measures, 125-29; benefits of, 125; drawbacks of, 125-27, 129
quantitative observation of technology learning habits, 115, 124-38
quantizing method, 73

race-related inequalities, in STEM education, 167-69
Radio Arte (Chicago), 18, 48, 59, 61, 65, 68, 78, 80, 81, 87-89, 92, 93, 101, 188, 190, 198, 210, 214, 223, 235, 245-46
Rafalow, Matthew H., 34-35
Ramos-Wada, Aida, 169
Rankin, Joy Lisi, 30, 217-18
reading technologically, 89-92
repertoire, building, for management of frustration and boredom, 63, 68-73; blocking out distractions, 70-71; breaking down tasks, 69-70; enlisting help of others, 71-73; pivoting, 69
responsive learning contexts, 60, 197-98
Ridgeway, Cecilia, 9, 202
Riegle-Crumb, Catherine, 169
Rising above the Gathering Storm: Energizing and Employing America for a Brighter Economic Future (National Research Council), 38
Rockman et al (educational research company), 239, 246

safe places, failing in, 60-62
Sandvig, Christian, 75
Santo, Rafi, 246, 248
Sanzenbacher, Beth, 76, 246
school technology teaching scales, 177-78, 177t
Scholastic Achievement Test (SAT), 126, 219
science, technology, engineering, and mathematics. *See* STEM education

Second Life, 26, 48, 215, 216, 234, 246-49
self-concept, 12, 169
self-efficacy, 58-59
self-regulation, 63-64
Shauman, Kimberlee, 165-66
Shedd Aquarium (Chicago), 238
Shetterly, Margot Lee, 205
shortcuts. *See* efficiencies
sine qua non of technology learning, 58-60
Small, Mario, 231
social efficiency logic, 17, 25, 26, 36-40, 41, 211-17
social mobility logic, 17, 26, 31, 37, 38, 40-43, 211-16
Souls of Black Folk, The (Du Bois), 210
standardized testing, 32, 126, 145, 150, 177, 199
Stark, David, 75
STEAM education (science, technology, engineering, arts, and mathematics), 46, 234, 280n87. *See also* STEM education
Steinkuehler, Constance, 92
STEM education (science, technology, engineering, and mathematics), 3, 4, 5, 8, 12, 18-19, 20, 24, 209, 214, 218; addressing inequalities in, 138, 164-71, 213-23; aspirations and pursuit of, 19, 151, 156-58, 159-69, 170; class- and race-related inequalities in, 45, 167-69; DAS and aspirations in, 159-60, 160f; gatekeepers and inequality in, 16, 165, 174, 178; gender-based performance and, 8-9; gender inequality and, 165-67; lower-income families and, 168; occupations, gatekeepers and, 174; racial disparities and, 21, 39, 45, 168; reconceptualizing goals of, 18; research in, 12, 18, 38, 41, 130, 149-50, 157, 160, 169, 171; US, efforts to address inequities in, 138, 165. *See also* STEAM education
stereotypes, 7-8, 44-46, 48, 114, 138, 149-50, 167, 171, 173, 174, 199-201, 202, 211, 233-34; addressing, 174-75, 204-6; Asians and, 266n7; negative consequences of, 174
St. Rose, Andresse, 218
structures, educational program, changing, 198-99
Stuck in the Shallow End (Margolis et al.), 32-33
Sutton, Rosemary, 212

Tai, Robert H., 157
tasks, breaking down, 69-70, 84, 184, 187

tasks, gender, devaluation and, 202-3
teaching strategies: for design logic habit,
191-94; for efficiencies habit, 195-96; for
management of frustration and boredom,
184-87; for use of models habit, 187-90;
for willingness to try and fail, 182-84
techies, seeing hidden, 219-23
Technicolor: Race, Technology, and Everyday Life
(Hines, Nelson, and Tu), 21
technological ability, belief in "natural," 20-21.
See also technological instinct
technological change, 5, 10, 18, 23, 27, 33, 36, 43
technological competence, 3, 4, 16, 26, 32, 36,
45, 115, 175, 202, 205, 210; assumption of
natural ability and, 13, 107, 113, 172; bias
and, 149, 206; continual learning and,
10, 199; developing, 223, 262; equitable
society and, 17, 25, 27, 33, 43, 215, 218, 219;
gatekeeping and, 25, 152, 171, 175; habits
and, 44, 49, 51, 97, 101, 194, 195, 205, 206;
inequality and, 26-36; measurement of,
128; past understanding of, 5-9, 24, 32, 171,
273n13; recognizing and certifying, 167,
215; redefining, 3-5, 20, 25-26, 36, 102, 105,
112-13, 139, 161, 165, 171, 196, 199, 202,
204, 209
technological instinct, 4-5, 8, 44, 86, 105
technological learning, 6, 37, 87, 103, 174
technology, as "guy thing," 8
technology education: access to, 34, 211, 219;
gatekeeping in, 106, 219; equitable society
and, 33; logics for, 17, 38, 42, 211-14, 216;
pursuit of, 156, 159; reform and, 144, 219;
rethinking goals of, 105, 215, 216, 220
technology learning, 3, 6, 9, 23, 26-27, 46, 87,
102, 119, 147, 169, 171, 172, 190, 210, 234;
context of, 18, 61, 143, 144, 168, 175, 176,
181, 221, 247, 253, 261; DAS and, 130-38,
140, 148; development of, 86, 139, 154, 156,
221; for an equitable society, 24, 26, 36, 43;
failure and, 63; gatekeeping and, 176, 197,
205; habits and, 4, 18, 19, 20, 25, 36, 43, 45,
51, 54-55, 61, 63, 64, 68, 72-75, 84, 86, 96,
97, 104, 105, 106t, 109, 113, 114, 115, 120,
124, 129, 139, 143, 149, 151-53, 158-63, 165,
167, 170, 171, 175, 179, 180, 196, 202, 205,
217-19, 231, 235, 252, 260, 261, 262, 264; for
individual advantage, 36, 40-43; inequality
and, 24, 28, 105, 114; interest and, 114-24;
language development and, 89-92, 236;

making more inclusive, 197-99, 205,
213-19; for markets, 36-40; persistence
in, 184; as process, 7, 12, 16, 24, 33, 64-65,
69, 73, 86, 184, 187, 206; readiness for, 33,
105, 129, 138, 150, 173, 176; sine qua non of,
58-61. *See also* general technology learning
habits
technology-specific habits, gender and, 102-5
technology teaching scales: friends, 178-79,
180t; home, 178, 179t; out-of-school, 180,
181t; school, 177-78, 177t
tech savviness, 86, 113-14, 130, 145, 234
tech-savvy teens, 4, 17, 45-51, 113-14; identifying models and, 75-78; seeing "good,"
144-49
tech skills, 4-7, 10-14, 17-18, 20, 24, 27-29, 32-
45, 49, 51-52, 56, 59, 64, 68, 75-77, 79-80,
82, 86, 90, 103-4, 107, 113, 128, 138, 148-50,
156, 173, 181, 199-202, 209-12, 221, 235, 238,
239, 242, 244-47, 250, 254
teens' futures, 151-52; five habits and, 151-71
think aloud, 109, 115, 123, 255, 287n8
Thompson, Clive, 200-201
Thorne, Barrie, 175, 198
Tibbs, Carrie, 65, 66, 72, 190
Tichavakunda, Antar, 210
triangulate, 132, 258
tricks of the trade, 96-102; importance of
learning, 98-100. *See also* efficiencies
Tu, Thuy Linh N., 21

*Unanticipated Gains: Origins of Network
Inequality in Everyday Life* (Small), 232
Unlocking the Clubhouse (Margolis and Fisher),
32-33, 213
Unmarried Couples with Children (England and
Edin), 231
Unzueta, Tania, 88
Urban Promise Academy (UPA), 1-3, 24, 174,
207-9, 220-21, 242, 249
use of models habit, 4, 18, 55, 73-83, 84, 91, 93,
94, 95, 96, 98, 103, 105, 106t, 110, 120, 123,
133, 146, 151, 172, 182, 183; apprenticeships
as, 74-78; DAS scoring for, 132; design logic
and, 95, 146, 191, 193, 195; distribution of
DAS scores, 134-37, 136f; distribution of
scores by gender, 139-40, 142f; efficiencies
and, 99, 101; instructors as, 75-76; mental,
developing, 81-83; using multiple, 78-81;
online resources as, 77; peers as, 76-77; in

use of models habit (*continued*)
program structures, 77–78; teaching, for addressing gatekeeping, 187–90, 196. *See also* design logic habit; efficiencies habit; management of frustration and boredom habit; willingness to try and fail habit

Varma, Atul, 259
Veblen, Thorstein, 44, 210

Weber, Max, 44, 210
Weeden, Kim, 157
What Video Games Have to Teach Us about Learning and Literacy (Gee), 90–91
WhyReef at the Field Museum (Chicago), 17, 47, 75–76, 235, 238–39, 246, 250. *See also* Field Museum
Why So Few? Women in Science, Technology, Engineering, and Mathematics (Hill, Corbett, and St. Rose), 218
willingness to try and fail habit, 4, 18, 55–62, 63, 84, 94, 96, 103, 105, 106t, 110, 111, 117, 121, 123, 151, 161, 163, 172, 182, 194; DAS scoring for, 132; distribution of DAS scores, 134–37, 135f; distribution of scores by gender, 139–40, 141f; teaching, for addressing gatekeeping, 182–84. *See also* design logic habit; efficiencies habit; management of frustration and boredom habit; use of models habit
women, in computing, 201–3. *See also* gender
workplaces: gatekeeping and inequality in, 25, 197, 200; recognizing inequality in, 199–204
Wright, Leticia, 222–23

Xie, Yu, 165–66

YOUmedia Chicago, 18, 47, 82, 101, 150, 185–86, 195, 196, 198, 223, 234, 235, 236–38, 258
Youth Movement Records (YMR; Bay Area), 17, 48, 60, 61, 66–67, 68, 69–70, 73–74, 78, 79, 93–94, 97–98, 187, 188, 191–94, 198, 210, 223, 235, 242–45